Praise for *My First Thirty Years*

"We should all be as fierce, loud, and convinced of our own self-worth as Gertrude Beasley was. This story of a justifiably angry woman living ahead of the world she lived in will resonate deeply today."

—Soraya Chemaly, activist and award-winning author
of *Rage Becomes Her: The Power of Women's Anger*

"Gertrude Beasley's 1925 memoir grabs the reader by the arm and holds tight, speaking with a voice as compelling as if she had just put down her pen this morning. Feminist, socialist, and acute observer of both herself and the world around her, Beasley gives us stories that illuminate the costs of poverty and of being a woman. To read *My First Thirty Years* is to be in conversation with an extraordinary mind."

—Anne Gardiner Perkins, author of *Yale Needs Women*

"In a voice as compelling as it is sinister, Gertrude Beasley recounts a hardscrabble upbringing, transcending time and place to bring to life her story of overcoming brutal circumstances in the search for a different way to live—even if her own success was partial. This long-banned memoir is one of the best coming-of-age stories about being poor and a woman—another way of saying, being human—in twentieth-century Texas. *My First Thirty Years* is a damn good book, and it deserves a wide audience."

—Mary Helen Specht, author of *Migratory Animals*

"*My First Thirty Years* is a literary gut punch. Gertrude Beasley takes us on a harrowing journey into an early twentieth-century Texas childhood filled with brutality, sexism, and racism. How she survived it, much less wrote about it, is nothing short of miraculous. This book, and the world it depicts, will haunt me."

—Gloria Norris, author of *KooKooLand*

"*My First Thirty Years* is a brutally graphic personal memoir that was censored, suppressed, and nearly forgotten. This reprint will finally enable people outside of library special collections to read and honor this memoir by an indomitable and almost erased Texas heroine."

—Dr. Sylvia Grider, coauthor of *Texas Women Writers* and senior professor emerita, Texas A&M University

"It is utterly impossible to sequence the genome of the Southern woman in the early twentieth century without Gertrude Beasley's revolutionary memoir *My First Thirty Years*. Beasley's nearly lost masterwork is an essential bit of DNA whose importance cannot be overstated. Let the rejoicing at its rescue and reissue begin!"

—Sarah Bird, award-winning author of *Daughter of a Daughter of a Queen*

"Gertrude Beasley wrote one of the great modern autobiographies, but it was immediately suppressed. Widely available at last, it is a shocking but moving feminist exploration of growing up in America."

—Bert Almon, author of *This Stubborn Self: Texas Autobiographies*

"From its unforgettable first sentence, this brilliant, bitter memoir of West Texas girlhood in the 1920s sears itself into the reader's imagination. Published by an avant-garde Paris press in 1925, banned, forgotten, remembered, treasured, buried again, and finally made available in this new edition, Gertrude Beasley's memoir is invaluable to our understandings of modernism, feminism, sexual violence, and Texas history. Beasley is a born storyteller. I could not put this book down."

—Lisa Moore, Archibald A. Hill Professor of English and professor of women's and gender studies, University of Texas at Austin

"For all of the celebrated obscene books of the 1920s, there are none like Gertrude Beasley's unsentimental autobiography of her family's hardscrabble West Texas existence in the early twentieth century. A truth-teller who enters and exits her coming-of-age story raging at the sexual, psychological, racial, and sociological facts of her existence, Beasley details an American story so shocking, the book was suppressed immediately and has only just come back into print."

—Allison Pease, author of *Modernism, Sex, and Gender* and professor, City University of New York

"Gertrude Beasley provides a uniquely raw and unvarnished account of growing up poor, abused, and female. And yet, her story is also about the power of education and of achieving professional success in the face of impossible odds. Throughout this memoir, her voice rings out, reminding readers of the struggles that women had to rise above in a culture that placed little value on their bodies, aspirations, and even lives."

—Dr. Celia Marshik, professor,
Stony Brook University

"One can only marvel that Gertrude Beasley survived her family and childhood: reading her riveting, astounding dark memoir is like reading *Little House on the Prairie* while having a nightmare. *My First Thirty Years* has simply not been on the scholarly map of Western women's frontier writing and life narrative, and it will transform how we understand the genre's contours and history."

—Cathryn Halverson, associate professor,
Minot State University

"Before William Faulkner's *As I Lay Dying*, and long before Dorothy Allison's *Bastard Out of Carolina*, Gertrude Beasley inaugurated the twentieth-century American genre of 'white trash' literature with this 1925 memoir, a coming-of-age story of sexual violence and sexual awakening, economic deprivation and deep-seated shame. Now widely available for the first time in nearly a century, *My First*

Thirty Years tells the frank and brutal story of what Beasley calls a 'typically American' family, a story we have long resisted hearing."

—Pamela L. Caughie, author and professor of literature and women's and gender studies, Loyola University of Chicago

"Beasley's steely narrative tones describe the childhood poverty and sexual trauma in rural Texas that drove her to pursue a graduate degree at the University of Chicago and to embrace the ideas of Margaret Sanger and Emma Goldman. A socialist, educational reformer, journalist, and above all, a feminist, Gertrude Beasley and her unjustly neglected life story have finally been restored to the American cultural panorama of the 1920s. Before being forcibly committed to a psychiatric hospital, Beasley declared, 'I was going to go on and on and on.' This beautiful publication of *My First Thirty Years* ensures that she will do exactly that."

—Urmila Seshagiri, associate professor of English, University of Tennessee

MY
FIRST
THIRTY
YEARS

MY FIRST
THIRTY YEARS

a memoir

DISCARD

GERTRUDE BEASLEY

foreword by NINA BENNETT
with MARIE BENNETT

🅢 sourcebooks P.O. Box 668
Park City, Utah 84060
435-615-5600

Published by Sourcebooks
P.O. Box 4410, Naperville, Illinois 60567-4410
(630) 961-3900
sourcebooks.com

Originally published in 1925 in France by Contact Editions. This edition issued based on the paperback edition published in 1989 in the United States by The Book Club of Texas.

Library of Congress Cataloging-in-Publication Data

Names: Beasley, Gertrude, 1892-1955. author.
Title: My first thirty years : a memoir / Gertrude Beasley
Other titles: My 1st 30 years
Description: Naperville, Illinois : Sourcebooks, [2021] | "Originally
  published in 1925 in France by Contact Editions. This edition issued
  based on the paperback edition published in 1989 in the United States
  by The Book Club of Texas"--Copyright page.
Identifiers: LCCN 2021013092 | (Trade Paperback)
Subjects: LCSH: Beasley, Gertrude, 1892-1955. | Women
  teachers--Texas--Biography. | Women journalists--Texas--Biography. |
  Poor whites--Southern States--Social conditions. | Victims of family
  violence. | Feminists--United States--History. | Modernism (Literature)
Classification: LCC LA2317.B42 B42 2021 | DDC 371.10092 [B]--dc23
LC record available at https://lccn.loc.gov/2021013092

Printed and bound in the United States of America.
VP 10 9 8 7 6 5 4 3 2 1

FOREWORD

Gertrude Beasley is furious. She survived soul-crushing poverty, sexual assault, and wild dysfunctionality from the very family members who were supposed to keep her safe. She somehow retained her dignity and sense of self, escaped the toxic environment of her childhood, and scrabbled up the social ladder. Having faced so much in her first thirty years, she had zero patience left for anyone who would presume to have a say in how "women like her" should behave. Do not, she seethed, romanticize small-town life. Do not flatten survivors with demeaning pity. And above all, do not tell us to "get over it" and quietly conform to your vision for what a satisfying, fulfilled life should look like.

Gertrude's prose is fierce, unapologetic, and aggressively intelligent. She pulls no punches and will not go down quietly. If she were handed a microphone at a women's march today, mainstream media and even some fellow protesters would shift uncomfortably at her combative fury and her vehement hatred of her childhood surroundings. Her rage, as she acknowledges, is scarcely contained: "I shall protest against having been brought into the world without any heritage—mental, moral, or physical—to my dying day."

The 1920s were in no way ready for her. While booksellers, literary magazine editors, and others within the publishing world took up the cause of other modernist authors who defied social convention and faced censorship, such as James Joyce and Ernest Hemingway, Gertrude "was without funds, a woman with no husband, and abrasive. It was easier just to put her away," explained Alice W. Specht, the Abilene librarian who, eighty-one years later, finally solved the mystery of Gertrude's disappearance.

Gertrude and her memoir were erased so thoroughly that it took sixty years for her writing to start recirculating amongst academic literati and another twenty to discover her whereabouts. Only now, finally, almost a hundred years after it was originally published, will general readers be able to access the audacious book that cost Gertrude her career and her freedom.

A LIFE WORTH TALKING ABOUT

Edna Gertrude Beasley was born on June 20, 1892, in rural Coleman County, a portion of West Texas where cattle drives and clashes with the Comanche had by then given way to the legions of small family farms that were gradually proving to be economically and ecologically unsustainable. She was the ninth of thirteen children born to an unhappy, abusive marriage. Her father, a violent alcoholic, uprooted the family frequently; her mother's bitter vitriol was constant. It was a childhood marked by fear, hatred, and barbaric physical, sexual, and verbal abuse. Gertrude's first memory, at age four, is of an adolescent brother holding her down in the horse stall attempting to rape her. A sister is fondled by a circuit preacher, another is beaten by their father until she defecates blood, and a brother is whipped for being "caught in the barnyard with the old cow."

Finally, when Gertrude was about eight years old, her mother pretended to take the children out to pick cotton and instead ran away with them to Abilene, the nearest town, and obtained a divorce. Though indisputably an act of bravery and self-preservation, the divorce was yet another source of shame, a family secret that threatened to strip the Beasleys of any semblance of respectability. Gertrude learned that white lies and discretion were key if she wished to be judged on her own merits.

She was undeniably intelligent and ambitious. The only Beasley sibling to take an interest in school, she was accredited to teach elementary school at age seventeen and worked in rural schools during alternate semesters while attending college in Abilene. Then, at age twenty-one, she left West Texas to pursue a master's degree in education at the University of Chicago.

Chicago plunged Gertrude into the heady environment of suffragettes, birth-control advocacy, the emerging field of "sex psychology," and socialism—then perceived to be a viable electoral alternative in those days before the 1919 Red Scare. She got involved in protests for equal pay for female teachers. She grappled with Freud's theory that childhood exposure to sexual overindulgence or sexual frustration thwarts psychological development. She attended lectures by Margaret Sanger,[1] the founder of Planned Parenthood, who argued that birth control could help women like Gertrude's mother become more than mere objects of lust, an "instrument of satisfaction." *My First Thirty Years* is a forceful vindication of Sanger's heretical notions that sexuality should be discussed with more candor, that women have sexual drives, and that sex should be an activity of "confidence and respect." Gertrude's entire lived experience to date was proof that free speech constraints and a destructive approach to sexuality degrade women and ruin lives. She also attended lectures by Emma Goldman, a Chicago feminist/anarchist who asserted that the patriarchy was just as toxic a hierarchy as state power and class divisions. These intellectually riveting ideas and the powerful women who presented them transformed Gertrude into a strident, articulate activist undaunted by authority figures (much to the exasperation of her later employers).

It was in Chicago that Gertrude began writing for newspapers, producing increasingly pointed critiques of the public education system. Within two years of completing her master's degree, she left

---

1   In an example of dispiriting foreshadowing, Margaret Sanger's insistence on distributing contraceptive information to women led to criminal charges in 1915 for "the circulation of obscene literature and articles of immoral use" in violation of the federal Comstock law. A decade later, this same law would be used to justify the confiscation and destruction of Gertrude's memoir.

teaching for a career in international journalism, relocating first to Japan to write for *The Far East* and then to China for a secretarial job at the Rockefeller Foundation's Peking Union Medical College. She wrote about her travels in Japan, China, and Korea for *National Geographic*. In Moscow, with a front row seat to the Bolshevik takeover of Russian civic life, Gertrude wrote that tsarist sympathizers were "as sterile and emasculated, socially and intellectually, as the average Southerner in America." At least one of her articles was published in *Birth Control Review*, a journal edited by Margaret Sanger.

In 1925, Contact Editions, a small avant-garde press in Paris, published a limited run of what would turn out to be Gertrude's only surviving book, her memoir titled *My First Thirty Years*. Contact Editions was at the center of Paris's 1920s expatriate scene and specialized in sharp, controversial pieces, including debut works by Hemingway and Gertrude Stein. Robert McAlmon, the publisher, would later recall in his own memoir that "only two authors got 'temperamental' and they were both Gertrudes, Stein and Beasley." He went on to describe these uncompromisingly fierce women as "megalomaniacs with an idea that to know them was to serve them without question in all their demands." With such a cohort of daring fellow modernists, Gertrude seemed to be at the start of a memorable career.

Initial reactions to her book were favorable. H. L. Mencken, arguably the most influential American literary critic of the era, deemed it "the first genuinely realistic picture of the Southern poor white trash" (remember, *My First Thirty Years* was published an entire year before Faulkner made his debut with *Soldier's Pay*) and observed wryly that Gertrude's remarkable coming-of-age story most likely "comes out with a Paris imprint because no American publisher would risk printing it." *The New Yorker* categorized it as "a naughty book" but also "an amazing one." The British Nobel laureate Bertrand Russell, whom Gertrude had first met in China, called the book "truthful, which is illegal."

Within the next several months, the book's distribution came to an abrupt halt. Britain, where Beasley was living at the time, banned the book for its obscene material. More than half of the copies from the limited run were seized and destroyed by Scotland Yard or U.S. Customs. The few that made it to Texas were yanked off shelves by Texas Rangers, purportedly on the orders of Governor Dan Moody, whose mother-in-law was unflatteringly portrayed in the book as having an affair with the prominent Baptist preacher at Gertrude's childhood church. Even sixteen years later, in 1941, the Texas legislature's un-American activities committee summoned a rare book dealer to explain his decision to sell a copy of Beasley's memoir to the state's flagship university in Austin. The book was promptly removed. That book dealer, who managed to place three additional copies of *My First Thirty Years* in university libraries throughout the state, later explained to famed Texas folklorist Al Lowman that "there were folks here in Texas who tried their damnedest to suppress" Gertrude's book.

The visceral reaction to *My First Thirty Years* points to more than distaste for her scandalously blunt style. Gertrude's life story directly threatened the treasured fictions to which Americans were increasingly turning for comfort amidst a rapidly changing world. The country was urbanizing at a breakneck pace: farm boys were becoming factory men, newspapers breathlessly reported on violent labor confrontations and women's rights protests, and, of course, the First World War had just shattered minds and geopolitics alike. Scrambling for a sense of stability, readers embraced a vision of the Heartland and frontier families as emblematic of all that was wholesome and patriotic. When *My First Thirty Years* was published, Willa Cather's nostalgic, uplifting depictions of hardworking prairie homesteaders had just been awarded the 1923 Pulitzer Prize. Laura Ingalls Wilder was about to draft the first of her wildly popular Little House on the Prairie books, a seductively cozy children's series on pioneer family life. Norman Rockwell was nine years into his tenure at the *Saturday Evening Post*, already famous for his bucolic images such as *Gramps at the Plate* (1916) and *Mother Tucking Children into Bed* (1921). Turn-of-the-century frontier families were being flattened into a romantic, increasingly mythologized morality tale that glorified the purifying benefits of hard work and married life. Gertrude's evisceration of this myth, her grim resolve to showcase over and over again the literally unspeakable inhumanity of her childhood, challenged more than the social mores of polite society—it questioned Americans' core assumptions about what a "fulfilled life" should look like. Contemporaneous novels that portrayed frontier life as emotionally and morally degrading for married women—such as Edvart Rølvaag's *The Giants of the Earth* (1924) and Dorothy Scarborough's *The Wind* (1925)—sidestepped obscenity laws only to fall quickly into obscurity. American readers didn't want to know.

The authorities in London had tried unsuccessfully to deport Gertrude in 1925, shortly before the publication of *My First Thirty Years*, on the grounds that she was writing "an indecent book on American life." In 1927, during an altercation with a policeman who was attempting to turn her out of her lodgings for unclear reasons, Gertrude broke her window with an umbrella in protest and was promptly arrested and committed to the mental ward of Holborn Hospital. She was released to the American consulate on condition that she leave the country. From the ship en route to the United States, she wrote a rambling letter to the U.S. Secretary of State claiming that she was in danger, that the British authorities and "certain people in Texas" were conspiring "to destroy me as a writer and a personality and have me put to death."

Then Gertrude vanished.

REDISCOVERING GERTRUDE

In the late 1980s, beloved Texan novelist Larry McMurtry was at the height of his influence. *Lonesome Dove*, his grim, unsentimental take on the cowboy Western, had won the 1986 Pulitzer Prize—an Emmy-winning four-part miniseries was in the works—and prestigious universities were inviting him to speak about demythologizing the Old West. Faced with a tsunami of public attention, McMurtry attempted to channel at least some of it into an obscure, out-of-print memoir written by a fellow West Texas native. *My First Thirty Years*, he wrote, "is one of the finest Texas books of its era; in my view, the finest."

McMurtry convinced the Book Club of Texas to produce a deluxe five-hundred-copy run of the memoir in 1989. The edition is exceedingly handsome, with Claire Van Vliet's spare woodcuts and an afterword by McMurtry that established the book's importance within the historical, regional, and feminist literary canons. The few copies not purchased by Book Club members wound up in university libraries, largely in Texas. A copy will occasionally find its way to a purveyor of rare used books; these days, the asking price is typically in the hundreds, if not thousands, of dollars.

Though few members of the general public ever saw McMurtry's 1989 edition, it caught the attention of those two underappreciated shapers of young minds: librarians and literature professors. Alice W. Specht, then a librarian at Abilene's Hardin-Simmons University (Gertrude's alma mater), threw herself into a decades-long quest to solve the mystery of Gertrude's disappearance. It was Alice who unearthed Gertrude's school records and magazine articles, even clippings from the *London Telegraph* about her British deportation hearing and a copy of the letter she wrote to the U.S. State Department during her final transatlantic crossing.

The 1989 reprint also caught the attention of Don Graham, the leading historian of Texas literature. Graham became almost evangelical about Gertrude's memoir, integrating selections into his UT Austin literature courses, profiling her in regional magazines, and referencing her memoir whenever possible. Graham kicked off a 2000 *Texas Monthly* article with, "No other book in Texas literature is quite like Gertrude Beasley's little-known memoir. She belongs in the first rank of Texas writers." Ahead of the 2003 Texas Book Festival, he gushed to an interviewer, "Beasley just gives one of the best, most damning portraits there is of a pure-dee white trash family." He went on to explain that Gertrude was a pioneer in the confessional memoir genre and one of the most daring modernists in the English language. When W. W. Norton & Co. approached Graham about publishing an anthology of Texas literature, he included the first ten pages of *My First Thirty Years* and decided to target a general readership rather than an academic audience. Though her complete memoir remained largely inaccessible outside of university libraries and rare book collections, those passages dangled Gertrude's dark, complex prose before a new generation of twenty-first-century readers.

In 2008, the mystery of her disappearance was finally solved. The advent of the internet and the digitization of handwritten historic records led to a breakthrough. Shortly after the 1930 census was made publicly accessible online, a Beasley was found listed among inmates living in a mental institution on Long Island. Alice Specht, the librarian in Abilene, worked with Gertrude's grandniece to obtain a copy of the death certificate from the State of New York. We now know that within ten days of her ship docking in New York, Gertrude was committed to Central Islip Psychiatric Center on Long Island. She was thirty-five. This was an era when medicine was used to police polarizing women. Those who called into question society's inflexible ideas about how women ought to behave ran the risk of being declared insane and imprisoned in a lunatic asylum without recourse. Unlike Nelly Bly, Gertrude had no powerful, well-connected backers to lobby for her release. She died in that hospital of pancreatic cancer at sixty-three and was buried quietly on the property. She could not have been silenced more effectively.

RESTORING HER VOICE

My first encounter with Gertrude occurred shortly after I moved back to Texas in 2019. Looking to reacquaint myself with Texas's complicated self-image, I stumbled across the pages of Gertrude's memoir in Don Graham's *Lone Star Literature* anthology and, like so many others before me, couldn't let go.

Gertrude's story showcases the superhuman bravery that it takes to extricate oneself from a toxic environment and the psychological scars that survivors then carry throughout their lives. Aggressive pride and ambition coexist with deep-rooted shame. Hers is a story about reclaiming power and a determined pursuit of dignity. By the end of her book, her voice becomes defiant: "I promised them and myself that if things didn't go to suit me in Bellingham I was going to raise hell; you had to kick and kick hard in this world."

Her worldview remains discomfiting, even a hundred years later. Gertrude took pride in meting out pitiless corporal punishment to master unruly rural schoolrooms. In addition to bestiality and attempted sibling rape, she speaks about consensual sexual play among children. She has little grace for others who have endured equally hard lives, including her mother. Most jarring of all is the blunt, racially demeaning language that permeates her family's conversations and the more subtle, unconscious assumption of white supremacy that surfaces in her own narrative voice. *My First Thirty Years* forces readers to experience racist rhetoric as both insidious and quotidian, a painful exercise at a time when twenty-first-century Americans are reckoning with the appalling frequency of police-instigated racial violence and white supremacist–inspired domestic terrorism.

And yet, twenty-first-century readers also understand the power of righteous anger. The Black Lives Matter protests and the #MeToo movement have taught us something about marginalized Americans wielding their stories like pickaxes to tear down harmful silences. *My First Thirty Years* depicts a real life in all its ugly, messy complexity; Gertrude practically dares anyone to attempt pat moralizing. It is our responsibility to listen closely to her story. As she herself wrote in an article for *Hearst's International-Cosmopolitan*, "My generation of women have been great warriors in a mighty battle, in a battle so horrible that if they told the truth about life it would take away the last breath of the censors."

It is egregious that this woman's story remains largely inaccessible, a legacy of her strident refusal to adapt to social convention. Over the past year, the women in my family banded together to restore Gertrude's voice: my mother-in-law, Dominique, championed *My First Thirty Years* within Sourcebooks; my sister-in-law, Marie, meticulously prepared the digitized 1989 text for reissue. For the first time ever, *My First Thirty Years* will be widely available to American readers.

"Watch me!" wrote Gertrude. "From now on I'm going to tell people what is what!"

Yes, you are, Gertrude. Let me pass you the microphone.

Nina M. M. Bennett
Dallas, Texas
2021

Thirty years ago, I lay in the womb of a woman, conceived in a sexual act of rape, being carried during the prenatal period by an unwilling and rebellious mother, finally bursting from the womb only to be tormented in a family whose members I despised or pitied, and brought into association with people whom I should never have chosen. Sometimes I wish that, as I lay in the womb, a pink soft embryo, I had somehow thought, breathed, or moved and wrought destruction to the woman who bore me, and her eight miserable children who preceded me, and the four round-faced mediocrities who came after me, and her husband, a monstrously cruel, Christlike, and handsome man with an animal's appetite for begetting children.

It is perfectly clear to me that life is not worth living, but it is also equally clear that life is worth talking about. Perhaps talk is the greatest thing in the world. If I could destroy my bump of curiosity, I would go on this January day to the river at the Kremlin where Russian churchmen are said to be carrying out religious rites (a piece of idiocy which prevents life from being worthwhile) and throw my body into its icy depths. But I have curiosity, fear, and that potent enemy of death known as hope. Besides I have enough money (U.S.) to keep me going for nearly two years…

The first flood of consciousness in life, the first milestone of our miserable existence here, stands out, I think, before an intelligent mind. I remember mine. I was lying on my back on the hard, dirt floor of the stalls in my father's horse lot. My hands were being held by my older brothers and my feet also, I think, and the great weight on my body seemed about to crush me. God, what an awful thing! Would the consciousness, the struggle for breath, which seemed about to be pressed out in case my frame broke in, my ribs stuck into my entrails and heart, ever return! Thus was I first made conscious. The rest was only a dark whirl; perhaps the wind was blowing, and it seems to me now there was laughter. My oldest brother, then about sixteen years old, though he was very small for his age, was trying to have sexual intercourse with me, although I was only about four years old at the time. Of recent years I have been startled at having this picture come into my mind and said, "God, what if I had really been crushed to death!" But I answer now that perhaps it would have been better. I remember distinctly that between the ages of four and about nine, each of my five brothers older than myself tried at one time or another to have sexual intercourse with me. Although I feared and hated my three oldest brothers, the two just older than myself, being nearly my own size, brought me no fear, only shame in case we should be found out. In fact, I think when the three of us were exploring the field of sex together, watching and talking about animals in their sex acts, and using all the childish expressions concerning sex life, that I was quite as interested in our childish efforts at sexual intercourse as they were.

—←❦

There are some things which I remember with pleasure about the house and surroundings where I was born, pleasurable merely because of the form which the picture takes in my own mind, for I assure you there is nothing in the content of my early life which I should care to remember. I put it down here because I can't forget it, and because I want to see what forms it will take as I talk about it… It was a two-roomed shack; that is, a large boxed house of one room with a small side room, divided into a kitchen and what my mother referred to as a "shed room" for the boys. The stalls, pigpens, and cow lots were some distance from the house, as was also the field planted mostly with cotton, cane, and corn in the spring.

I received my first impression of the beauty of spring here; I remember beauty and light. For although my mother already had ten children to cook for, and all the rest of it, before we left Coleman County, Texas, she had time to cultivate flowers. I think I can honestly say that one of the little flashes of admiration which I early felt for her lay in her ability to give, what appeared to me, such a great number of names of flowers. Then there was song in that age when I was four, impressed upon me in a singular way on the occasion of my mother's catching a dear little hummingbird which sang about her potted and tin-canned flowers just without a low door of our house. I remember how she screamed and chattered about it; calling it sweet and dear, as she put her hands over it when finding it in the blossom of one of her flowers. It stuck in my soul; here was something lovely, something which the hands of a woman, who so often appeared vulgar, coarse, and ignorant to me even when I was a mere baby, put in to a fly trap with the tenderest of care and assured us, a whole brood of round-faced children, that in a few days it would sing. Here was my first conscious moment of beauty. The sun shone brightly that day. But it was not all delight, for my mother screamed too loudly when she caught the bird, and I felt she was giving us an exhibition, as the saying was, she was "putting on"—there was a note of affectation in her voice. This incident also saddened me, for the bird did not sing and was let out "to be free" by the same hands. I felt the same strong emotion, this time to weep, and also wondered if the pretty speech about letting the bird "free" was quite sincerely stated by this woman, my mother, whom I doubted, hated, sometimes admired, and greatly pitied.

There were many, many emotional experiences which registered themselves in my consciousness, and were stored away in memory during this first year of conscious recognition of feelings and events. For example, I quite understood that my parents did not get on; indeed, I think I felt their great hatred for one another. In fact, my mother used to hiss so and pooh, pooh so, with the corners of her mouth a way down when talking of my father and his family, that I wondered at him and feared him, so much so that when he came in at night, sat by the fire, held me on his lap, played and grunted over me, I wanted to respond rather contemptuously. If he asked me very ardently, "Hug yer daddy's neck, tight, tight," I would do it very slowly for I was wondering if it were not true that he was one of the meanest men who ever lived. My mother had already suggested it in my presence scores of times at this early age, and the statement that "the Beasleys is the sorriest people that God ever made" was not only written in my brain but in my soul. Then, too, I knew that my father beat his animals unmercifully, a thing which terrified me; and that he sometimes beat my brothers with as little concern as though they were cast iron. One day, this same year, I remember, one of the boys ran to the house from the field and cried out frantically to my mother, "Maw, he's killing ole Mary." I feel now how it saddened and frightened me. The old mare which he had been driving at the plough had suddenly sulked and he had beaten her with chains until her body was full of welts, and finally with a stray stroke had knocked one of her eyes completely out. My mother ran about with her apron over her arm in a frenzy and finally disappeared from the house in an effort to stop him.

And then he could swear so loudly and in such earsplitting tones, "Hellfire!" "God damn it to hell!" and the like, his god-damning usually rendering me perfectly stiff and dumb; the whole household was usually silenced with his oaths. Although my brothers swore and all of us said "God" and "God Amighty" whenever we chose, nobody could begin to put the cutting swiftness and frightfulness into oaths as the head of the house did.

Many things crowd into my mind now of the happenings of that first year of memory, at four or perhaps younger. Going to town was always a big event for my mother, who went a few times each year to buy clothing for herself and the family. One of the most humorous events of her preparation was the putting on of her corsets. Being inclined to be stout due to excessive childbearing, having been pregnant every second year since she was eighteen, her waistline had naturally disappeared. My three oldest sisters were the instruments for putting her into this vice. First, the corsets were unlaced as far as the strings would allow and then the three girls would stand around her as required, holding her at the waist, while she craned her short neck over her ample breasts in an effort to put the hooks into the eyes at the front of the corsets. Then someone pulled the strings at the back until she called out enough and the corseting was finished; and everybody was in good humor unless some one of the girls had chanced to laugh, or to cause her to laugh, to shake her abdomen so as to prevent the "hooking." Then someone was liable to get a large smack, and she would turn to nagging and scolding, perhaps saying that everything went wrong whenever she went to town, besides, "yer Daddy never wants me to go nowhere." On this occasion I think she was going to Coleman City, the town where she wanted to put my oldest brother and oldest sister at school, for she, at least, always considered "ejication" important. But my father declared that they would only get into "devilment" and so the plan was never carried out, in spite of the fact that my mother declared many times after I grew up that there was money enough to put them to school for several months that year, as there had been a large cotton crop harvested. I remember sitting near the fireplace on one of these occasions, at a very early hour in the morning, watching her dress, and asking her not to forget my tea set, for it was in the late fall and she was to buy the Christmas things.

There was more laughter in those early days and perhaps more happiness on the whole than at other times in later life, as I was less conscious of the conditions under which we lived. We lived near a German settlement, my older brothers and sisters attending the country school with the children of these families. And the tales they used to tell! This is, of course, only a vague impression, my memory of those days being largely dependent on the many rehearsals given in the family of the humorous and interesting occurrences of that time. I have a picture in mind of my mother getting on a stout old mare, with one of the girls sitting behind, going to pay a visit to one of the funniest of the German families. She sat on a sidesaddle, the only kind of saddle she and my sisters ever used, with a long flowing skirt of black cashmere, her round figure and the squatty old mare making the figure more plump.

But the tales on her return were what stirred one. The old German woman and her daughter had showed them everything of interest, even taking them into the cellar and serving them all the

delicacies known to German peasants and middle-class immigrants
to America. But in conversation they had got things woefully mixed.
It was their Teutonic bad English and their total lack of compre-
hension of the misuse they made of English words which caused all
the merriment. They came home roaring with laughter, and as they
rehearsed how the old woman had tried to explain that her daughter was menstruating, my mother shook and laughed until the tears
streamed down her face, my oldest sister being convulsed with laughter too. Of course, I did not understand the meaning of menstruation, I only understood the little obscene words which were used.
I cannot imagine that these people were consciously obscene. They
merely used the words which their native neighbors had taught them.
In fact, my impression is that the Germans of this community were
the most civilizing force in that section of the country. Some of my
happiest memories of those early days are of the visits which my parents paid to these German families where special teas were prepared
for the children, cookies and various delectable cakes being served
from toy tables, out of pewter dishes and real tea sets for children.
Then there were dolls and numerous other toys to add to the merriment, the best time of all being at Christmas when two or three
of the German families and ourselves shared the festivities. I cannot
recall that these children were ever obscene and I never heard that
they attempted sexual intercourse among themselves, or knew all the
little crass and unclean words with reference to excretions, urine, and
sex which were known in my family, and which I found later in life

were used by many native American families, that is Anglo-Saxons of the old South. The heads of these families were exceptional farmers often becoming well-to-do after a few years; the wives kept immaculate houses and were renowned for their cooking and care of the children. They sent their children to the district school and came to be reckoned among the most reliable and trustworthy citizens.

—◄✳

There is a picture of my father in this first year of memory; he was in the early forties, being thirty-eight when I was born, my mother being thirty. He was about six feet in height, slightly stooped shoulders, and of a good build. His face, I should say, was typically American, full and heavily bearded; his eyes as blue as indigo; teeth sound and well-shaped, though discolored by tobacco; a high forehead which his hat bleached, contrasting with his bronzed cheeks which were high and angular; his head was inclined to be round rather than square, a little high on top (which my mother always maintained was the best proof of his great conceit) and crowned with thick black hair. Two pictures associate themselves in my mind; one of my mother lying on the floor with my younger brother, her tenth child, who must have been two years of age and who was asking to be suckled. She presented him with a large breast, the nipple and front of which she had colored with soot, for she had been told that the baby would reject the breast under such conditions, and that this would prove a convenient method of weaning him. Seeing the black on her breast, he became very angry, refusing to suckle and throwing himself on the floor, kicking and bumping his head.

It was in the midst of this scene that my father appeared, having just come from some one of the neighbors or the village where he had been shorn of most of his beard, the chin whiskers and the mustache being taken off, leaving a frill of sideburns at each side of his face. I remember his broad smile and regular teeth and particularly the deep dimple in his chin, the last being a sure sign of deceitfulness according to my mother, who was then fond of contemplating an old diagram of the head and face, and who recalled frequently a sitting which she and my father had had with a would-be phrenologist. My impression is that as he passed out of the house, my mother made some derogatory remark about him, suggesting that such traits were especially prevalent among the Beasleys. I think I can honestly say that I recognized the words "conceit" and "deceit" at the age of four, these words being associated with my father's dimple and his receding crown, though I did not, of course, know their meaning, but I understood perfectly well that my mother had no intention of conferring a compliment on the head of the house when she used such terms.

—≺✦

The older children went to writing school in the summer; I remember my oldest sister and second brother receiving some praise, but my oldest brother was exceedingly slow, treating writing as a drawing lesson. All of these things are a part of my first impressions: appetites for food and sex; enjoyment of light, laughter, and color; a small consciousness of the relations of my parents; the fact that my oldest sister was quarrelsome and obstreperous with my mother; that I did not like my three oldest brothers (I feared, mistrusted, and hated them at times, chiefly because of their treatment of me which I look upon now as pure rape. There was no play about it.); that I liked to see things flying as when one rides horseback; that I liked climbing and to smell flowers. Though I often said "God" and "God Amighty" as by-words, I think there was never any idea of even inquiring what they stood for.

—←*

Before I was five, my father sold the place in Coleman County and loaded the furniture on a couple of big wagons, prepared and equipped for camping; and taking a small herd of cattle and horses set out for Scurry County, a distance of about 200 miles to the north. My mother was terribly saddened at having to leave the old place, for even though the house was very small and inadequate for a family of twelve, she had gradually made it livable by papering it with various newspapers and pictures and decorations. She had collected a number of homemade conveniences, and, I have no doubt, was about as happy there as she has ever been in this life. Besides there were her good German neighbors whom she had finally come to know almost intimately during the seven or eight years in Coleman County, and others like the McDermotts and other native Americans who had come out from the old States. But the time came when we had to "pull up and move."

This trip did not require a very long time or else my memory is very dull with reference to it. I recall the cold; brush heaps piled around the herd after they had gathered and lain down for the night; fires being made to keep the cattle warm and those for preparing the food; black pots, skillets and kettles; my mother's rolling out the biscuits by hand; that the food was good to eat; and that I did not like the mineral water which we were forced to drink. There were days of camping in the open in Scurry County before the house on the "four sections" was completed, and it appears to me now that the time must have been the spring for there were sandstorms covering everything with a coat of dust. Finally, the house was finished, at least to a degree that we were able to move into it. My mother was displeased—the corners of her mouth sagged lower and lower at this "boxed house" without weatherboarding and ceiling, except insofar as a floor had been put into the loft forming a second story. There were small windows in the second story comprising one large room, and a ladder-like staircase leading up to it from the outside of the house. How yellow and new it looked in the sun! The rays against the windowpanes, sometimes gold, sometimes flaming red, formed one of my first delightful mysteries.

Life was reorganized here. The cattle were put on the range; a small field was cleared which required hard work, cutting of timber and grubbing the roots before the field could be prepared for planting; postal connections were established with Wheat, Texas, where my father also obtained groceries for the family; acquaintances were made, and the Beasley family became a part of the community.

There was a little new schoolhouse a few miles from our place where my older brothers and sisters attended school for a few months during the year and where, at the age of five, I was permitted to go for two weeks. The first day, accompanied by my mother's brood, possibly the entire eight of them older than myself, I made the long walk of two or three miles, doing it with the greatest delight and curiosity. I had been warned not to speak aloud in school, and so observed all regulations with the greatest seriousness. After I had asked the teacher, a young fellow, not much older than my oldest brother, the names of some of the large letters written in the front of my primer, and had been astounded by his loud voice, I would return to my bench and proceed to name as many of the letters as I could and then go back to ask another question. My brothers and sisters were proud of showing me off as another specimen of our illustrious family, and with the usual enthusiasm that ignorant children show for "little sisters," two or three of them came and read the first page of the primer to me. And as they pointed out the words, I found they were photographed on my mind much more indelibly than the letters. I never mixed them and was never in doubt from that day to this about such words as can, see, baby, and so on which appeared on that first page of my primer.

The teacher had nothing to do with this first lesson; some one of the Beasley children, having put his finger under these words, shouted the pronunciation of each in a hoarse whisper in my ear. During that day I would fasten my finger under certain other letters of the alphabet and then march up before the teacher and putting the book as near his face as possible, without in any way moving my finger from under the letter, I would inquire, "What is it?" Once I stumbled over his feet as he sat with his legs crossed at full length before the fire, and losing the position of my finger on the page, was in great consternation as to what I should ask him. He laughed at my stumbling over his feet, at my excitement in finding the letter, and called out in such a big voice, "Don't you know G? your name begins with G—" that I was frightened almost to tears. I returned to my bench, reproaching myself, feeling that perhaps he thought I was an idiot. (This word idiot was one of the most familiar in my early vocabulary, the pronunciation being known to me as ee-di-ut. My third brother would say of my third sister in his funny slow drawl, whenever he was in any way displeased with her, "Maw, Immer (Emma) acts lak' an ee-di-ut." People were described as talking like an ee-di-ut, laughing like an ee-di-ut; and my father often declared that my oldest brother *was* a damned ee-di-ut, an exact prototype of one of my mother's brothers.) But before the day was over, I was called before the teacher to "recite" my lesson. I read; the whole school stopped their study to listen, the Beasley children putting up their ears with special concern and sort of radiating, as I imagine now, "Well, what do you expect?—she belongs to us—we are all like that only we don't find it necessary to tell anybody about it." The teacher questioned me about the words separately and finding that each was securely imprinted upon my mind, he praised me and sent me to my seat.

That afternoon we walked home over great pastures of dry, gray grass in a warm sun, my second and third sisters sometimes holding my hands as we skipped or walked, crunching the stiff grass. It was a golden day for me; for there we were, traversing this great stretch of pasture land, with schoolbooks strapped on our shoulders, dinner pails and milk bottles carried by hand, our feet sinking in the grass and rebounding as one's foot does when running on a straw mattress, as we used to do sometimes in the "shed room" when our mother was not looking. Every step was full of joy; there were grunts and a few words as we crawled under the barbed wire fences, one holding the wire to prevent our clothes being torn; we finally reached the threshold of our little shack where my mother was doing some baking, I think, by the fireplace. (It occurs to me now that this was a different house, being far smaller and a much older house than the new one which I have described.)

Sometimes we almost stumbled on the doorstep on arriving after such long scampers, out of sheer fatigue. Boys were panting and unstrapping their books, and no doubt asking for something to eat as was invariably the rule, when one of them drawled out, "Maw,

Gertrude can read." I will not say that this simple statement made me happy merely; there was an exquisite sensation of pride and satisfaction; something had transpired in my mind that had amounted almost to a physiological change; besides I could open the primer and read it again if I wished to. There was more talk. I see the mother of these healthy, round-faced Beasleys, a stout, almost corpulent woman, then about thirty-five, who held her back and neck so straight as to be almost stiff, getting up from her position at the fireplace, sniffing and turning her head with a gesture of satisfaction as she looked at her offspring and beginning, "Well, I knowed so-and-so—" and then, "W'y, she'll be a-teachin' school by the time she's sixteen." (From the time I began to be cognizant of words I wondered about this "w'y" which I could make nothing of but a plain "y." What did it mean? I used to count down the alphabet to this letter and then recall that my oldest brother said, "Y, I don't know," when asked something. But I still remained puzzled.)

My mother wore a loose-fitting garment of dark blue cotton, I think, as was often the case, perhaps shaped as a bask at the back and loose at the front, over which she usually wore an apron, sometimes white, sometimes of the same dark color as the dress. This was a convenient mode of dress for her, a woman who had borne a child every sixteen months or two years during the last nearly twenty years, for she had only to loosen the band of the apron and readjust the bask a little to accommodate her expanding body during pregnancy. She stepped quickly and with decision, short paces if sometimes a little

16

awkward, mannerisms which some people admired; but if anyone had asked me what I thought of her I should probably have replied that she was too plump and her feet were too flat.

I was allowed to go with the rest of the children to school for two weeks that year, during which time I read many pages in my primer and no doubt acquired what was referred to as the "swellhead," for I adored being praised. I recall distinctly a daydream which I had about this time. There was a great gathering of women among whom I was the principal figure, as I am eventually in almost everything I dream of, sitting or standing in some open space, all dressed in white, including myself, and all intensely interested in my directions or speech or whatever was happening. I can only suppose this to be the heavenly host for whom I am to sing the contralto. At any rate this was the beginning of my various ambitions which have gradually consumed me during the last quarter of a century and not virtually incapacitated me for supplying my quota of seven sons and six daughters (no twins) to the state.

Many interesting, sad, and barbarous incidents happened at school. Jack Mabey, the teacher, was quoted as saying my second brother was very bright at arithmetic and that my third sister was "as quick as powder," which made me the slightest bit jealous. One day my oldest sister came home from school early, having left at recess in the afternoon (this was one of the days when I was not in attendance), her big, blue eyes red and inflamed and her cheeks stained and swollen from crying. I remember she sat down at the kitchen table, the kitchen and dining room being in one, and cried aloud as she fumbled with the oiled cloth and told how the children had "made fun" of her and how some of the older girls with whom she did not get along teased her about the teacher. She blubbered and writhed and my mother only hissed and grunted, her chief method of punishing Willie, for my sister was named after my father William Isaac Beasley, for her "longheadedness." The truth of the matter was that Willie was in love with the teacher (I knew it then as I know it now), and was hurt in a way that a girl of seventeen is likely to be wounded in such matters, and was pouring out her sorrows to a woman, who, although her mother, was unable to act the mother's part, because for several years past they had quarreled and exercised their spite against one another like enemy children. This incident aroused a curious emotion in me, for I realized that my sister was sorely hurt and yet I had known almost instinctively, had taken it in with my mother's milk, that there was some great virtue to be attached to being loyal to one's mother. I think it made me sad perhaps because I could not understand it. I don't understand it now either; science has not discovered everything.

The little school was full of shocks as well as interest for me. One day the teacher had to punish one of the Lockhart boys who refused to comply with the teacher's regulations. I see a boy; I think he was wearing long trousers, clinging to a long-slatted bench, quarreling and struggling with the teacher who was lashing him with a heavy strap, cutting at his fingers which clasped the slats of the bench. There was a big story to tell at supper that night and I remember that one of the boys closed the narrative by, "An' Maw, all the little girls wuz cryin' out loud." Then the law was laid down and that was, as was repeated many times afterwards, "If enny of you young uns ever cause that teacher enny trouble and he 'as to lick you and I find it out, I'll double the dose when you come home."

⟵✦

This community near Wheat, Texas, was full of religious people, people who followed the debates between the Campbellites and the Baptists, who delved into the profundities as to whether or not baptism was essential to salvation. On such occasions, long-haired preachers were invited to the country homes for chicken dinners, such a gathering being necessary every spring or summer to quicken the souls of men and supply the tooth of the parson with the best jelly and the most delicious chicken pie the housewives were able to prepare. Once I rode behind my oldest sister who went to pay a visit to a nearby neighbor. The woman asked her which church, Baptist or Campbellite, her parents belonged to. "They don't belong to no church," said my sister while the woman looked surprised, "they are free thinkers...Ma believes something from both of them." I was immensely pleased that my sister knew such a big word as free thinkers, though I had no conception of its meaning.

Then the three oldest children used to go to Sunday School on

Sunday afternoons and to "singing," the latter my father referred to as a courting school. Nearly all the older children had Sunday suits, and my oldest brother was supplied with cravat and four-inhand, which he guarded in his small brass-knobbed trunk as an old maid watches after her love letters. Sometimes when he was ready for "singing," his great plaid tie, of various colors, showing at his throat, my mother looked on him with great admiration. I seem to hear her now, "I don't cair what you say, that he's an idiot or what you please, he's got more good mother wit than all the rest of the boys put together—looks a powerful lot lak' yer uncle Mack." (The word "mother wit" used to awe me, I suppose my mother used it to describe a reproduction of her personal characteristics in her boy.) To look like the Ficklins, my mother's people, was to be at once immune from all the arrows and slings of the tongue of this plump and apparently harmless matron, who sometimes seemed to feel the greatest antagonism towards her offspring for no better reason than that they greatly resembled their father. My oldest brother acted as a sort of spy, and I think exercised his office with some fairness, for my mother, as I was aware that he reported the conduct of the younger ones at school and church to her, my mother rarely going anywhere, at least not frequently enough to know all the details which daily and weekly transpired concerning her children.

—←✦

Then, one day something happened. I stood at my mother's bedside early in the morning, and although it was July, I seem to have been cold as I shivered there in my bare feet. A red, soft, little wad lay near her and wriggled a little. I was astonished. Besides my mother looked very ill. An itching desire made me want to stroke its hair, but I was not permitted to touch it. The drawl in my own voice sounds in my ears now, "Maw, where did you git that little baby?" She answered that the doctor had brought it to her during the night in his saddle-bags. Nearly everyone in that section of the country rode horseback and usually carried a pair of bags attached at the back of his saddle. I can't recall that it occurred to me to question this baby-in-the-saddlebag theory. She talked a bit to herself saying that the poor little thing's head was "mashed out of shape" a little but that she would rub it back in place. Perhaps it would not live, and then she enumerated her babies, with the perplexity of a sick woman and with a note of sadness as she spoke. This was the eleventh one.

But the baby proved to be very much alive, growing and requiring a lot of attention, and I was made its nursemaid. A little chair was bought especially for me, in which I used to sit and rock the baby during the long hours when practically everyone older than myself was at work in the field, while my mother prepared the meals and did all the sewing and patching for the family. Fancy what the patching alone amounted to. There were five boys to "patch for" and make over old trousers for, besides my oldest sister never learned to sew at an early age and so my mother had to make all her clothes until she was almost grown, as well as those of the other girls and the babies. Sometimes she would work into the night after the whole household had been snoring for hours.

We stayed here until the second crop was gathered, I think, and my father, finding the "grubbing" too difficult and requiring too much time, or the grass too dry, or the summers too hot, or the cotton crop too little, or the water too mineral or "gyp," or that the horses were getting "locoed," or the cows didn't bear calves fast enough— something or other was always wrong with the big central taps of the resources of life—began to talk of "pulling up" and going to look for another place. Although my mother was never what I should call a happy woman, as my earliest remembrances are of how she had been "dragged down" and how hard life had been since she had been in the Beasley family, she became more depressed and almost melancholy at such talk. If there was anything wrong with the farming, there was wood to be hauled to the townspeople; there was "freighting" to be done, that is hauling goods from the railway center to the little country town; besides this was a great cattle country, my father having already a small herd of young cows and a number of horses and mules, the young stock and especially the "calf crop" in another year would make farming only as a minor industry, unnecessary.

Months passed and the cotton and maize were harvested. I picked my first pounds of cotton at odd times when my mother or some of the others took care of Martha Washington, for that is what my mother called her having about "run out" of names by the time the fifth daughter arrived. One day my father returned from town after selling the cotton; he walked with a slight stagger but seemed in the best of spirits. That is, a smile, if a little bitter, nevertheless curved his lips and radiated his face as he sat by the fireplace and told what his wife considered vulgar (in the sense of obscene) stories. But we children were always a little terrified; whether or not he smiled had no special significance for us, as he was just as likely to turn to storming and swearing the next minute if anything angered him. My mother was angry and pouting, hissing and turning the corners of her mouth down, "I declare to God, there's never been no woman mistreated as I've been." Some of the older children whispered, "Pa's drunk." All talked little or in hushed tones, and my parents did not speak to one another. I felt that I was thinking and acting just like my mother, at least I would have liked to have assumed her attitude as I walked about the room near the fireplace; and if I registered any other emotions at this time, they were fear and sadness.

—←✶

Other remembrances at this place occur to me: one being my oldest sister's first real sweetheart, a country boy about her own age, whom my mother declared was a half-idiot, who just had to shake hands with my sister every single time he came, no matter how often, and every time they parted. Sometimes they sat in the kitchen and talked and I remember this farewell handshaking was rather lingering and caressing... My mother sometimes made the most extraordinary delicacies for birthday and Christmas parties, my third sister receiving a huge coconut cake for her birthday this year, making some of us jealous, particularly myself, as I had never had a birthday cake in all my life (not even to this day if I remember correctly). But my mother explained that this was because Emma's birthday was near Christmas when she had to do the holiday cooking anyway...

A certain old parson used to come to us for dinner once in a while; I recall him in connection with his kissing this same sister who was rather playful and would talk back to him when he teased her. He used to take her in his arms and kiss her white neck, getting his whiskers tangled with her light-colored braids. Once in this tumble he bit her a little too hard and made her cry; then she would have nothing to do with him. This incident gave me a tremendous sensation. There was some sexual feeling mixed with it. I understood much of my mother's comment concerning it and felt something strange in the expression on her face when she told my sister to keep away from the old preacher.

Another thing which stands out in my mind was a hat which my father purchased for my mother, an incident which she repeated for years, just as she repeated a similar incident which had occurred several years previously. The hat was either all red or trimmed with red, I forget which; at any rate red was a color which my mother thought a woman of her years, some of whose children were already grown, should not wear. At least when my father presented her with clothes or hats with color, she was always of the opinion that she should be dressed in black and lavender. She "ripped and snorted," to use my parents' expression with reference to their quarrels, until he took it back, and would talk aloud to herself, apparently when no one was listening, about the time (when the seventh child was a baby) when he went to town and bought her a hat, all covered over with the most ridiculous flowers, as gaudy as a nigger's bonnet, which cost sixty-five cents, for she was clever enough to look at the mark on the ticket. This he brought home, being himself half drunk, and presented to her. This was the way she was treated; no woman had ever lived who had had to put up with what she had had to put up with.

Then there is a story of some one of us talking in his sleep, which recalls also that in one of these primitive houses, my feet, at least my heels, were never warm during the whole winter; some part of me, usually my lower extremities, seems to have been cold at all times during a stretch of several months.

⟵✦

Well, the place in Scurry County was sold; that is my mother had to acquiesce and sign the deed or the contract or whatever was necessary, and then the family moved again, this time to Mitchell County, another small distance, settling near Cuthbert, Texas. The Beasley family went through the same round of living; there were crops planted and harvested, cotton to pick in which all were engaged except my mother, and myself and the two babies younger than myself, for at this period I was still the "nu'se." (My mother never put the "r" in the word nurse. She would say, "One of these children'll have to nu'se the baby for me.") I chafed under this duty but was usually amenable to reason and accepted it when I was reminded by my mother and second and third sisters that I also was once a baby and had to be rocked, though I considered it rather cruel of them to mention such unpleasantnesses. My sisters went into great detail, in describing how one sat in a big plain stiff-backed chair holding me, the other pulling the chair back and forth with tremendous jolts, while I cried and did all the things which babies do to keep little girl nursemaid sisters from having a moment of peace from breakfast until dark. Indeed, they both thought they might have scars on their backs, bruises which this stiff-backed chair had made.

But it was not all drudgery, for after several months the country school opened and I with the others attended for four months. During this time, I "went through" the first, second, third, and a good part of the fourth readers, and if no one took any particular interest in me or praised me, it did not matter so much for I was immensely pleased with myself. For I could not only read with a voice loud enough to attract the whole school, but I memorized long passages, I could spell, and I could write; and it gave me the greatest happiness. I remember that most of the children used to have great fear and stage fright but at this time I had no such fear; I was only too delighted at an opportunity of speaking, besides it made me popular.

It happened again. My mother bore another child at this place, another girl, making six boys and six girls. This happened in July also, just two years since the last baby was born. I remember it distinctly, it was very hot; I entered the room where my mother and her red baby lay, having just returned from the neighbor's. My two oldest sisters were there also. "This is the last one," she said in a voice angry and quarrelsome. My father entered the room and said something, it seems, about the medicine left for her, to which she made answer in a way showing her full hatred and contempt for him. Not daring to "storm at her" in his usual way for her talk, he went and sat on the porch, hung his head, grew a little smaller; and it seemed to me that I wanted to sneer at him also. This is the first time I remember seeing my father defeated in their horrifying and disgusting domestic relations.

Sunday School was introduced to me at this time, being held in the little church not far from the schoolhouse and some two miles from our place. When the school was not in session, the Sunday School took its place for me. I remember weeping copiously if I were kept at home, just as, later on, I used to cry if anything happened to detain me from school. My attitude towards the two schools was about the same, only of course we did not jump the rope and run and yell at the Sunday School, but the pleasure for me was the same. There was reading of Bible stories and memorizing verses, the latter of which I adored speaking before the class, as I was sure to attract some attention and gain some praise. I think the word "sin" had no relation to me as yet, and so I was rather free and quite happy. Once, though, I remember going away from the house disturbed, as my mother suggested in my presence that perhaps my father would kill her someday when we were all away at Sunday School. My parents, I remember, were having the usual quarrel and my mother was pouting and refusing to answer when he spoke to her, "acting the damn fool" as my father would say.

—✦—

My father used to work sometimes in a blacksmith shop in Cuthbert, Texas, and it occurs to me now that he always had a small shop of his own on the farms where we have lived. Once he perfected an old hack, a sort of buckboard, which he or someone suggested my mother should have to go to church in. This vehicle had a plain straight bed, enough room for three seats supported by springs, and wheels which seemed especially delicate to me as we had been accustomed to go about, to singings, to Sunday School, to town, to parties or wherenot, in an old farm wagon with thick, stocky wheels, whose axles oozed with grease. In my childish fancy, I could see that conditions were looking up for us and thought we should certainly be held in much greater esteem by the neighbors for having such a new and thrifty-looking vehicle. A curious picture is associated in my mind with this vehicle, and that is of my mother now exceedingly fat, this being just before or just after she had borne her twelfth child, dressed in black and wearing a black grandmother's bonnet with a small frill of lavender at the front of it, getting seated with much difficulty in this hack. She was still a few years under forty, perhaps thirty-seven.

———

The older children had many friends in the community, were liked by almost everyone and, it seems to me, must have had a very good time. They went to "singing dances" where they danced the old square dances, the round dances where the couple waltzed or two-stepped together being held as indecent; courted and were courted; and took part in all the life of work and play in the community. I remember well what happened to my second sister. The four children older than herself having "gone with the girls" and having had many beaux, it was now time for the second daughter, a girl of square build and large bones, the brunette of the family (for she had black hair, skin almost olive, and gray eyes), to enter the field of lovemaking.

It happened at school. My third sister and myself were waiting for her to come out of the schoolhouse, as the school children having been let out had nearly all started well on their way home. And when she did not answer our call we went back to the window of the schoolhouse, and my sister pulled herself up at the window to see what the second sister was doing. She took a long look and then slid back to the ground, a little startled and perhaps a little jealous, saying,

"Yes, I'm gonna tell Ma on her…letting Doc kiss her." After a bit the boy and girl emerged looking rather sheepish, as we explained later, and we were all off for home. I don't remember that I had any part in relating this story to my mother, perhaps I helped to verify it. But when my father came in from his work at sundown, my mother after some words and sniffing as though she expected the whole lot to turn out "wrong" if a tight rein were not held over them, said to my father, "Now, Bill, you've got to whip that child… Some of these children'll be ruined etc. etc. She's been lettin' Doc Handley hug and kiss her," and she puffed and said she was not able to do it herself. This sister was always tremendously willful, and it is my recollection that, when she was questioned about this affair, she would not answer. So my father took the whip which he used on his horses and began striking her, and because she was angry and set her teeth and would not cry, he beat her "in an inch of her life."

I think I did not witness all of this terrible scene as my mother sent us out, but I followed my sister to the privy afterwards, for the toilet house was built several yards from the house, after my father had finished his work on her. I could see blood on the excrement from the side of the privy as I passed which terrified me, although I had been in the toilet with my oldest sister when she was menstruating and fancied I knew what was happening to her. I pushed the door in and there she sat trembling, with drops of water falling from her nose. "Get out o' here, you little fool," cried she, and banged the door on me. If I had gone in with an attitude of saying, "I hope you won't kiss any more boys" or telling her she ought to "watch out" (with the slightest smile on my lips), I not only felt myself to be low and mean, but I wanted to weep with her now. She was not yet fourteen, yet her body had assumed the curves which puberty brings, and she was full of sentiment and capable of great emotions... Although there was talk of matches being made for the two oldest children, neither of them came off, the only thrill of this sort for me being their description of the schoolmaster's wedding which they had attended.

—≮≉

A year or two passed at this place and my father having found everything wrong with the land, stock, water, people, government, and whatnot in Mitchell County, it was decreed that the Beasley family, now consisting of fourteen people, a man and his wife and six sons and six daughters, must move again. This time the whole family was to be taken "prospecting" as my father did not know where we would "settle." There was quarreling over signing the deed of sale as my mother did not want to move, but finally this transaction was agreed to and signed, and all was made ready for travelling. Everything was sold, the place, the stock, that is cows, pigs, and the horses not needed for travel, the sale amounting to $3,300 as I remember it. I recall the day we started; it was for me another experience with a mixture of feelings. Because my mother was unhappy at going, I too did not wish to appear too eager, and when my father asked if I did not like "moving" when I climbed up beside him on one of the big wagons, I wanted, I think, to wear an expression like my mother's and to deny that I did, but I hear my answer now in my mind's ear the almost invariable, "Yes, Sir." I always felt the least bit of warmth when he addressed his children as "son" or "daughter," the girls, from the baby to the oldest one, were always "daughter" unless he happened to be in one of his rages. So when on this morning he spat his tobacco far and, reflectively, took down the reins from the brake of the double sideboard wagon, climbed up to the high seat and asked, "Daughter, don't you like travelling?" I can well guess what my answer must have been.

Our caravan made quite a long train, for there were some three wagons and a hack besides a few extra horses; one wagon had a grub box attached and all the necessary utensils for camping, all having bed springs arranged at the top of the sideboards, being the beds for my mother and father, the girls and the babies; while the older boys slept on the tent which they used as a sort of sleeping bag. When we were getting packed up for the moving I felt a sharp pain of sadness, as I often did from the time I was conscious; this time it was in connection with putting away in the bottom of the wagon all the old schoolbooks with the exception of one or two which were left in the wagon as sort of play things and which I soon grew tired of. The wind was blowing, that is a sandstorm was raging, I think, at the time packing was being done; I sometimes feel a chill when the picture comes to my mind.

For a whole year my father "drug" his family around, as my mother termed it, travelling towards the Southwest and covering a course of several hundred miles before we had finished. There was camping in the open; black skillets and pans were hauled out and placed over a blazing fire or over an outdoor stove, if we remained in a place long enough for such an arrangement; a large jar full of sourdough was produced for making the bread, sometimes baked, sometimes prepared as pan cakes; and other requisites as to food were had. Nothing was ever quite happy in those days in spite of many pictures of scenes and experiences which appear to give some pleasure; there was always some mixing of fear, embarrassment, shame, or sadness in practically everything which came to me. One of the scenes which I recall, as our covered wagons made their way to the Southwest, was the country about the town called Paint Rock, where the riverbanks and hills were of red sandstone. I remember the many questions, "How far is it to Paint Rock?" etc., asked of those whom we passed in the road, and that my father sometimes halted the caravan for an hour or two, standing with his foot on the axle of the wheel, spitting his tobacco far, and exchanging comments of the country and asking questions. He would stand there in his high boots, big gray Stetson hat and talk, while my mother would be hissing and quarreling in the next wagon, and wondering why we did not move on, and why on earth any decent white man wanted to drag his family around the country in such a fashion. And she would sometimes add with sniffs or slurs or sneers or tears that at least she was "not raised that way."

At some one of these places, I remember we stayed for several weeks. Here an old man who was referred to as an infidel used to come to our wagons to talk. There was talk of a god or the lack of a god, as the case may be, and then this old man was always predicting the world's destruction and saying that a comet or something was going to destroy the world, all of us. This was a great terror for me which was made all the more real because there was no one in this whole lot of thirteen people to whom I cared to confide my fears. I simply kept silent wondering how this thing would ever turn out, would fire begin to rain on the earth someday? And in the evening I would climb into the big wagon to go to bed and would lie there seeing great red blazes, the whole heavens one great rolling fire, trembling sometimes for hours with the most intense terror which racked and exhausted me until I was able to sleep. The slightest excitement sent me off into the wildest imaginations and yet there was no one among us who could do more than interpret the primer or the most elementary book, not to speak of imaginative stories.

For some weeks we were camped in a great grove of trees below San Angelo, a beautiful country with streams and green pastures and pecan groves. My father talked of buying some land here, and I remember my mother dressed up to go out and talk with the landowner about it, but my father declared the man was trying "to skin" him out of all his money and so the matter closed. We frequently met other "campers" who visited us and whom we sometimes visited; occasionally some townswoman would invite us to come and talk. Once when my mother went out to see a neighbor, she chose me to go with her. In secret I wished terribly that the people would think that I was the only child my mother had, and I think if I had been more intimate with my mother I should loved to have told her to make believe in some clever way that I made up the sum total of her progeny and that considering everything by and large we were very extraordinary people; it seemed to me very fitting that she should have just one child, myself; the picture was complete when she and I walked off together. That same time we almost stumbled on a rattlesnake and I was frightened almost into a convulsion. I recall distinctly that something sympathetic came out of my mother when she saw my terror, it was either what she said then or what she said afterwards to the family, that made me know that she sympathized with my tears on coming so near to the ugly, hissing snake.

Here my second brother quarreled with my father; there were a few loud words and earsplitting curses exchanged; my brother now about seventeen threatened to leave. All of this, but nothing happened.

Travelling through all that beautiful stretch of country towards the southwest of Texas, passing groves and banks and rocky streams and hills and great stretches of pastures and fields, we came at last to a little town, as yet not much more than a post office and a few stores. Somewhere near this town, Eldorado, in Tom Green County where we were camping, I remember that my father and brothers brought many good things to eat to the camp, among them being honey, which was brought in in gallon pails, former receptacles for molasses. Sometimes it was wild honey which they had actually found themselves and sometimes they bought of others who had "smoked out a honey tree." It seems to me now that there was always plenty to eat during these days of journeying and camping—rabbit, cottontail, the young of which is more delicious than chicken; meat such as veal, beef, and pork which they secured from time to time; and a few times there was venison, the meat of wild deer. In those days, food was frightfully delicious to me and the wild meat, fish, honey, syrup, and occasionally milk which was brought to the camp together with the hot bread, cooked in the open, and the steaming coffee, seems to me now everything which hungry people require.

~✦

Here my father saw a chance to earn some money; at least so he said (but my mother afterwards declared that he wanted to stay in Eldorado because there were plenty of saloons) and so he secured a small house for the family, he himself working part of the time in a blacksmith shop, and later he and the older boys using the teams for working the road. My mother also did not wish to be idle; besides there were three daughters old enough to do considerable work and all were anxious for pin money. One day I went with her to a large house, near the town, where a ranchman lived. The dwelling appeared to me of colossal size inasmuch as there were two stories with big windows and a large roof, the white painting and the window blinds giving it a certain dignity. There was a large yard and garden and a small pasture where two young spotted deer were playing, a pair of most adorable creatures. But with this I could not be proud and natural; my heart and nervous system were cramped.

There was some stifling embarrassment; my mother was going to talk with the woman of the house about doing her washing. I remember how I hated to go out to the backyard where a great pile of dirty clothes was lying; afterwards my mother complained that she was treated like a servant and I think she changed her customer, for cowboys about the country used to bring their shirts, cuffs, and collars to be laundered, most of the work being done by my older sisters. My father objected to this work, if I remember correctly, and cursed and swore, though he swore about so many happenings, that it is difficult for me to differentiate as to the occasions; my second brother also put in a word of protest. But my mother replied that my father never gave her money, moreover she never knew what funds he possessed. Besides, "all work was honorable," a phrase which she used in talking the matter over with my sisters. I liked seeing these cow-punchers come to the house, but I hated the reason for their coming.

There was a great dance hall in the town where young and old met almost every Saturday evening for the usual promenades, square dances, the waltz, schottische, and two-step, this being my first observation of two young people dancing together. The floor was waxed and so slippery that it gave one a fright to walk on it. I think it was the Fourth of July dancing which my mother allowed us to see. There was much whispering between her and my oldest sister about how some of the young women of the town and surrounding country behaved, and about the shamelessness of girls who wore their dancing frocks so low at the front as to show a part of their breasts. Then there was horse racing, swearing, and whisky drinking, all of which were special contributions to the life in Eldorado.

In the midst of all this an evangelist appeared to tell the people of their wickedness. They made a great tent and the people came for days and days to listen to his descriptions of how God damned people's souls and how it was necessary to repent and the like. One Sunday afternoon, after a long day of feasting and preaching, the parson called on the people to testify, that is he would point out this one and that one saying, "And what is your cross, Sister? Or Brother, what is *your* cross?" A woman testified and said she had lost her husband who had recently died, and that she had two sons whom she wished to bring up for the Lord, but it was very difficult. This was her cross. While she was saying this in a loud tremulous voice with tears in her eyes, my face was also streaming with tears which I caught up quickly as soon as I saw the preacher was pointing towards the place near the rostrum where my father with a few other men with skeptical faces were squatting. That is, he was apparently sitting on the heel of one boot with the hands on the opposite knee, perhaps whittling a piece of a tree or playing with his hat. At this age (about eight years) or even before, I had begun to feel embarrassment for practically every member of the family, and my father was no exception, for I felt ashamed of what he might say when the time came for the finger to be pointed at him. "Brother, what is your cross?" asked the evangelist. My father deposited a great mouthful of tobacco juice in the soft dirt before him and said simply, "Sir, all trials and temptations." This astonished me for I had never heard him talk about trials and temptations in my life; in fact, I had never heard anyone use such words. Afterwards my mother sneered—in secret, of course—about his words, and insinuated that it was all hypocrisy, that the Beasleys were all like that; for example "ole Doctor Beasley" (my father's father) would go to church and Sunday School, pray and testify in public, and then go home and beat his wife.

——

After several months in Eldorado, we were loaded up again and started back to central Texas. The old "grub box" was again attached to the back of a double side-boarded wagon, which held the victuals ("grub"), usually consisting of plenty of bacon, coffee, sugar, and other staples and a large crock, a stone pot in which the yeast worked its miracles with the sourdough. This jar of yeast was absolutely necessary as we sometimes travelled for days without being able to get milk for the making of bread. Then the furniture and bedding were all stacked in and the bows put on the wagon and then the sheets, for they were as usual the "prairie schooners."

I recall an incident at this time or possibly before which was to me a form of torture. This was getting up in the mornings. I slept on a little square, at the head of my parents' bed in one of the wagons, which was covered with my mother's favorite old featherbed. In the morning the boys would get up before sunup, unhobble the horses and mules, harness them, and roll up their ducking tent on which they slept, while my mother and sisters made their beds and prepared the breakfast. After all this was well underway my second and third sisters (who seemed to take a great delight in torturing me as did also my brothers) would come and crawl up to my place in the wagon to wake me. If one has never been very, very sleepy in one's whole life and has never slept in a warm bed in the open air, soft and invigorating as I remember that to have been, it will be difficult to describe this torturous incident. For example, my sisters would come and rouse me; I would answer, and then go back to sleep. Suddenly they would come again and pull my hair, consisting of three or four little brown pigtails, tickle my ribs or the bottom of my feet until I became so angry that the tears streamed from my eyes; or worst of all uncover me in that cool, dewy, morning air which requires blankets during the night, and sprinkle cold water on me. I don't know why I was so sleepy, perhaps it was because I stayed awake in the first part of the night just because I was afraid or cold inside me. Perhaps I was tired from thinking about hell and seeing those great red flames which were lapping up the earth after the manner of the predictions of the old "infidel." At any rate, I wished some punishment not unlike hellfire visited on my sisters, for I wished they were dead.

During these mornings the sun rose on thick stiff grass and low bushes trembling with dew; a curious sound accompanied by its echo might be heard, but the Beasleys were generally oblivious to all except the breakfast and the "making of their tents." My mother was generally angry during these journeys as "she was not brought up that way" and was always reminding us when my father was not listening that only a low, mean man would "drag his family around" like that, that he had often cursed her and "threatened that he would bring her to sufferance." My father was usually silent, unless he was at the boiling point of anger when he stormed and cursed. Once in a great while there was a fight between some of the boys, or some one of the older ones struck the little ones on the head or gave him a terrible kicking... My second and third sisters whispered together a lot about being thirteen or when one of them would be or was thirteen.

One day about this time when I was asleep in a tent or in some house or old wagon yard, as was often the case when we were camped, my second brother, who was then, I think, nearly twenty years old, came and lay by me and tried to wake me for some sexual communication. When I woke and saw his penis which he had laid against my legs, I was frightened, perhaps at the size of it as much as anything, and filled with disgust and shame—shame that almost consumed me with frightfulness and horror. I cried out at first and my brother seemed frightened (although we were alone in the room) and then I turned away from him and feigned sleep; he left me and went to his own bed. I remember that I had a strong sexual desire at this time, a desire which I experienced at the age of five or six when sexual energy was so great in me that I used to press something against myself trying to obtain gratification, but this desire was also accompanied by great shame and horror that made one's flesh shrivel up or appear to crack as with some dreadful malady.

The vow which I made to myself then was similar in seriousness to me to an experience which I had when I was twelve (some three years later) which I afterwards referred to as my "conversion." And that vow was that in spite of my desire, this thing should never happen to me again; in three years I would be twelve and then the next was thirteen; and although I did not know what being "thirteen" meant in any special way, I well understood from my sisters' whisperings and significant glances that something important, perhaps awful, happened to one then; I would keep away from all this. Besides I had a great deal of contempt for my three oldest brothers; I could spell better than any of them unless it was my second brother, and on one occasion I had "spelled down" the whole lot of them. Then my fourth and fifth brothers, a few years older than myself, were no longer of great sexual interest to me as competition had already developed between us not only as to who could read, write, and memorize with greatest efficiency, but also as to our physical strength. From the age of seven or eight to about eleven, I used to have from time to time terrible fights—fist fighting, hair pulling, and the like—with these two boys, in which bouts I often proved a very good match for them. In fact, I think the intense and consuming sex energy which I felt at my earliest recollections, at four years or perhaps even before, which was far greater, consuming far more of my conscious desires than that of food hunger, began to diminish as soon as I learned to read at the age of five. At least it appears to me now that, during those first few months of reading, my sex energy was held completely in abeyance.

To end the journey, we finally arrived in Nolan County where my father bought a lease of a section of land near Roscoe, Texas. He had spent most of the three thousand dollars which we started out with, so my mother explained later, and had not enough money to buy land and was forced to rent a farm for a time.

—✦

The year in Nolan County was full of torment. My oldest sister was always "in the outs" with my mother; they quarreled in most furious tones calling out to one another, "You are a liar," in some of their disputes. Sometimes my sister would cry for a whole day at a time and go for a long walk in the pasture alone. Other times my mother would hold forth for a whole afternoon with her daughters recounting some terrible and disgusting dispute with my father, telling how he had treated her when she was pregnant with such and such a child; or how his people had acted, or how his sister "ole Alice Beasley" had taught her children when they were very young and helpless all the devilry of Satan and his hell. (Here she was referring to my father's sister who had invited and encouraged sexual intercourse among the oldest children. My mother said that Alice Beasley had showed the children when they were very young everything about sexual matters.

In fact, though she was several years their senior, she had had sexual relations with the little boys, my oldest brothers.)

Once when she was recounting her experiences in the Beasley family, my father appeared at the door, having come from the field to get a drink of water. He evidently had listened while he was drinking, for I remember his fierce eyes startled me as he put his head in at the door and just stared at my mother for a minute. Then he went away and after a few minutes returned again only to hear my mother's harangue as she and her daughters quilted or patched. This time he swore and "popped his fists" at her for talking about "his people" in this manner. My mother acted like a guilty schoolgirl—smirked after he had gone and said it was all the truth.

The older boys went away during the year to help drill wells. I remember being astonished at my mother's kissing her third son on his return and that one of the young ones said to me in great amazement, "Did you see Maw kiss Rush?" The babies were the only members of the family who received any kisses at our house. After a time the others returned, full of stories of how the third brother, a tall young fellow, about six feet in height, of eighteen or nineteen years, had entertained the drill hands with his jokes and stories and how they had all nicknamed him "Rusty," some calling him "Irish." This latter appellation was given him because of his dark auburn hair, large blue eyes, and reddish complexion which they imagined had something to do with the funny stories he told. I do not remember his stories, I only remember that we laughed a great deal at what he said, particularly at the second table (all the little ones had to wait for their meals until the second table) where he often sat at the head. If it were supper we usually munched on sour milk "clabber" and corn bread, and between the great spoonfuls of this mixture in large glass goblets which we brought to our mouths, there was much cackling and loud laughter. Perhaps it was only because he had said that if he married a slim wife, he would surely feed her "condition powders," a medicine given to lean horses to fatten them. Often the amusing expression on his face betrayed a joke and we laughed when he had said nothing. It was the same at the time of my earliest recollection, at three or four years, when a whole row of little Beasleys sat on a bench before an oil-clothed table with goblets and spoons and laughed at his remarks about what he was eating or how he was eating.

During the winter months the country school began and after a little while none of the children seemed especially interested except myself. It was like cutting me with a knife to say that I could not go to school or attend the Sunday School. One morning it was cold and sleeting and no one wanted to go to the little schoolhouse some two miles away. Having moved them with my tears, my mother decided that my third brother should accompany me. I remember how we were wrapped up, with books strapped to us and my brother with the dinner pail; and how my mother spit at the door (for she sometimes took a little snuff which she explained was for her bad teeth), sniffed, and told my brother to take care of me. Before we started, she faced him squarely with, "Do you understand me Rush...I want you to take care of this child…treat her right." "Yes, ma'am," replied my brother and we set off. I was afraid of him and kept about two arm lengths from him all the way, for my mother's securing from him this strict promise made me wonder whether she knew what he once did to me when I was a baby back in Coleman County. It happened about the time of my first experience which I have already related, and I thought I should never be able to use my legs again. I seemed to have shriveled up while he became a giant.

At this school I learned "to do fractions," studied geography, and before the year was out had skimmed through a fifth or sixth reader and was allowed in the Texas history class. I contrast now my attitude and interest in school with that of my two older sisters. I was nearly always seriously at work, or competing with someone or showing off. They spent most of their time giggling which annoyed the teacher tremendously.

⟵✦

Although my father always had a violin and was considered quite a good fiddler, we had never owned an organ or a piano. So after the first crop was harvested, the girls having picked a good share of the cotton, my mother and sisters began to beg of my father to buy an organ. It was finally purchased, but my oldest sister who was most anxious for it seemed incapable of learning to play it. In fact, she was never brilliant a moment in her life. My second sister was discovered to be the musician of the family, that is she went about it seriously. My third brother who sometimes played my father's fiddle, could play the organ "by ear," as could also my third sister. I recall that as soon as my second sister had shown me some chords, my father asked me to accompany his very jiggy pieces which he sawed out on his old violin. How proud I was when they screwed the stool down so that my feet could touch the pedals and stretched out my fingers over the chords on the keyboard! But I was jealous of my second sister, a girl now about sixteen years old and six years my senior, for she was going to take lessons. I was relieved somewhat, though, by the promise of my mother, always a very thrifty woman, that as soon as my sister learned the notes, she would teach them to me. Then there was a singing school where I learned the square notes and could sing the second part, the alto of many of the absurd, evangelistic songs which were flooding the country churches at that time.

My sister paid for her music lessons in wood, most of which she chopped down and loaded herself and secured one of the younger boys to drive it to town, Roscoe, where her teacher, Mrs. Underwood, lived. She learned the notes and could play several pieces and her teacher praised and encouraged her a great deal. One Sunday the Underwoods (the music teacher and her husband) were invited to dinner. I remember all the cleaning was left until the morning of their arrival. My mother was horrified, angry, and almost in tears. For everything was in such a mess that they would think us totally uncivilized. There was a great spot just before the front door (over which the visitors would have to pass for entrance) where my father had urinated during the night. This he always did in spite of my mother's pleadings, naggings, or protests. Then he chewed tobacco and would spit all over the stove, which had to be cleaned. If he blew his nose without the use of a handkerchief while he was standing in the door or near the house, he would wipe his fingers on the part of the house nearest him. If he cleared his throat while in bed, he spat on the nearest wall. All this in spite of twenty-five years of protest from my mother who wanted to be and often succeeded in being the essence of cleanliness. She would work and talk and nag and end it all by saying, "Cleanliness is next to godliness." The place had to be cleaned up by eleven or twelve o'clock when the visitors were expected; and they set me to scrubbing off the spots on the front entrance which showed very plainly, as the house was almost new when we moved into it; and I put some new dirt over the place in the yard. The inside of the house was put in order and the dinner prepared. I remember what shame and embarrassment all this gave me, especially when I found that my efforts at cleaning the front wall would leave the yard immediately in front of the door perfectly muddy.

The visitors entered the living room where my father sat—cross-legged with the baby in his arms, his hair roached high and whiskers combed unusually well—to receive them. He rose half forward, shook hands with them, then sat and resumed his tobacco chewing, depositing mouthfuls this time in the ashes, while the others took their wraps and gave them seats near the stove.

The husband began to question my father about affairs of the day—it seems they had met in a blacksmith's shop in Roscoe—and the way in which they received his answers made me think they had considerable admiration for him. At any rate the music teacher seemed especially pleased with him, though this could have been for other than the reason I had assigned, which was that she looked upon my father as a clever and well-appearing, perhaps even handsome, man. It was one of the few times, perhaps the only time, during my first ten years when we lived with my father, that I felt any pride in him.

My sister finally had to give up her lessons as she had a desperate quarrel with my father about the wood, the cutting of which he objected to. I remember how angry she was and how finally she was saddened by this incident.

Everything became sad or desperate; my parents were quarreling furiously or not speaking; my oldest sister was always crying; my mother was threatening to separate from my father; all were in a quandary. My oldest brother declared one day that there was going to be a killing over all this; and as for myself, I was frightened almost into prostration, so much so that I would forget what I was told to do. Once when I had forgotten what my mother had directed (and I assure you it was because I was thinking of the terrible and awful conditions under which we were living) she slapped me, striking the side of my face with so much force as to turn my head to the side and almost wrenching my neck. She screamed at me, saying I was going to be just like Willie (my oldest sister), and to be like Willie was to be like "that ole Alice Beasley," my father's youngest sister; and to be like "that ole Alice Beasley" was to be the lowest type of female my mother was capable of conceiving of. I will not say that at the age of ten years I understood everything just as I have written it here, but the central thought of nearly all her insinuations, against whomever they were directed, was perfectly clear to me.

———≺✶

In the midst of this awful family strife, though the worst of it came afterwards, my mother's thirteenth child was born, a plump healthy boy, her seventh son. We were sent away to the neighbors overnight and returned the next day to find an addition to the family. I think I was the first to enter the room. The first thing which I noticed was a large blood stain on the floor near the bed which had not been thoroughly washed up. Then I looked at the woman between the white bed clothes. "She is dead," I thought. Then I looked again, and I saw that her eyes moved. Her hands and face were completely lacking in color; there didn't seem to be a drop of blood in her body—the body of an ordinarily corpulent and red-faced woman. The blue lips parted and she told me to come and look at "your little brother." After a bit she began to talk to herself or to whomever would listen to her something after this manner: "Now I know how bad I look... My God! I wish you could-a seen that child's face when she looked at me...she was as white as a sheet and her jaws jes' dropped... She thought I was dead…I shore come mighty near passing over and Ole Doctor Geiger told yer Daddy so… He told 'im that he guessed if the men had to bear some of the babies there wouldn't be so many… Yer Daddy just hung his head like a sneak… Said *his* wife had had five, but, my God, thirteen!…" It was like having a corpse revive and speak.

My mother had two ardent and loyal friends in my second and third sisters. I think they would have gladly died for her, or murdered their own father on her behalf if they had found it necessary. They, of course, knew about the arrival of this child, my mother having confided and talked over many things with them; they had taken over the entire management of the house, chickens, cows, etc., under my mother's directions, months before the confinement. So they continued, assuming the office of nurses in addition. My oldest sister did not speak to my mother after returning from the neighbor's and would not look at the baby for some time afterwards. She scolded that my mother had continued bearing children, though they were all growing up in ignorance; and would talk at length in this way, in spite of the fact that she never showed any ambition or desire to improve her own education.

I had seen baby clothes being made but was told they were for the neighbor's baby, and at another time was informed that they were for my little brother; this without any further explanation puzzled me, but if I questioned too much I was sure to be sent away with a smack. But here was the baby. The mystery was solved.

After a few weeks when my mother was better, she instructed

the two girls—about the ages of fourteen and sixteen but of stocky, robust physiques—to sleep in the same bed with her, one on each side. It seems to me now that I have heard them talk of putting the poker and a heavy shovel at the head of their bed, so that in case my father ordered them to go away they would have weapons for defense. About this time, either shortly before or after, my parents came to the final break. It happened this way. My mother was bathing the baby before breakfast one morning and going through her usual rigmarole out loud of how badly she had been treated since she had been in the Beasley family; and was doing what she called in other people, "throwing out slurs" about the man who had begotten her children and who was lying in a bed in the same room. Finally, someone dropped the water basin, or somebody received a good slap in the face and was sent away crying, which roused my father who sat up on the side of the bed, began putting on his clothes and swearing in most violent tones.

In his fury he exposed himself and I caught a glimpse of his private parts, the size of which frightened and awed me. He was cursing my mother and saying, "I never have cared a damn about you…I ought to have my goddamn throat cut for ever living with you." My mother replied quietly that she had known that for many years, and then she began raising her voice and shouting that she would never live with him another day if he cut her throat that minute! A terrible scene of talking, shaking fists, and threats ensued, but my sisters backed themselves towards pokers and knives in the next room, the kitchen, and my father did nothing, though on several occasions during their twenty-five years of married life he had struck her or choked her.

If the days which followed were terrible, the nights were more frightful. My father would sit in a chair at the door until midnight chewing his tobacco and occasionally grunting and calling out "God damn it to hell!" (It seems nothing of any importance now as I write this phrase, but twenty years ago a single oath from my father would throw me almost into a spasm.) My oldest sister went away to Roscoe to work as a sort of housekeeper for a merchant's wife, the chief storekeeper; and my mother conceived a plan of getting away from my father by taking the whole family on a cotton picking tour into Taylor County. So we loaded up again and set out for another trip, though I am almost sure that my mother said she would return after the cotton picking season was over. It seems to me that some of the older boys remained behind with my father to finish "putting up the feed stuff" and then joined us later. After we had all assembled, there were only twelve of us; my second brother had left home before this time and my oldest sister stayed on in Roscoe as a servant, a cook, or a housekeeper, perhaps all in one, while my father was left alone at the farm. When we did not return in a few months he came in search of us. We had camped at a big cotton farm some distance from Abilene, where my mother afterwards bought a small place on the outskirts of the town. Here we had been gathering the cotton for some weeks when my father appeared.

What consternation there was among all of us! It was as though the bottom had fallen out completely. We ran to the house, for my mother was living in the same house with the wife of the owner with whom she had become very friendly. It was as though I was going to the gallows. I ran until I was out of breath and then I was shaking all over. My mother told the woman what had happened. She looked at me and said, "But look at this little girl; she is nearly frightened to death…she will never be more pale when she is in her coffin." Many times afterwards my mother recounted how astonished the woman was that I should have been so worried and frightened, and turned away with tears in her eyes.

⤚✶

We finally settled at Abilene, about the beginning of the year, and as soon as the house and affairs were in sufficient order, all children of school age entered the city school, that is the South Ward. I was placed in the high fourth grade with children of my own age, although in the last country school I had attended classes with students much older than myself. My two brothers just older than myself were placed in the first and second grades, and my sister nearly six years my senior was placed a half grade lower than myself. I was put out at being placed lower than I had expected but, I remember, I consoled myself by saying that I had only attended school about thirteen months in all my life and, of course, this accounted for it. I found many worries, as the teacher, a large, severe woman, demanded many forms of work, especially in arithmetic, which I did not understand. And there was not a soul at home who could help me. I wept a lot over this and finally begged the teacher to allow me to remain after school for some special help. I stayed with the teacher so much, sometimes for two hours after school, that she used to look upon me with some curiosity and asked why I did it. I told her, and she repeated it to many people, that it was because there were so many children at my house who disturbed me so much as to make it impossible for me to prepare my lessons. (There were four children younger than myself, and two boys just older, all loudmouthed, noisy children, none of whom ever looked on any phase of schoolwork seriously; not to mention the others.)

Then, too, I was very nervous. I dreaded the first day of school. The teacher would call out my name so everyone could hear. Maybe everyone would recognize it as a very bad name... Anyway my mother had always contended that the Beasleys were the sorriest people who ever lived. Perhaps when the teacher called out "Gertrude Beasley" they would not hate it so much as laugh at it. And ridicule was more cruel than death. Besides she would ask about my father, and perhaps I would have to tell her aloud before everyone. I was not sure what I should say; would it be better to say simply "he is not living," meaning, of course, that he was not living with us. One of my brothers said he was going to say that he was dead. But my mother finally decided, though she had once suggested it herself, that it was a sin to say that he was dead; though it was quite all right to say that he was not living and then, of course, if one were compelled to explain, one could. Then another question which I abominated was telling the number of children in the family for, although nearly everyone had large families in those days, a family of fifteen as in our case was rare and sometimes called down on one—as the least addition to one's natural embarrassment—a great deal of laughter.

The first months at Abilene were troubled by visits from my father who was never allowed to enter the house but usually stood in the yard or sat on the back porch where he was able to talk with the older boys. Sometimes he was cursing and threatening, other times weeping copiously. Once he asked to see all the children and we were ushered out to the back porch. Again I was trembling with shame and fright. He noticed it and softened into tears while he asked, "W'y, daughter, are you afraid of your pa?"

One day we came home at noon finding my mother weeping almost hysterically; her eyes and cheeks were red and swollen. When she wept I, as many of the others, often wept with her. This time she seemed so hurt that my face was streaming with tears too when I inquired, "Mother, can I do something for you?" (Soon after we arrived in Abilene, finding that nearly all children said "Mother" instead of the long drawn out "Maw," we began to use the former word also.) She told me choking and weeping that there was nothing I could do and then she added: "He plead with me so this mornin.'" I know how I wanted to hear every word my father had uttered but I dared not ask. What did she mean, "He plead with me so…?"

But the first awful chapter of my parents' obscene life together was closed. My mother obtained a divorce. She had talked it over with a Judge Beal of Sweetwater previously, had told how cruel my father had always been; how he had come home in the middle of the night, had cursed her and threatened to kill her. This happened many years previously, nearly twenty. Many times my mother repeated how the lawyer answered her; "W'y Mrs. Beasley, fiad-a been you I'd-a hid behind the door with a gun and a-slipped a bullet through him." She went "before lawyers" in Abilene and told them what she had had to put up with. One of them, a young thunderer, took my mother's case and outlined a procedure. The count which Mr. W. B. Lewis, my mother's attorney at Abilene, brought in the divorce suit was nonsupport. This was the easiest means of gaining her suit and hurt her pride least. Three children, two sisters and a brother aged sixteen, eighteen, and twenty, being my mother's fourth, fifth, and sixth children, appeared in court to swear to my mother's testimony, which was that the family had not been adequately provided for during the past year or so.

My mother gave thanks to Lewis, whom she looked upon as the "smartest little ole man she had ever met," for many years. He had released her from her demon, the sorriest man who ever lived, whom she always had meant to leave. She hadn't done it because she thought it was such a disgrace; she had no place to take her children, and she was afraid he would kill her as he threatened. Twenty-five years of married criminality, official monogamous prostitution, between a "damn fool woman" and the "sorriest man that God ever let live" ended after becoming the parents of thirteen legitimate bastards. I never have understood how my parents could be so heartless. I shall protest against having been brought into the world without any heritage, mental, moral, or physical, to my dying day. What force I have is pure accident, it seems to me. I shall not discuss the riddle of accident here. Then to add to my fury, even as a child, my mother would quote the Bible in defense of her action, letting her eyes show that there was something far worse than she had ever told in connection with my father, saying, "He that provideth not for his own household is worse than an infidel"… "it says worse than an infidel."

My father was never told of the pending suit for divorce; my oldest brother, according to my recollection, told him after the decree had been granted and warned him that the lawyer said he should keep out of the yard.

—✦

After a few months the whole lot of us, including my mother, came down with the measles. We had to call in two doctors from the town and finally, when my mother fell ill, secured a nurse, a woman sixty-four years old who was a marvel of strength and endurance. The first doctor, a man of some sixty years, became enamored of my mother, and then or later there was talk of a second marriage. In the autumn we returned to school, but none of the children older than myself reentered. My two brothers just older than myself never liked school and rebelled against going. Then my third sister began work at a telephone office and my second sister continued her services in the house of a music teacher in Abilene where she received her board, lodging, music lessons, and a little money.

I had to take the examinations before entering my class as I had missed the finals. The day these were completed my teacher and the principal of the school were walking on the playground and came to where I was standing to question me. The teacher asked how many children at my house had had the measles. They laughed at so large a number. I used to think that people employed such questions as a method of hurting me. Then she told me in the presence of the other little girls who "passed" me at school, but with whom I was never very friendly, that I had excellent marks on all my papers and would be able to enter the class with the others. I was happy especially as she had praised me in the presence of my classmates.

Many terrible things happened during the first two or three years of my mother's separation from my father, some of them so terrible that I was sometimes quite exhausted for hours or often for several days on account of the nervous strain. One evening about nine o'clock after all the younger members of the family had gone to sleep, my mother entered the room where the boys slept with a heavy horse whip in her hand (with my two older sisters standing about the doorway armed in some way, I think) and began beating my fourth brother, a boy about fifteen years old, who had just undressed and gone to bed. He cried out to her at first to stop but she was sufficiently armed and reinforced so that he had to take "what was coming to him." I was poring over some schoolbook when this awful crash came, and the thunder and distress of my mother's voice, the lash and crack of a heavy whip, called me to the door where I could see and hear. "Oh, God, I have a notion to take a gun and shoot you," cried my mother in a frenzy, her face dripping with tears and sweat.

At first my brother pretended that he did not know why she was beating him. Then my mother said she had caught him there in the barnyard with the old cow. She kept calling out to her God to witness what she was saying and telling the boy that the most merciful thing she could do would be to kill him. She kept lashing him as he rolled about on the bed clad only in his underwear until he cried out half daring, half begging, "Kill me, I wish you would take the gun and shoot me." Finding herself exhausted she stood in the room, weeping and explaining to my brother that if he lived to be a man, he would thank her for the lesson she was trying to teach him. She went on, "I have knowed for years that some of you older boys was doin' things that no human bein' ought ever to be guilty of. That's one reason why I left yer ole Daddy, because he would never help me to raise you children right."

She became more quiet and explained to him that such a thing was not only a crime in the sight of God but it seemed to her, she couldn't quite remember, that it was a criminal offense punishable by death in the old days. She had talked this over with my oldest brother who had asked some man who knew about such things and she was perfectly sure that there was a law on the criminal statutes of the state of Texas making bestiality a penitentiary offense. She secured some sort of promise from him that he would never do such a thing again, but she also assured him that she would never attempt to beat a boy as large and as old as he again. The next time she would turn him over to the officers and "let the law take its course."

Afterwards she and my two sisters went into the kitchen to talk; my mother was telling them about having caught my third brother, who was then about twenty-one years old, at this same disgusting thing. She added with a deep sigh that she was so glad the three oldest boys had gone away (during the first two or three years my three oldest brothers worked or farmed near Abilene, but afterwards they went to quite other sections of the country), for she was getting afraid of them, especially the third one; she had lain awake nights praying to her God asking what to do. Then she added in a whisper, "I was just scared nearly to death before that old cow's calf come... God, I didn't know." At such times she would sit perfectly dumb for a minute, then jump up from her chair brushing a whole stream of tears from her face with the corner of her apron and start towards the door saying, "Emma, pull that curtain across there; Corrie, see if that other door is locked; I thought I saw a man's face at that window the other night; I declare to God, sometimes I think this will kill me."

The next day we would start off to school and perhaps when we were just ready to go, or were just taking the last sop of molasses at breakfast, my mother would start up with, "You children, hear me, don't you ever tell ennybody what happened here last night. If ennybody asks you, you tell 'em this or you tell 'em that or you tell 'em you don't know. Don't you ever dare breathe a word about what goes on in this house…about yer ole Daddy or about how some of these children has acted. If I ever hear that you have told these little Scott young uns or a child at school enny of the troubles that we have, I'll beat you in an inch of your life." Then she would say in a half whisper to one of the older ones, "My God, I wouldn't have enny respectable person know about this thing for ennything in this world. It's the biggest disgrace that could ever befall enny family." Sometimes threats from my parents rendered me rebellious and angry at heart but this time I was glad of my mother's severe attitude, for I, too, was afraid someone would find out what had happened the night before. I would watch anxiously the expression on the faces of the neighbors' children when we met in the street on the way to school and wonder if they had heard anything or would ask me any questions.

⤙＊

One evening during the first year or so at Abilene, when the three oldest boys were still at home, my mother received an urgent call to come to a neighbor's telephone several rods[1] away. The operator read

---

1   A rod, a unit equal to 5.5 yards or the length of a standard canoe, was a commonly used measure of distance on the American prairie. The rod was particularly convenient for nineteenth century surveyors, homesteaders, and fence builders, as the eighty rods added up to exactly a quarter mile. Today, barbed wire still comes in eighty rod spools.

a telegram over the wire stating that my oldest sister at Baird, Texas, was dying and asked my mother to come at once. All the older members of the family with my mother assembled in the kitchen to discuss the matter. (Bits of this whole story were told from time to time afterwards in the family. I assemble the facts here as best I can.) As usual everyone was excited and talked in whispers; my mother was skeptical. She drew the corners of her mouth down and said she was not going to be a fool; she was not going; perhaps it was only a plan of my father's to get her away from home to kill her. (For many years during the twenty-five years my parents lived together and during the time they were divorced, a period of nearly twenty years up to the time of my father's death in 1920, my mother seemed obsessed with the idea that somehow sometime my father intended to kill her.) Besides why was my sister at Baird? She did not know she was there.

But something had to be done. It was decided that my second brother, then about twenty-two, and my third sister, about sixteen, should go by the first train to ascertain what was the trouble. It required only a few hours to reach this town by train and my brother and sister soon found themselves in the station at Baird inquiring for the address the telegram had given. My brother asked a man at the station where the place was, explaining that he and his sister had to go there immediately, as there was someone there at the point of death whom they had to see. My sister said that the man looked her over very carefully and then exclaimed, "But God! Man, you can't take your sister there." Then the man drew my brother aside and explained that the house he was asking for was a house of prostitu-tion. My sister was left at a hotel for a few hours while my brother went to find the sick one. Afterwards he returned with a railway ticket for my sister and told her she must return home by the first train. He wanted to be very steady but broke down under her ques-tions and finally told her how he had found her, my oldest sister, in this house of ill fame in the throes of childbirth. She was crying out as she rolled about on her bed, asking God to forgive her, saying that she was going to die and finally that she wished she would. "I have never seen anybody cry as Reuben cried; it just seemed like it would kill him," I remember my sister saying.

I do not remember that my mother expressed any sorrow for the fate of my oldest sister, though my second and third sisters were crying and they all seemed at times angry about what had happened, disgusted and disgraced. "Disgraced…disgraced…disgraced," the repetition of this word rang in my ears. My second sister would choke up with tears and then say, "Now, we are disgraced. We can never be ennybody; there will always be that to be throwed at us; and some ole low-down dawg of a man will always be trying to take advantage of us on account of it." The four oldest children then at home and my mother would stand in the kitchen for hours after supper and talk in whispers; and maybe my mother would begin to lecture about the low-down Beasleys and how hard she had tried to raise her chil-dren right and then somebody would speak up and say, "Don't talk so loud, Mother, maybe somebody is listening."

This idea of some enemy or suspicious person with his ear at the keyhole, or the possibility of seeing a man's face at the window, threw me into my usual state of fright. Then, too, I only got snatches of their conversation; I was nearly dead of curiosity mixed with a sort of shame and fear. Finally, when they were about to break up one of these conversations, I could stand it no longer and so asked one of my sisters, whom I was most friendly with, "Tell me, Corrie, is Willie dead? Is she going to die?" "No, you little fool, get out o' here," she scolded. Then my mother directed one of the girls to go with me to the other room saying in scurrilous tones that "she is all ears and eyes." I was less afraid of her occasional slaps and thrashings if possible than her words. For example, I dreaded being told that I was "jest lak' some o' the rest"; or that I was going to be "lak' that ole Alice Beasley"; or that was the way "yer ole Daddy al'ays done or tawked." (I say this although I believe that I was scolded and beaten less than any member of the family.) I remember being escorted to an adjoining room, on one such occasion, and told to undress and go to bed; and when my sister returned to take up the conversation with my mother I overheard, "Mother, Gertrude is jest shakin' all over an' as white as a sheet." From my earliest recollections I was always very sensitive to any form of human sympathy (perhaps only another form of egotism); my throat was choking me a little and my eyes were full of tears when I heard them talking about how afraid I was, my mother saying that sometimes it just looked as though I was going to die of fear, when my father came around and wanted to see and talk with the children.

After a few days my oldest brother went down to Baird to see if he could be any help in taking care of my oldest sister, and I finally wormed out of my second sister what the trouble was. She told me in a blunt sort of way that she guessed I was old enough to be told (I was about twelve) and said, a little hurt and disgusted, "She is in the family way." I had heard the phrase before but had no complete idea of what it meant. So I asked, "What does it mean 'in the family way'?" "You little fool," she responded, looking angry and a little sad; "She is going to have a baby."

I imagined then (as I often do now when people tell me precious or horrible tales) that I knew what attitude she expected me to assume in receiving it and no doubt I lived up to her expectations in the serious way in which I received this bit of information, though I think the result was a further stinging of my curiosity. I do not remember, however, that I thought anything about asking about her husband or if I could see the baby when it came, etc. etc. I felt that the correct attitude to take was that of the sister who had imparted this information, namely, that this was a terrible and horrible thing but that the worst thing about it was that we were all disgraced. I felt this way or at least assumed to feel this way in spite of the fact that I had a very inadequate notion of what a house of prostitution was and what a great difference it made to the average person for a girl to have a baby without having been married. I had once heard my mother and the oldest children talking about some fancy women who had come to Roscoe when we lived in the country near this town; and

I once overheard them talking about a young woman in the community whose father took his gun and went to the man with whom she had been keeping company and told him if he did not marry his daughter he would kill him, with the consequence that the wedding took place and a baby was born after two months.

Soon my brother wrote that my sister's baby had arrived, this bastard as my mother called it. Here was a new word. What did they mean by calling a baby a bastard? I thought vaguely that it must be some horrible cripple or monstrosity, although the correct meaning was arrived at after I had heard many attempts to define this word. It was a child who had no name, who had no father; when a woman has a child without being married to a man, she gives birth to a bastard. Then to show the infamous depths to which birth under such circumstances carried a man, someone in the family had once heard a man in great anger call another a goddamned bastard; this was told under whispers and it was concluded that it was the worst thing you could call a man.

My father with the aid of some "missionary" women who had found my sister in the house of prostitution secured a small two-roomed house and took my sister there, where I believe the baby was actually born. For three weeks after the child's arrival they thought every day would be the last as my sister had what my mother thought to be "milk leg" from which she almost died. As soon as she was able, she wrote to my mother. I remember one line of the letter which ran about like this: My darling little baby is lying here on my arm. My mother was emitting a few p'shhhs; (her nose nearly always turned up more retroussé and the corners of her mouth went down when she wished to show her contempt or disagreement) as she opened and read the letter. I am pretty sure that I felt myself in agreement with my mother; "my darling little baby"—anyway it was a little silly to write in this way; I had no special use for babies, especially for babies who cried and filled their diapers with excrement; I had stood over whole tubfuls of the baby's "clothes" (which my mother pronounced "klaws") and shaken off the worst in the water; then secured a tub of clean water and continued until the baby's diapers were rid of all their dung and ready to be washed with the other things. I did nearly all of this disgusting washing for the eleventh and twelfth children. My mother had taken notice of my attitude when her twelfth child was born, for she often repeated the neighbor's story of the way in which I received the news that I had a new little sister. My reply had been, "God Amighty, another baby for me to nu'se!" Both she and Mrs. McGuire had laughed until they cried over this.

If my sister asked my mother in this letter to forgive her for having brought her grief, she did not beg ardently enough, for it was clear that it was wholly unsatisfactory, and my mother was more determined than ever to turn Willie from her door forever. One of the remarks which she made brought a strange picture to my mind, a picture which I was unable to reconcile at that time with the idea of a baby. The remark was this: "She tawks lak' it's an honorable child." The word honorable troubled me: I saw a vague image of a man apparently well-groomed and wearing a white standing collar and a black tie. The only thing I can think of now, by way of associating the word "honorable" with such a mental picture, is the probability that someone in white collar and black tie had been introduced at school as the Honorable So and So.

My mother soon worked herself up in a state of indignation, anger, and tears, and she recited or preached once more for the hundredth or thousandth time what an unruly and longheaded child Willie had always been; that she could never do anything with her and that when she corrected her, her father always took her part. And after she had recalled some of the worst disputes they had ever had, and the "disgraceful sassy way in which she had talked to *her* mother," my mother would sum it all up by saying, "yer Daddy al'ays thought she was so smart and I was such a fool." As much as to say, now we can see who is the fool; we perceive now who has come to grief.

Then directions about answering her letter were given to my second and third sisters, my mother speaking in the tone of a lawgiver saying that the two girls were to write my oldest sister as follows: that she had disgraced all of us and that they never wanted anything to do with her again; that she could never darken our door again and that my mother wished never to see her. I know how tense I was while she was saying all this and how I felt relaxed, as though some burden had been removed from me when my mother told the girls to add that if my oldest sister would go off (which she pronounced "gwaff") to some "rescue home" for five years and actually live right and prove it to everybody, perhaps we would see her again sometime.

One day during this awful strain, my mother took down the family album from the shelf and looked through the photographs. There was one of the four oldest children, three boys and a girl, taken in Coleman County when my sister was about sixteen. The girl was photographed in a white dress, standing at the side with her hand on the shoulder of one of the boys who was sitting. How funny it looked when the girl had been carefully cut off leaving only the hand on the shoulder! The other three, my mother was going to have enlarged, as an old travelling photographer had been to see her and had made a bargain to do some work of this sort very cheaply. Then my mother took out the only photograph of my father, a small tintype of about two inches by three inches. The photograph had been made of him with sideburns and the cheeks and eyes had been tinted a little. His hand with only one finger and a thumb (a source of great embarrassment to my mother) showed in the picture. (This loss of the first three fingers was due to an accident which he had had when a boy near Corsicana, where my grandparents lived. He was playing with a six-shooter, which he did not know was loaded, during the absence of his parents, and had discharged it, blowing off three fingers, I believe, on the left hand. I think someone laughingly called him a left-handed fiddler; he held the bow as he played in the left hand, his "good" hand being required for the strings.) Taking the small tintype and the photograph of the girl which she had cut off from the others, my mother started to destroy them and then put them away in an old book. It seems to me that she took them out later and burned them. The incident caused something within me a little like the collapse of my nervous system.

After some days the photographer returned with the enlargements of the photographs, among which was one of my grandfather, my mother's father, Thomas Ficklin. (I can't recall that I have ever heard this name except among my mother's people, it may be a rare name, or it may merely be misspelled.) This brought my mother once more to recollections of her father, and a lengthy description to us children of what a just, honest, gentle, and virtuous man he was; she would stand before his portrait and talk something after this manner: "No better man ever lived. I tell you there ain't no better blood ever flowed than the Scotch blood." Then she would explain that his father was the genuine article as he was born in Scotland and came to America in seventeen hundred and something. "Just look at that sensitive nose and them eyes. He was the kindest man I have ever known. I never heard him say a cross word in his life." Then she would interrupt herself with some explanation of how he once scolded "yer Aunt Maggie fer tawking and laffing too loud" while in conversation with some young man, I think perhaps a Beasley; or she would sidetrack with a description of how he once had an argument with "yer uncle Mack," after the latter had returned from the Civil War and was either feeling very cross or very cocky, this altercation amounting almost to a quarrel. But he had never scolded her, and she had sat in his lap until she was nearly grown. "W'y I must-a been twelve years old before I quit settin' on his knee." At that I would want to interrupt the story with questions as we frequently did; I wanted to know if one were nearly grown at twelve years.

One evening we were given a long story of my grandfather's religious experiences. He had been converted at the age of twenty. My mother would go on: "An' he was a religious man too. Though he wasn't one of the emotional kind and he couldn't stand having people shout, he was sure that he had been regenerated; he said the morning after he had made peace with his Savior, the sunshine was brighter, the flowers was more beautiful an' the birds sung sweeter than they had ever sung before." And invariably when she would come to "an' the birds sung sweeter," her eyes would fill up with tears and those of us who listened usually followed her in brushing our own away. (I am astonished now at the amount of emotional energy the members of my family have spent on such occasions. I believe it must indicate a very primitive state of development, probably combined with an extraordinary nervous strain.) My grandfather, my mother's father, was born either in Georgia or in South Carolina and afterwards moved to Alabama where my mother was born, being the youngest in a family of twelve children. He was an overseer of a large plantation in Alabama, having many negroes working in his fields and rice plantations, and some thirty servants for the house, kitchen, and garden.

We used to be entertained for hours (this after my parents' separation) by my mother's stories of her childhood; of the sayings of her negro "mammy"; of the carriage which her "own mother" had for going to church in; of the little seat at the back for the "nigger" boy; of magnolias and of chewing sweetwax; of a white woman who once gave birth to a negro baby; of a very wealthy mistress who used to have the negresses beaten with straps and whips, if she found her white silk handkerchief soiled after brushing it over the pots and pans; of a pig which was half negro; of the little schoolhouse which her father had built for her and her brother and sister; and of the system of private education where children were instructed by tutors (My mother would stretch her eyebrows as though to give you some understanding of herself without the use of words, and then with a quick turn of the head she would say, "I never had a nickel's worth of free schoolin' in my life; my father al'ays employed a tutor for us children, until we broke up the old home to come to Texas. T'hum, I never went to the ole free schools."); of how she had never turned her hand to work until they came to Texas; of the trip by railway to Navarro County, Texas from Salem, Alabama when she was fourteen years old; of a young man named Smith, a Yankee, and about ten years her senior, who had come on the same train with them and who had been in love with her; of how uncouth she had found the native Texans; of difficult financial straits and hard work; of the old parties and square dances; of meeting my father from whose description I gathered the impression that at one time, at least, she had looked upon him as a sort of Beau Brummell, and many other things.

Then perhaps she would wind up the talk by referring to her

father again, saying she had never heard him swear an oath in her life (the Beasleys were the worst people she had ever known for swearing); he had the sweetest voice she had ever heard, and the mildest eyes she had ever looked into; he had said on his deathbed that there were two places the doors of which his head had never darkened; one was a fancy house, and the other a saloon. He was an awful fine man though he could neither read nor write, only being able to sign his name, as my mother would explain, to deeds and documents; he never made a great show of making love to his second wife, though he often sat for hours holding her hand. Then, "You can't find many people these days, who live as he lived." Though I think I discounted these statements a little, and I am sure I always doubted people who praised their parents (undoubtedly because I never had any keen joy out of acquaintance with either of my parents), I sometimes stood before my grandfather's portrait in awe, for it seemed that his face and long white beard must resemble a little my vague idea of God.

⤙❦

One day, during the first year of our life at Abilene, some ladies of the Baptist Missionary Society came to see my mother about enlisting us in the Sunday School. The South Side Mission Church was very near our house and these ladies were anxious to swell their numbers by adding the children of the Beasley family to their list. On such occasions my mother was very vague; I feel now that her pride and sensitiveness, to what people said to her or what she imagined they were saying about her, resounded in me like the strains of a chord which one string transmits to another in the same instrument, the latter tone often swelling and vibrating with even greater force. I knew she was sensitive about the number of children she had, more especially since my oldest sister had been cut off from the family, "disinherited"; that she did not want it known that she was divorced, that is, she preferred to leave some suggestion with those who questioned her about the head of the family to the effect that my father had died; she might just say, "He is not living," sort of under her breath, and be ready to nod her head if the other person ventured that he was dead; and that she was very sensitive as to our ignorance and poverty.

Many of these crossroads in morals and psychology I met with her under the most acute nervous strain, sometimes almost jumping when the missionary women would ask her questions. After my mother had explained to them that she was trying to keep her children of school age in school, but she did not know if she could buy the proper clothes for them to attend Sunday School as nearly all of us required new hats, the church ladies then suggested that their society had many hats and that if my mother wished they would send her a lot so that she could make a selection of those which she needed. She acquiesced in this after explaining that she had never received any help from anyone and that nearly every member of the family was able to work and hence was not in need of any form of charity. Afterwards several packages of hats and old clothes arrived, some of which we kept; and all of us were ashamed to wear them. I was proud of having a new hat but I nearly burned up with shame at the thought of anyone knowing that it had been "donated"; I felt very shy walking into the Sunday School and facing the woman who had visited us and learned a good deal about us and who knew just where that hat came from.

Afterwards the missionary women would come to ask us about becoming religious. This brought up the conversation about my mother's conversion. I had never known before that she laid any claims to religious experiences. When the missionary women (of the Ladies Aid Society of the First Baptist Church, Abilene, Texas) asked her if she had been saved, my mother related what she called her conversion, occurring at the age of twenty years, after her second child was born. She had lived far in the country, perhaps eight or ten miles from Corsicana, for several years after she and my father were married; he had gone away and left her alone very often, going to town by horseback when it was still dark in the morning and some-times not returning until midnight. And how she had suffered from just being alone! From hearing the slightest noise or from fear of the darkness! (The tears would roll down her face as she talked. At such times, it seemed to me that a few tears were not enough; I wanted to cry out with my tears like a child being beaten.) She would walk the floor in broad daylight in such terror that she would think every breath would be the last one; this until her nails and lips were as blue as indigo. She would close by saying, "Ah declare to God, I don't see how enny woman could stand what I've stood." It was at such a time that she had made peace with her God. Some of this she had told the missionary ladies, but she related the story to us many times in great detail and once she added that with all her terror she was very, very sad, for she had already begun to see that *He* did not care for her.

Then the missionaries began coming for personal prayer meetings and began asking us all in turn, "Don't you want to be saved?" "Don't you want to follow Jesus?" "Why don't you give your life to Christ?" Almost any member of the family with whom they talked would swell up and shed tears. One day when one of the missionary women began to tell me about Christ, how He had come into the world to save the lost and ended up by saying, "Daughter, wouldn't you like to have a better life?" I left the room, my tears splashing on the floor; and I heard the woman say that I was a very tenderhearted little girl, and that my mother ought to encourage my becoming religious.

So it went on; my third sister was the first to declare that she had been converted. She was working as a maid and cook too, I believe, for a sanctified Methodist woman and was prevailed upon from two sides; the mistress of the house held prayer with her, and she was visited by the missionary women too. One day she came home sobbing and blubbering, for she was the champion weeper of the whole Beasley connection, and announced that just that afternoon she had been converted, had given her life to Christ and was going to be a Christian for the remainder of her days. (Perhaps I shall be led into unwarranted statements if I try to tell how I felt on this occasion, but one must make an attempt. All of these various situations affected me in much the same way, whether it was bestiality among my brothers, the fact that my sister was going to or had already given birth to a bastard, an account of the godlikeness of my grandfather; my mother's hatred of my father, or getting converted, or a thousand and one other things; they all filled me with dark confusion. Mentally, I was sadness and anger and pride and ambition with a lot of competitiveness all shot through with fear.) "God…God Amighty…God, why does Mother say she hopes Emma will stick to it." The way Emma and Mother talked to one another showed them either very insincere or very ignorant. Perhaps it was neither, I don't know.

After several months of urgings and suggestions that I should become a Christian, with shock after shock of embarrassment or fear or shame or something, as keen as though one had cut my flesh and pricked at a nerve, I decided upon an incident which I called my conversion. I had been told by my Sunday School teachers, and it was borne out by my mother, that if I asked God very, very earnestly to forgive my sins He would do it and then everything would be settled. (This in spite of the fact that I knew the way in which my mother received petitions from my father, or how she took it when my oldest sister cried until her face and eyes looked as though they would burst. These incidents in connection with forgiveness: my mother would hiss and say, "He knows he's guilty; she knows she's to blame.")

I had misgivings about asking for forgiveness. One afternoon, I returned from school to find one of the missionaries at our house again. It was after she left that I prepared to make peace with my God. I sat in the baby's high chair and tried to think what I should say. I went through something like this: "Oh, God, forgive my sins; I want to be saved; I want to go to heaven with all the good people." And when I raised my head I was ashamed, for I felt very stupid speaking or rather whispering there into thin air, embarrassed that no one had heard me. I was a little frightened: fancy, I had prayed and there had been absolutely no change. Then I decided to pray to Christ, anyway he was the one who could save, and I had always had a lot of interest in Him, having seen many colored pictures of the Savior. So I told Jesus that I wanted to give Him my life; that I wanted to follow Him; that I wanted Him to forgive me and all of that sort of thing, just as the Sunday School teacher had prescribed. And when I had finished I had tears in my eyes and went and looked out of the window and saw a cluster of light gray clouds in a blue sky, and I imagined I saw a shadowy figure of a man in flowing pink garments. I felt better: I felt changed and I called it my conversion. I ran out into the yard, finding I had been alone in the house, and wondered if anyone would take any notice of me. But no one knew about it and I had no desire to tell anyone—I would guard it as a secret like giving birth to a bastard or my mother's divorce or something like that.

Now, I imagine, though this may be considered irrelevant sociological material, that what I should like to have had in the way of a religious experience would have been something like this. The teacher would have called to read the Sunday School card on which was a picture of the boy Christ, telling me some of the interesting things about His life and then pointing out how similar I was to Him. She could even have said without exaggeration that I looked like Him with my short hair and clear eyes; that I was a very bright little girl (nearly everybody agreed on that point) and that no doubt I was going to be clever like Christ. She could have gone a step further and said that since I was going to be a woman and was born so many years after Jesus that perhaps I might find something new, maybe something better for humanity or at least more intelligent or more beautiful.

I feel sure that any reference to myself as becoming an intelligent woman with perhaps greater powers than those of an intelligent Man would have met my approval. For I was well aware from my first conscious moments, when I was about four years old, that the general idea of their mental superiority prevalent among men was fallacious. I regarded myself as an infinite improvement over any of my brothers; in fact, over the combined mentality of the entire family. If my conversion had occurred as I suggest, I think it likely that I should not have been ashamed of it; there would have been no hurting of my pride, an approach towards breaking my spirit; and I should likely have told my mother in a simple but glorious spirit that the Sunday School teacher says I'm doing very well in her class: she thinks maybe I shall be clever like Christ. But as the thing was managed, I had to go the way of the damned and sinful at the age of eleven or twelve, as though I were to blame for the hideous misfortune which had already overtaken me. As a result, I never volunteered to relate my new experience to anyone. I began to stand up when the teacher or superintendent would ask the "saved" to rise, but I was hesitant, and if questioned too intimately, would sit again as though the incident were not certain.

—⋆

A variety of things were happening at school. There was plenty of competition, thrusts at one's pride, and occasional doubting of my own powers. Sometimes I almost wept when I compared my hesitant way of reading or my difficulty with lessons with the rapidity with which I learned at one of the country schools when I was seven years old. Then I read through the first four grades of readers in four months, and learned a lot of other things. But now everything embarrassed and fettered me. Sometimes my tongue appeared not to work and I wished I could drop through a crack in the floor. My hands were too large, at least the people at home thought so, and then the wrist bones protruded too much. If I held a heavy geography book up to read, I felt every eye in the room on my wrists, which gave me so much pain that I was often relieved at the idea of dropping dead.

One day at recess, when the little girls were all gathered at the toilet, a small outhouse several rods from the building, our teacher entered. She waited her turn, looking at the walls and seat of the privy. The whole place was written full of obscene words and drawings in colored pencil or crayon, and then on the seat, which had apparently been done only the night before, were carved a half inch in the soft pine in large letters these words, "Fuck me you whoar." The teacher tried to suppress any change in her countenance and each girl seemed for the moment dumb. I felt that all of them were horrified like myself, and would have been glad if the earth had opened and swallowed the last one of us. I looked at the inscription on the seat once more, and as always on such occasions, something happened to keep me from dropping dead. I thought: whoever wrote that misspelled the word "whore"; I had seen it in the Bible, and then I had heard my mother whisper it many times. Whispering or hissing or facial expression or expression of the eyes always added degradation to persons who uttered such words, and made the hearing and seeing of symbols or words more poignantly obscene, shameful, or, as some would have said, "sinful." The other word I knew as connoting sexual intercourse, a word which I had sometimes used in conversation and sexual play with my two older brothers, when I was a very young child. There was a drawing of a man and woman in coitus and the walls and door were littered with such words: shit, a common word for excrement; piss, for urine; cock and pussy, which stood for the sex organs of a boy and girl; tird, for hardened excrement; fart, for breaking wind or letting off gas from the intestines; ass (This is the old English word arse, but it was always spelled and pronounced ass); the rectum; and other words relating to bodily discharges and sexual matters. (I am surprised that I write all these so easily, for when I look at these words all spelled out I wonder at their power at bringing fear and degradation, and the sense of something I am unable to describe to a child's mind. Then it lasts far beyond childhood. Several years ago a woman of my acquaintance, who was looked upon as an educated person, on coming out of a toilet room, began a conversation with me about her work by using this common word referring to excrement as an expletive. I felt as though she had struck me and then insulted me; besides I was nauseated. She regarded the expression of my face and apologized, saying that her mother always used that word to express her disgust.)

In the classroom as well, there were many cases of obscenity, especially during the first two years of my schooling at Abilene. The boys were seated on one side of the room and the girls on the other, so that signals and placards were used. Sometimes a boy would pretend he was going to expose his sex organ, or he would prop up his geography book and make signs with his fingers about sexual intercourse, or hold up a paper with the word for the same printed on it, and would grunt or cough to try and make some girl look at it. Almost invariably the little girls would turn their eyes on their books and pretend not to see the signal or reclam; an older girl used to laugh about it and get pink all over. One boy older than the rest of the class seemed to think of nothing else. He was dull at his studies though active physically, and caused the teacher, as well as his parents, a lot of trouble. My will was sealed against all such people. Although I sometimes had some contraction or movement in the region of my sexual organs, which was nothing more or less than sex desire, I put down all such feelings with the greatest ferocity and regarded children whose mouths were full of smutty words with disdain.

To illustrate how difficult the times were for us, during the first few years of town life, I shall mention the farm work and gardening which we continued to do during the cultivation seasons. The first summer we went by wagon to a large fruit farm near Clyde, Texas, to pick blackberries and dewberries. This place was a half day's drive or so from Baird, where my oldest sister had been, and as far as I know may still have been. I know that the question as to whether or not anyone there would know about my oldest sister was constantly before the minds of my sisters and mother. Had anyone there, by any chance, heard about Willie's having been in this house of prostitution in Baird, and if so, how would they look upon my mother and her daughters? Of course, this did not affect myself as I was only a child; but I knew, I think, what they were wondering, thinking of how they meant to meet any "slurs thrown at them on account of what someone else had done."

At first the whole family was engaged in gathering berries, basket after basket and crate after crate being filled. After some association with the man and his wife, my mother developed a good deal of confidence in them, she and the girls having lived in the proprietor's house, and left us to carry on for a few weeks while she returned to

Abilene to look after the place. The boys slept in the wagon while my third sister and myself slept in a room adjoining the sleeping room of the man and his wife. And one day, when my mother was away something similar to what had been anticipated did happen. The proprietor came to my sister's bed in the night, and put his hand on her breast, for he had only one arm, and tried to arouse her sexually. She told this story several years later, saying she was afraid to mention it to anyone at the time, for fear of grave trouble. Having struck him a good blow, while still lying in bed, she told him that if he didn't get out of the room, she would knock hell out of him. When any of the women of the family were aroused, they could use phrases of this nature to as much advantage and with as much force as a man. Besides they were about as strong physically. Being afraid his wife would wake, he crept out of the room. The next day in the berry patch, when my sister had been crying all day, he mentioned this to her, and she told the landlord that if she reported this incident to the family, that even if her brothers failed to act, that her mother would bring a gun there and kill him, as she had had all she could stand in this life. The man tried to defend himself by saying that he had heard about her older sister at Baird and ended by asking, "And how was I to know?" She replied, she said, that if anyone ever banned her on account of what someone else had done, that she was going to take a gun and shoot that person herself. I used to become very excited over such statements, but after a little reflection I usually decided that it would never happen. All of this aroused disgust, pride, curiosity, suspicion, and a multitude of other feelings; and sometimes I formulated in my own mind just the opposite theory from the one presented.

Another means of livelihood was the large-scale gardening which the family did. My mother rented a five-acre patch including an orchard and gardening plot, where we were employed during the summer and after school hours in the spring and early autumn. The garden was located at the north end of Abilene adjoining the campus of Simmons College, then a small private school for both young men and young women. The red dormitory where the girls lived especially attracted me. How I should have liked to go away from them all and live among girls all of my own age, and of course studying and understanding the things which I understood! One day some girls who were out walking came into the garden and one of them, recognizing my mother, came and kissed her. She was an only daughter of the people for whom my oldest sister had been working at Roscoe. Did she know how Willie had acted? Perhaps she had not heard, but everyone there knew. Anyway, it had not made her less friendly towards my mother. And how it pleased her: "She come and kissed me as big as anything...got an awful nice, honest face, that Beulah Edmondson," my mother would say. Then she baked a cake and took it to Beulah. I thought my mother was flattered because this girl had been friendly with her. Afterwards, when the girl married, my mother would remark casually, but with pride, "She married the Professor of Music and then they went off to Germany to study."

When the vegetables were harvested, my mother would drive about the town peddling them in an old hack, which she drove with a straggly horse. One day I came upon her at noon when I was going home from school for my lunch. She was just stopping in front of the house of the little girl whom I was walking with, and the little girl had called out, "There's your mamma. I must run in and ask if mamma wants anything today." I don't remember that I stopped to talk with her; I recall the sharp tinkle of the bell she rang; her face was very, very red, radiating anger, and I had never noticed before how fat her hands were. This short-waisted, shortnecked woman, with largish breasts, in plain dress and poke bonnet was almost a caricature, sitting on the seat, holding the reins with one hand and ringing the bell with the other. I did not want to hear her talk to the woman; I nearly always wanted to leave her presence when she talked with people, that is, with those who spoke simple English correctly, and Mrs. Christopher had been educated to be a teacher, I think. It was always that way. When we lived in the country, I dreaded having the teacher come to see us, for there was not a member of the family who could use the simplest forms of speech correctly. Besides I had heard teachers laugh at the language of some of their patrons, the excuses they wrote for their children; and what would I have done...? Maybe I would have turned into something like smoke; or struck them perhaps with a big rock; called them the worst name I could think of like doggone black fool; or maybe my body would have fallen into pieces; maybe anything...but it is quite likely that I should merely have cried.

There were many vicissitudes, petty squabbles, quarrels, and heartaches mixed with the difficulties of getting a living. My mother had a "terrible" time getting her children to take an interest in education. She wanted all of them to take up some form of business study. My oldest brother was either too stupid to learn, or else he had been told that so frequently that he had come to believe it. He could draw out his name in perfect letters, W.T. Beasley or Wiley Thomas Beasley (he was named for his two grandfathers); but when it came to writing, one would think his form and spelling that of an idiot child. He would say to my mother in the most pathetic way, "I'd lak' awful well to know somethin', Maw; but you know I ain't very quick at learnin.'"

My second brother looked upon himself as extraordinarily clever, like myself in that respect. He declared that he wasn't going to waste any time at a business college as he could work any problem (in arithmetic) in existence and he could understand anything he read. What more did one need? He knew everything he needed to know. Fancy, he thinks he knows enough, I was saying in disgust to myself, probably repeating a platitude of some one of my teachers to the effect that one should never cease learning. As to my third brother, even my mother remarked that he could hardly write his name; and there was no sign of his wanting any improvement of his condition. My second sister, Corrie, worked in the house of her music teacher, an educated woman who corrected her English and demanded that she study grammar along with her musical history. She had learned many of the correct forms for: I seen, I taken, I throwed, and the like, and would tell how severe Mrs. Tate had been with her for not knowing the correct forms of the most common verbs, besides the multitude of other mistakes.

My third sister, Emma, did really start at the Business College, which after a few weeks developed into what my mother termed a courting school, as the teacher and my sister contracted a love affair to the alarm of my mother. She was always whispering that she was afraid Emma would go astray like Willie. She would make a wry face with a mixture of scorn and interest, and say in a hoarse whisper, sometimes to herself, sometimes to me alone, and sometimes to whomever would listen to her, "She's just crazy about the men, and they are all crazy about her, too." Sometimes when my mother looked and talked in this manner, I would feel something in my sexual parts contract or move; and the same thing would happen if I saw the Professor holding my sister's hand. Though once I had some feeling of annoyance or fatigue when he held her hand so long; it was at a Punch and Judy show, the man standing at the side of the buggy in which my sister was sitting, holding her hand for a stretch of two or three hours. I believe this was one of the occasions that my mother sent me along, as she did not want my older sisters to go out alone with men at night. Then my fourth and fifth brothers were out of school and worked in the country or in the town, and though my mother exerted every effort to get them interested in the night school, she never succeeded.

—✦

Myself and the younger ones attended the public school daily. We practically never missed a day except for sickness; besides the teachers were severe and we had to show good reasons for absence. At any rate I should have felt very abused and downtrodden if I had ever been detained at home. It was as heart-breaking as keeping me away from the colored cards and Sunday School of the little country church when I was a child of six or seven. I was pretty happy then as no one had succeeded at that time in getting any idea of sin into my conscience, my chief source of unhappiness then being my parents' quarrels.

The companions whom I chose to play with at school did not wish to play with me. (I get a lump in my throat when I think of it.) Sometimes the cleverest and best dressed little girls called me into their games, but it was usually to take some small part and if anyone was to be ruled out I was the one to step aside. Sometimes I imagined the discrimination was made because of my clothes, for, if they were clean, they usually had no style and were often made of old ones. I felt that everyone knew I was wearing some dress of my sister's made over, or, in a few cases, clothes which had been "donated."

The little girl who lived next door was of a very ignorant and scrubby family of cotton pickers and small workmen, that is the father engaged in blacksmithing during the winter. This child would run to catch me on the way to and from school. At first I was friendly with her, but the teachers and students laughed at her bacon-greased, yellow hair and her queer manner of speech so much that I came to be ashamed to play with her. (How often have I found during these thirty years that as soon as I became well acquainted with a person, or approached anything bordering on familiarity or intimacy with them, I, at the same time, became ashamed of them!) I used to feel a sort of shrinkage and burning of my whole being when this girl would approach me in the presence of others and begin to talk in a voice which sounded more like that of a distempered calf than a human being's. If we were alone it did not matter so much; I was usually friendly with her. One day when we were playing together in our backyard, riding broom sticks, she began to talk to me about sex matters. She said she had had sexual relations with her brother (we were both then about eleven years old); and asked me if I knew that I had a rather large opening at the place where one urinated; and then when we were sitting astride a bench she poked at me with the end of the broomstick through my underwear and recommended that I take a mirror and look at myself. As far as I remember I was very careful to conceal from her the idea of having had any of the experiences which she referred to, while at the same time being perfectly willing to let her prod at me with the stick. I believe someone must have almost discovered us at this, as I have a recollection of terrible fright and shame.

On the question of sex with other children, I was as silent as a sphinx; it was in the same category as the name of my oldest sister whom I never mentioned. (I have never told a soul my oldest sister's story; and even in the family her name is always mentioned in a whisper. Once when I was twenty-two or -three years old someone mentioned the name Abigail, and I remember that the words came out as though my head and lungs were a vacuum, "One of my sisters has Abigail as a middle name." I felt sheepish and wondered if the person were reading anything in my face.) The use of disgusting words, or references to any part of my own body in a slighting way, or suggestions about puberty or sex which I did not understand, stirred me with indignation and often threw me into a sort of tantrum mentally, which I was not able to express physically, for fear of a box on the ear. For example, my mother would talk for two or three hours on what vile mouths the Beasleys always had, repeating what "yer grandma" (Beasley) had called her oldest children. One of these hyphen words was equivalent to saying one was a donkey that continually poured out excrement (i.e. shit-ass); it could have referred to a person with his buttock covered with dung. I never heard it explained. Another was a name for a worm which works in bodily refuse, (i.e. tird-worms). These are only two of them; there were others. And just after my mother had expressed her disgust in grunts and phrases, for people who used such language, she would call some one of the children one of these names and then fall to laughing about it, as though it sounded clever coming from her. At such times something surged through me like violent hatred; and once when she smacked me and struck me with a cloth which she asked me to put into the ragbag, I wanted to call down curses on her, to spit and bite, but I only cried.

And to further add to my disgust and degradation she called out, "Put this in the ragbag, it will do to go between your legs." This was like ridiculing me for not knowing about menstruation. If I were "in the pouts," as she would say, about anything she would sometimes tease me with such remarks, "I think she's got a flea *on* her crotch"; or if she said, "I think she's got a flea *up* her crotch," I would feel some sex movement in me mixed with the most violent hatred of her.

Although I think the idea came to me many years later, I once had a picture in my mind of kicking her shins for talking to me in this way. Once she said a thing to me which gave me the sense of the bitterest insult, it was much more devastating than a physical blow, for it appeared to be without any sympathy or any pity. Already when I was ten years old my nipples had begun to swell and when I was eleven there appeared a very small lump under them, sufficiently inflamed so that I felt it when I lay flat on my stomach on the floor. I never mentioned this to anyone in spite of the fact that it troubled me a lot. But I was immensely curious, uneasy, and a little melancholy when I thought of it. One day when I was in my underwear my mother noticed my sprouting breasts and remarked that they looked like "little risings" and said that after a while they would be as big as pincushions. I was so incensed that I began to blubber and cry, and before I could control my tongue had called her a fool. On such occasions I would have relieved my feelings by calling her "old fool" and "old devil," but I was afraid of her thumps and short blows on the head as well as some moral force (I say "moral force" for lack of a better word) which said that one should not call one's mother such names. She would scold if I cried too much and say that I knew that she was only teasing me. When I was a little older she would sometimes try to tease me, and if I were angry she would act very, very hurt and sometimes have tears in her eyes, and say that she could never tease "these children" because we always swelled up like toad frogs and became angry. Then one wanted to lash oneself "with scorpions."

My aunt and two of my uncles (my mother's people) came to visit us while we lived at this first place at Abilene which we always called the "Willow Street house." My mother had paid down four or five hundred dollars at the start from cotton picking money and the four hundred dollars or so which my father had turned over to her at the time of the separation and divorce. Then she was to repay the rest in installments of ten dollars a month and eight percent interest. The relatives, I think, were pretty well pleased with the house; it was well built, of four rooms, weatherboarded, and painted. My father had never supplied her with such a house. I liked most my aunt, a woman about three years older than my mother. When she came my mother met her at the train in a carriage. It was a vehicle loaned her by a very "respectable" neighbor, who lived several streets from us, whom my mother met while peddling fruits and vegetables. I think the truth of it was my mother had offered to hire the carriage for meeting her sister, but the woman had refused saying she was glad to lend it.

Aunt Maggie, whom my mother called Sister Margaret, was a well-appearing woman who could have been said to have belonged to the big bourgeois class. All of her clothes were elegant according to our way of thinking, and even her underwear was properly cut and fitted. She wore the best of spectacles of ground lenses and gold ear rims. But what I liked most about her was her manner of speaking. She nearly always spoke correctly, that is I thought her construction was almost as good as my teacher's; but her accent was exceedingly Southern. She always called my uncle "Geo'ge," leaving out the "r" altogether; this made me want to laugh and I was a little bit skeptical. Once or twice I could see that my mother was a little miffed at something she had said, but on the whole she acted as though she had been transported to a seventh heaven with her sister. Once in another room my mother turned the corners of her mouth down and said, "Aw, she's never had to work—just look at her hands—and George Bragg cared something for her…he was so good to her—she only had five children." This gave me a vague impression, that a man was good to his wife, if he never struck her and never gave her more than five children.

I had overheard my mother tell my aunt that I was "awful smart in my books" and that the teachers had praised me. One day my aunt took my hand and said, "You are my little girl, just see what beautiful hands this child has—you are just as smart as you can be and

I know you are going to be a wonderful woman." This pleased me; I felt beautiful and clever for the moment; and had a sensation of my body growing with tremendous rapidity, like Jack's bean stalk, into some wonderful woman. Nearly everything about this visit was agreeable to me; the *Abilene Reporter* had told of my aunt's coming and the editor who was also the reporter had said that the meeting of these women who had not seen one another for seventeen years had brought tears to his eyes. Then Mrs. Christopher's kindness in lending the carriage had indicated that she thought we were pretty nice folk. My aunt had brought me no disagreeable ideas and no fears; about religion she merely said that she believed in a religion of work, and I can't remember any embarrassment about prayers; and she didn't insinuate or say so, though she may have believed it, that I or anyone else was lost.

On leaving my aunt gave a warm invitation to any who chanced to come to Dallas to come and stay with them; she even planned that Emma pay them a visit in the fall during the Dallas Fair. How happy my sister was when she packed her trunk to go—a small, old-fashioned trunk with a tray for a hat and the like, which belonged to my oldest brother. She had been working at the telephone office, earning five or ten dollars per month, and had bought a few clothes and remade a dress or two which had been given her. She went, met her cousin, a few years her senior and, as usual, fell in love. After Emma returned home they wrote the most caressing love letters, which alarmed my aunt so much that she wrote my mother in great indignation telling her that she would have to watch Emma, that if she didn't hold a tight rein on her she was going astray like Willie. This was a tremendous blow and my mother, too, was indignant; "You can't turn around now that this thing ain't said to you"; she even permitted Emma to send a very rebuking letter to Aunt Maggie telling her she was a "wolf in sheep's clothing." This sounded very stout and very brave to me. As always on such occasions, I seemed to have gathered some information. My mother took the attitude of condoning this affair by saying, "Why; in England cousins sometimes marry"; and then she poo-pooed about the letters (I believe my aunt sent them to her) saying they were childish and silly, a little like the kind of letters we used to write and send in one envelope to my uncle's children when I was very, very small; I think we sometimes called our cousins darling or sweetheart.

Then one of my uncles and two of his children paid us a visit. How embarrassed and ashamed I was during the whole time they were with us! Uncle was a religious fanatic and construed the passages in the Scriptures about speaking in unknown tongues and casting out devils in a literal sense. He would shout out, "Glory to God! Hallelujah!" and sometimes tears would be streaming from his eyes. I always dreaded the hour after supper, for he was sure to begin this terrible hour of prayer, long readings, crying out "Hallelujah," praying and weeping. Then I was afraid he would want to talk to me about being sanctified; it was not sufficient to have been "saved," one needed another dose for becoming sanctified and perfect. And how this worried me! I recall distinctly that several times in childhood my whole nervous system seemed to have been completely shattered; I was on the brink of nervous prostration. I did not like my cousins; they were, I should say, exceptionally stupid children, and if any disinterested person had asked me what I thought of my uncle, I am sure that I should have said that, between him and myself, I believed he was about nine-tenths idiot; he even told of having seen devils in the shape of large eggs come out of the mouths of sinful and possessed people, he being the instrument through which this miracle was performed.

My mother tried to borrow money from my uncle to pay off the installments on her property, as the place was liable to fall into the hands of the seller in case the notes were not paid promptly, besides the interest on the installments as they fell due amounted to considerable, as the interest was calculated on the sum still unpaid each month. My uncle talked very favorably during the visit about lending my mother money, but when he returned home the matter was forgotten.

Then a second uncle came. He was an elderly single man who had served under General Lee in the Civil War (on the side of the Confederates, of course). He would talk about carrying the knapsack, describe the drum beating, until one could almost hear its roll; the great number of dead; and how sometimes the army could be tracked by the bloody footprints of the men in the snow. If I recall rightly, he never held family prayers at all, said a very short grace at the table, and took the attitude that the religion of Glasgow (Glasgow was the name of his brother) was strictly for weak-minded people, though he shared the belief, like almost everyone in the connection, that he had been regenerated. One day my mother said to him in a half whisper that the children said they thought "the Old Man" was in town—all of us now refer to my father as the "Old Man" in contempt, fear, or hatred—camping near the small creek which ran just beyond our section of the town. Then she added that she hoped uncle Mack would not get excited if he came "around here." My uncle said quietly that he was the very man to see him, that he would give him a good straight talk. What a different meaning this statement held for me when my mother repeated what my uncle had said. I remarked it at the time. She would mimic his tone of voice and the expression of her eyes and face would set me to thinking that maybe some potent danger lurked in my uncle's words, words which would have given me small concern had it not been for my mother's interpretation. Coming from her it sounded as though my uncle might not only be on the defensive but almost at the verge of going out to start some horrible conflict with my father. And those little white cords, or whatever term we use in referring to our nerves, in me would contract and curl up until it seemed they would break. The question of borrowing money was presented to this uncle also; and as usual he thought he could help.

One day my father's covered wagon did stop in the plot next to our house. He drove in there before school hours in the morning and one of my brothers came in breathless, saying my oldest sister and her baby were in the wagon and that she wanted to see us; if my mother or the girls would not see her, perhaps my mother would let the little children come to the wagon and talk to her. As I remember it, my mother said that the older boys could go out and see her if they wished, but that she did not wish the little ones to know anything about her, consequently we were all herded into one room and the blinds pulled down. The doors were all locked, even though my father was still sitting in the wagon, and we sat or walked about in this dark room, my mother and myself peeking through a small crack which she made by pulling the shade out at the side. They stayed only a few minutes and then drove on. I was agitated at the thought of being late at school.

Here I find it difficult to distinguish between images and realities. I have a picture in mind of seeing a partial outline of my sister and of her baby as a side curtain of the covered wagon was raised; and yet as I think of this childish image which flitted through my mind then (the shape of the child in what I now believe must have been only my fancy was that of a regularly cut rag doll with arms extended), my mature intelligence tells me that it could not possibly have been a baby which I saw. It is likely my mind simply manufactured this image out of curiosity for knowing how my sister and her child inside the covered wagon looked. There was emotion and curiosity and something of hate, scorn, pity, fear, a little skepticism, and perhaps myriads of other mental states out of which to manufacture a picture of a woman and a baby. My creation, if it were merely a fancy and not a reality, was certainly not a happy one and far from beautiful. I wonder now at the influences which produced it. I seem to remember that my brothers said my sister was crying and said that God would forgive her for He knew her heart. This again, I am afraid, cannot be taken as authentic. It may be only that kind of imagination, which makes one what America calls a sob artist. I account for this partly on the ground of the stories which my oldest brother told of my sister's agony at the time of the child's birth, as well as for some weeks after. One of them was an account of how she wept and screamed (he thought she was going to die) when she read the letters from my second and third sisters, saying my mother had said she could never darken her door again; and their statement to the effect that they never wished to see her again unless, unless...she would reform according to their prescription.

―≮*

Time passed and I finished the fifth and sixth grades and was transferred to the old Central Ward School building, where the high school classes met. I was glad of the change because I did not quite like my teacher; she was often severe without reason and almost never sympathetic. I had left an adorable teacher in the fourth grade, one whom I would beg my mother to let me pluck roses for; and when I had run until my tongue was almost ready to hang out in trying to catch up with her and had placed a few red roses in her hand without letting the thorns scratch her, I was happy. How I loved those who were intelligent and who could and would teach me, provided they did not hurt me too much by scolding or sarcasm, or any of the other methods, and provided, too, they thought I was bright, at least made me believe they considered me clever. My new teacher was as gentle as a lamb, a noble and beautiful woman, and as tender-hearted as a child. If she ever reprimanded me I was sure to want to cry. One day she met my mother. The conversation with this teacher was quoted many times afterwards. For one reason she had been very, very friendly with my mother, and as my mother would remark, she was of a good family, was well educated and was said to be the most beautiful young lady in town when she was a girl. "Aw, it don't make no difference to real fine people, if you are poor or ignorant," summed up my mother. She would repeat their conversation in tones of satisfaction and almost affection; "Are you Mrs. Beasley? I thought I heard your name, and are you Gertrude Beasley's mother?"... She had said I was a lovely child...maybe she had put it in the superlative, for sometimes my mother would suppress part of her praise until another time. "She thinks you are awful smart and she said, 'you just mark my word, Mrs. Beasley, that child is going to make her mark in this world.'" Maybe this was only my mother's method of expressing what was said, as I do not recall hearing anyone else use the phrase "make her mark in the world."

One day a woman came selling a preparation for womb trouble, and as my mother had falling of the womb and said continually that she thought the change of life was "working on her" they would hold conversation for hours. When conversation became too intimate I was sent out of the room. During one of the visits, as this woman came several times, I heard enough to understand that my mother was telling her all about my father. And then for some reason she told her about Willie and said that she was at that time living with her father. I think she described how my father and sister went about the country in his covered wagon, as my father did not stay long enough in one place for them to become established in a house. He would do blacksmithing or carpentry work at a place for a while and then move on to some other town. I think he must have had to take care of my sister too, as my brothers, who were in touch with them occasionally, reported that during the first year after the child's birth she was unable to walk.

After the woman left, my mother worked herself up to a fearful heat of indignation; she was "puffing and blowing" to use her own expression. "In the name o' God," she began, "that woman asked if yer daddy was the father of Willie's child." Then she went on in the greatest distress telling how she had gone into detail and explained the whole affair to her (a man at Sweetwater who promised to marry Willie had ruined her), for fear that she might go away thinking it true, as such a thing was considered the "most awful" disgrace that a human being could be guilty of. A feeling of resentment crept into me; I felt that she had overdrawn her distress and I believed she had suggested the idea to the woman. She had not said so in so many words, but her remarks and facial expression "spoke louder than words" and I felt resentful. "But I thought that was what you were saying to her," lurked in my thoughts, when my mother would repeat the conversation. If I recall rightly, she said she told the woman about Willie in order to watch her facial expression to see if she had heard that she had a child who had "gone astray." Well she found out what people thought of you for telling things like that.

The first few years after my oldest sister's misfortune, my mother and sisters lived in a perfect hell, wondering if people knew about it and what they thought of us on account of it. I cannot be accurate as to the date when my sister married, though I think it occurred when the child was about a year old. Anyway, she did not try to keep in touch with my mother after she had been "thrown away" by her and my sisters, the result being that we did not hear of her marriage for several years afterwards.

When I was twelve, I used to have pains in my sides when I ran and would complain to my mother. One day she began talking to me in a tone of voice which one takes in quarreling, although the wisdom of her words seemed strong to me and I felt her sympathetic. Maybe she talked a little as though I wouldn't understand or wouldn't appreciate the service she was trying to render. "I've been afraid to talk in my life and then I was ignorant; but now I am gonna tell you children some things, and if you don't take my advice and ruin your health, you'll just have to take the consequences. You've got to quit running in these streets lak' a wild ass's colt. I expect you're getting ready to have your monthlies." Then she became quiet as though serious or sympathetic or maybe only an effort to impress it on me. "You have to take care of yourself when your period comes around." She did not attempt to explain this to me. I think she did not know how, as she had never mentioned such a thing to one of her daughters before, as far as I know.

⭐

The following summer I was thirteen and my mother and older sisters agreed that I should take a job and earn some money. I don't recall that I volunteered for work but perhaps I did. At first there was some talk of my taking a place in one of the stores as a shop girl; but there were too many people, older and more experienced. So my sister, who was working in a store, asked the proprietor of a small ice cream and soda fountain shop to give me work. He consented and I was taken on to serve ices and cold drinks to the customers. One day after I had been there a few weeks, a mulatto, a man perhaps forty years of age who had had both legs amputated to the hips and who stood on the sidewalk near the shop selling pencils, scoured in at the door on his crutches, placed ten cents on the counter, and asked for an ice cream soda. I remember that a great battle, vague and non-decisive, raged in my own mind, while I put the cream into the glass. But the proprietor was out and it did not occur to me to ask a member of his family who sat in the back of the store if I should do it. Anyway, the man had paid the money and I had put it in the cash drawer. But I was extremely nervous about the transaction. The mulatto acted as though he had been accustomed to getting ice creams there for a long, long time. When this incident was reported to the proprietor, he was very angry, and spoke crossly to me; and had his wife explain that I should never do it again. And then when he chanced to see my mother he explained to her the seriousness of the matter, as he thought he would not have a customer left, if people knew that "that nigger" had had ice cream at his soda fountain.

After a few days my mother made an excuse, saying she needed me at home, and took me away; or perhaps she thought the man wanted to be rid of me, and didn't want the embarrassment of having me fired. Anyway, I was not a success at his Soda Fountain. I despised dipping out spoonfuls of the cream and filling the glasses; and I was so embarrassed if men or boys spoke to me in a familiar way that I often did not know quite what I was doing. I felt as though I should drop dead if one of my teachers or some of my classmates who never worked in shops should come and find me there. I am trying to think what embarrassed me. Was it because people might think I was not a "nice" girl? Or would they know now that we were very poor? Or was I ashamed of being employed in so mean a shop? Was it because I was so ugly? The last was a source of a good deal of pain to me. I do not remember having had the thought that there was any beauty in me until I was past twenty-five years of age. When I was a very young child, I remember my mother once exclaiming, "My God, ain't she about the ugliest child you ever seen!" Then they used to call me

"Little Wiley," because my mouth was large and when I laughed my teeth showed in the same manner as my brother's did, the brother whom I thought was an idiot. I disliked this brother profoundly, was ashamed of him and hated being in his presence, though I was always tremendously sorry for him; and being told by the family that I was like him was an enormous blow to me.

My period did come, as my mother predicted, that summer. It was while I was working at this shop. My sister passed the soda fountain joint and we walked home together on the day it occurred. I told her about it, that something had been coming out of me all day, she was sure that I was unwell. She advised me to take care, not to run or get my feet wet; said every girl had to have it and it came every month. So that was what my mother meant by "your monthlies." I put everything together and saw that although I had dismissed all my mother said as though I understood, I really had not had the smallest conception of what was going to happen to me, in spite of the fact that I had seen the stained clothes of my mother and sisters during their periods. I was not alarmed, only a little disgusted.

That year my mother sold the house on Willow Street and we moved into "one of the best communities in town." It was on Butternut Street; on one side of us was a Methodist parson, at least his family lived there, he being a "circuit rider" was away most of the time. Across the street lived old man Warren and his wife and daughter, eminent largely because of his sons-in-law, though the old man himself owned a controlling share in the bank of which one son-in-law was president. Another son-in-law was in the real estate business and sold this place to my mother, and still a third was the pastor of the First Baptist Church. How we were warned and preached to before we went there! We were not to go into other people's yards without being invited; there was not to be too much loud talking and yelling; we were not to let people hear us calling one another fools, idiots, devils as we often did when we were angry. For she did not want people to think we had been brought up like a lot of wild asses' colts.

The real estate agent, Eugene Wood, made the transaction with my mother about the house, the Willow Street place having been sold at a profit of two hundred dollars, which made our share in the old house amount to eight hundred dollars as we had already paid six hundred dollars. This eight hundred dollars was transferred as payment to the Butternut Street place, for which we were to pay two thousand dollars, leaving an indebtedness of twelve hundred dollars, my mother guaranteeing to pay twenty-five dollars per month in installments with interest fixed at ten percent. How would she do it? Where there was a will there was a way. Why, she could make enough out of boarders to pay that amount each month...

The three oldest boys had left home and were farming or had become sort of migratory workers. We seldom heard from them and I can't remember that they ever sent any money home. But there were my two older sisters about eighteen and twenty or a little past and my two brothers between myself and them who had to have work as they had refused to attend the public school. I say refused, they were out of school age and, of course, hated to be put into classes with the small children. What my mother wanted them to do was to take a job which did not require too much of their time or energy and then to study at the Business College in the evening. Education was a thing which you couldn't take away from a person and a business education was about the most valuable thing a man could have, besides everyone should know how to earn a living. A person could always make use of subjects like bookkeeping and shorthand. My mother had heard many stories of how ignorant men had "riz" to high positions through their own efforts. Besides she was going to pay a visit to Uncle Glasgow and she believed she could borrow enough money to pay off the notes for a year or two so that my brothers would have a chance to finish a business course and get a job; and I believe she put it plainly "and help her make a living."

But they swelled up with anger at the idea of working and going to school too. Besides my brother, Sumpter, just seventeen months older than myself, always hated school, not only school but any form of studying; and Ruel's attitude, the next brother older than Sumpter by another seventeen or eighteen months, was not much better. I remember very well the different angles from which my mother attacked the problem of trying to get these boys into school. At first she tried to reason with them, to show them the advantages to themselves of an education; then she tried to coax them, that is she tried to "hire" them to attend, by offering to buy them stringed instruments. Afterwards she stated she had made arrangements for their tuition with the professor of the night school; and when they still sulked and quarreled and would not listen to her promises to take one of them (Sumpter) when she went to see Uncle Glasgow (I must confess that a visit to my uncle's would not have interested me either) and the stringed instruments were taken back as there was no money to pay for them, and the boys showed no interest in them, she threatened them. She told them that she would have an officer of the law "escort them to that school every single night." She was going to put them into the hands of the law if they resisted. Her threats were almost as strong as those of Peter the Great who rammed education down the throats of the Russians with the sword. She would show them that they had to obey her. Terrible quarrels and long sulkings ensued. Although from time to time the boys were without work, Ruel had a good job driving the dry goods wagon of the store in the millinery department of which Corrie (my second sister) worked. It was not considered difficult work and he earned twenty dollars a month. Sumpter had had jobs here and there and had lost them.

I do not know who was at fault in the loss of these jobs, but sometimes I know my mother blamed the boys. She often declared that she spent half her time hunting work for her children. One day when she was very angry and exasperated, she summed it all up as follows: "I know what's the matter with these boys. They want me to beat them and then they'll leave home." Sometimes she would say, "And if they go they can stay gone." Then she would weep until her eyes were "blood-shotten," wiping her face with the corner of her apron, and say that no woman ever lived who had had a harder life than she had had. There she had five sons who were already young men, "you might say," and all of them "strong, able-bodied men with brains as good as anyone's, if they would only work them," and not one of them wanted to do a thing for her… "There ain't a one of these boys that cares for me…they all think much more of their old daddy than they do of me… They show it in the way they help me"—she meant their failure to help her showed they did not love her—"… there ain't a one of these boys that wants to help me make a living or lift any of the responsibility from my shoulders." Then she would tell how good this young man or that person was to his mother, "Just look at the way Steve Powers works and takes care of his mother." Often Emma and I would weep too, but Corrie did not shed her tears so easily, in fact I think Emma could weep more easily than any of us.

As I recall, it all came out as predicted; they quarreled and fought and scratched until the boys finally used this as a pretext for leaving. I liked very much having the family "thin out"; I had come to hate my brothers, when they quarreled with my mother and their faces and lips were all swollen from anger and tears, more than ever. I despised them as I have despised few human beings. Fancy anyone saying that he didn't want to know anything, "not wanting to be anybody," refusing an opportunity to study and using my mother's threats and ill temper as an excuse for leaving her in this awful plight. Then these older boys, Ruel and Sumpter, would sometimes strike the little boys younger than myself (Roger and Major), the most terrific blows often on the head, or kick them or hit them in the stomach and send them away screaming. I used to be so angry that I wanted to kill them. I say kill, I am sure that if the blow with the force I wished it to carry had hit them it would have meant sudden death. But of course I could do nothing except quarrel with them and I didn't dare do much of that, for this would have thrown me in a tantrum of fury which gave me fear as to what the outcome might be. I had very little in common with these two boys when I was ten years old; and now at thirteen we seemed totally in opposition. I had not much conversation with them, they never said anything which interested me; and if they ever brought their friends to the house, they were sure to be boys whom I disliked, was ashamed of or laughed at. Once or twice my mother ordered them not to bring certain boys to our house again. The truth of the matter was they hadn't many friends; I don't believe they were friendly with a single boy in our street. Life there "among the best people of the town" was too restricted for them; so they rebelled, then quarreled, and fought their way out of it.

—≺✦

My mother thought she would be able to get a living and pay off the notes on the place by taking in boarders, with what little money the children were able to give her. With this in view, she fitted up the first two rooms with the necessary equipment. We all hated having the "front room" or parlor given over to boarders; my sisters, especially

Emma, would have no place for their beaux. But it was all arranged and sometimes as many as six or eight people were accommodated. A curtain was strung across one of the rooms and two men and their wives occupied it. At first, all went very well, then the boarders dropped off; my brothers were without work part of the time or had left home altogether; and my sisters, as my mother often remarked, could hardly clothe themselves. Corrie was receiving only five dollars a month (the first year she received no wages as she was only an apprentice, and for some time afterwards she worked for five dollars per month); Emma was getting ten or fifteen dollars per month at the telephone office. And both of them spent most of their earnings for clothing. Of course, they were good at making things over and at making their own hats, but it was easy to secure credit accounts and they often made bills which required months to pay. My mother did the same thing; she established accounts wherever she needed them and paid them when she could. In this way, when anyone of the family was in need he could be supplied. But it led us into great difficulties and threw my mother into a panic when anyone of the family was sick or out of work.

If the boarders were scarce or it appeared that they were going to be, my mother would ask among the neighbors or missionary women for sewing. That was a thing at which I could help after school and on Saturdays. I was permitted to use the machine when I was ten years old and by the time I was thirteen I had made or helped to make many plain garments, that is children's clothes and underclothing, as we did a good deal of "plain sewing." Besides this I believe I must have done the major part of the family washing. Roger and Martha, a boy and a girl younger than myself, helped me and often Corrie and Emma were forced to wash and iron their own as they required waists and camisoles two or three times a week, not to mention the other garments… How much I have washed! And in what quantities! For years and years, from the time my sisters began to "work out" until I left home at the age of twenty-two, I consumed all my surplus energy at washing. But if it was hard work I rarely found any embarrassment in doing it, as I could do it privately. I liked it better than "waiting on" the boarders, passing from the kitchen door to the dining room with plates of hot biscuits, or bowls of edibles or whatnot—this I despised. My mother was often irritated and scolded me on account of it, "It looks like it will kill her to have to turn her hand to wait on that table." Often she would send me out in a rough way and say she would do it herself. She learned to put most of the victuals on the table; then she would sit at the head and pass things around and go for the biscuits herself. But as to the washing, it, I had with me always; intermittent, that is a lapse of two or three days, but continuous. I washed and ironed before breakfast and after school and on Saturdays; and sometimes if I had been lazy or had not had time to finish all, I would have to iron on Sunday morning, especially if anyone wanted to go to Sunday School and had no clean clothes to wear. Then I used to be called up early in the morning to iron a clean waist for my sister before she went to the store. And if

I ever complained, as I am sure I did often enough, I was told that everyone in the family was working like a dog and that I had nothing to do but go to school.

At school I was completing the seventh grade and would enter high school. I had learned Texas history fairly well and had good marks in almost every subject: spelling, grammar, geography, arithmetic, and whatever else there was; and I had time to play some too at school as the teacher was not too severe. After two or three years with some of the same classmates, we became friendly, though I believe never intimate, and sometimes we joked or wrote silly notes. A young fellow in the high school used to walk to and from school with me and carry my books. He was the brother of one of the teachers of the South Ward and considered a bright nice boy. One day I went up to the seventh grade room before the bell rang at noon where we were all talking, I began to tease my desk mate about the mischievous boy, whom the teacher kept sitting in the corner for an entire month or more, who had been throwing roses at her. I would write on her tablet W.M. (the girl) plus C.S. (the boy) and remind her that he had called her an American beauty. But, she said, he had called me "that" too; I explained that that was after she had asked him if he meant herself or myself and he answered both. Then she began writing G.B. plus S.A.; and I pretended that I didn't know whom she meant. "You don't know and you walked with him this noon," she jeered. "But," I said, "his initials are V.A." "Of course," she went on in a voice full of disgust and contempt, "his name is Victor Anderson but everybody knows him as 'Stickhorse Anderson.'" This was the appellation the boys in high school had given him because of his length. "I know what you will do," she went on, "you'll be married by the time you're eighteen; but I—I'm going to finish school and be a teacher." For some reason this stung me deeply, and yet I felt that she or any girl must be jealous that a fellow so handsome and clever as Victor was walking with me.

⤚✶

In the midst of work, worry, and school, I found time to learn to play the organ. The instrument was a good one; everybody remarked it— the one my father bought with the girls' cotton picking money when I was nine years old. From the beginning I was taught some chords and gradually learned the notes, and now my sister, Corrie, who had studied for these years, would listen to my songs and correct me. She nearly always said my time was incorrect; and sometimes she scolded me and called me stupid or a "little fool." I learned some of the exercises and childish songs in the instructor and was soon playing the more simple of the religious and popular songs. As often as possible I practiced after school or after supper or on Sunday afternoons.

After a time, I had acquired quite a repertory of old songs and childish ditties and would play and sing for hours. I didn't mind my mother's listening and commenting though I think I should have been "self-conscious" had I known anyone else was listening. I liked the old sentimental songs; the more weepy, lovesick, and sentimental they were the better I liked them. Once after I had been playing and singing "Juanita," my mother came to the door with tears in her eyes, "Play that song again, Gertrude, and *sing out*," she said, trying to hide her emotion. Then I pretended I didn't know which one she meant, or perhaps I really didn't know and asked her which one. "Jewneeter," she would say, "I think that is what you call it." And sometimes I corrected her as though I were irritated, "Juanita, Mother, (Wahnita), not Jewneeter." She'd go back to the sitting room saying, "Well, then, Wahnita." And sometimes after I'd gone over the old rigmarole… "Soft o'er the mountains lingering steals the southern moon"…and through the last chorus, "be my own fair bride," she'd come in again and say, "Now, this time *I'm* going to sing. Just wait till I get my glasses on…and let me find the place." Then she'd go out making remarks like these: "Yes, sir, that's a pretty song… That's sure one pretty song."

I wanted to laugh or to cry when she came in; or sometimes I was irritated if she made too many mistakes. I was so conceited that I thought it did not matter that I made many errors in playing the piece; what mattered was her pronunciation and her tune. Once she sang "When You and I Were Young, Maggie" and did it so well that when she finished, I spoke coolly about it to try to conceal what I was thinking. (I wonder just what does lurk in a girl's mind on such occasions. She had sometimes held her countenance like that when I wanted her to praise *me*. Maybe I thought she sang much better than I ever would; and perhaps, too, with this was mingled some fragment of an idea that her voice was a little cracked and a little out of tune. Maybe also I thought she liked her own voice better than she should. I think I was amused, sad, afraid she was becoming conceited, jealous, and perhaps a little irritated…all at once.) She had told of having sung this song as a duet with Aunt Maggie at the country schoolhouse when they were young, she having sung the soprano, which she still pitched much too high for the key in which it should have been sung.

Most of the girls at school lived in other neighborhoods and as I never had very intimate friends among them, I played usually with the neighbor children who came to see my younger brothers and sisters. Generally speaking, the four younger children (Roger, Martha, Alta, Major the baby boy) were of no embarrassment or irritation to me. Now that I think of it; I never heard a vile word about sex from any of them. This is rather remarkable when I think of the conduct and talk of my five oldest brothers when I was between the ages of about four (my earliest recollections) and nine. My mother's influence and severity, I am sure, bore fruit. She watched everyone and talked plainly enough, though often with little of the frankness of the descriptive scientist. But they understood, or were deterred, as though they did understand. For one thing these children were never left to play alone for hours together. They were usually under my mother's eye. I slept in the same room with them, saw them dress and undress until they were twelve years old or so, the little boys sometimes sleeping with us girls, and there was never the slightest indication that they realized they were of a different sex from ourselves.

The younger children had a much more preoccupied life than the older ones had had, with their school and Sunday School and all the other diversions which one finds in town life. I think they had many more friends than I ever had, especially the boys. They had friends and apparently very warm ones among the well-to-do and so-called best families. Once the daughter of the millionaire district judge who lived a mile or two away in a great house on the lake came and begged my mother to let Roger come out on Saturday. She would say in her coarse voice, "Mrs. Beasley, Roger is the sweetest kid I ever knew in my life." I think the child had worked on their farm in the summer or perhaps she saw him at school; anyway they all liked him so much that he was being coaxed and begged to come out and ride their horses. And if I even looked jealous, my mother would console me by saying she was the ugliest girl she ever saw (in spite of the fact that she had an awfully good heart), and that she wanted somebody to play the tomboy with her, who could ride. Besides she was in a lower grade than myself, though she was a couple of years older. "You know, she's a laughingstock with her gross voice."

—*←*

During these years my sister, Emma, gave my mother a lot of worry. Too many men courted her at once. Sometimes it seemed that a different person called her up every day. She went to shows, out to dinner with them, and buggy riding. Once in a while, if my mother doubted too much, she would send me along with them—to my chagrin, or pleasure in eating sweets, or joy in driving, or sorrow. Sometimes in order to keep the engagement, Emma would ask Mother to let me go with them; but at other times both parties were decidedly angry. My mother would worry and talk to me, if there was no one else to listen. Once she said right out that she had been watching each month to see if Emma's sickness came on her; and then she went on to say that if a woman had a lot of men she would not be "caught up" anyway. Sometimes she said things of this nature directly to me, other times she would talk to herself, as though she were mad. Men were always sending Emma boxes of candy, from one-pound to five-pound boxes; I believe a few times she received ten-pound boxes. And how we young ones loved it! I see now how we stood around with watery mouths and hungry eyes; and if we put our hands in once too often, we were sure to get a smack. She had enough candy boxes to cover the entire floor of a room. A few times she received rather handsome toilet sets or pins, but my mother required her to return them immediately, or else as soon as they "broke up."

In spite of all the suspicions and dark talk which Emma aroused in my mother, she was pleased that so many people said she was pretty and that the men thought her attractive. I could see that. She would go over the conversation she had had with a very staid, religious, old woman who said Emma was one of the prettiest girls she ever saw…she looked so soft and tender that a man could just crush her in his hands… "If I had a daughter as pretty as she who had to go out and earn her living, I should be scared to death," the woman said. Then my mother would turn to saying that Emma was so much more openhearted than Corrie, she would tell what these fool men said to her, while Corrie had rather die than tell. So she would go on, worrying, gossiping, and suspicioning, until I was saturated with curiosity or hate. I stored away almost everything I ever heard her say about sex, although a good deal of it was very vague to me, like her remarks about menstruation. And sometimes I was thinking how I should hate her if she ever talked and whispered about me, as she did about my older sisters.

She gossiped to us girls about other people, that is she would repeat some story which the boys or someone had told her; and then she would bet this was true or that was so about certain girls or women. There was a girl, whose parents kept boarders and lived in the next block, who used to be on her tongue incessantly; she would bet that ole Ader (Ada) Kirk was not living as she should. Then she would repeat in her usual whispers and grimaces a story which she said she heard from my oldest brother—how he came into possession of it, I have no means of knowing. The story was that Robert Hardy, a young fellow next door, the brother of my much loved teacher, Mrs. Morrow, who was about as different from her as one human being could be from another, had "run this ole Ader Kirk out of town on the handle bars of his bicycle, one evening, and done what he wanted to…they said she bled lak' a stuck hog…" Sometimes my sisters would turn away nauseated and, when they could stand no more, say, "I know if Mother caynt say the nastiest things of enny-body I ever heard." (This phrase is a fair example of English as she spoke at home; I'm sure I have employed sentences or near sentences quite as unintelligible in the letters which I have written home during the past years. It seemed so much more natural and so friendly to use language which they understood.)

At such remarks my mother was sure to be miffed. Perhaps she would wait until the next day, the next week, or the next month; but she was sure to fly in a rage sooner or later and scold and talk and preach. She had worked and suffered, talked and preached to us about "these things" and now if anyone got into trouble, he or she needn't come to her for help. "I try to tell them and they act as though I was just a vulgar-mouthed old woman." (All of us used the word vulgar in the sense of obscene.) She would connect this incident with the hard times and the little help the girls were giving her and for days and days we would live in a perfect hell. Sometimes she would begin her "rearing and pitching," as she and my father both used to term their quarrels, because she was unwell, or because we children were not working hard enough, or because she could see no way to make a living.

⭒

I passed to the eighth grade, the first year of high school, the next year, and took up the study of Latin and Algebra along with

American History, grammar, and other subjects. No one in the whole connection, as far as I knew, had ever seen inside a Latin grammar or a treatise on Algebra. I have seen members of my family look in these books and then close them instantly as though afraid something would jump out of them. Perhaps they only thought I would scold them for handling my books. On such occasions I often frowned, acted cross or uninterested, or called them idiots, to keep them from seeing the pride in my eyes and the conceit of my countenance. I adored thinking I was going to study the higher branches.

One day while I was walking with my eighth grade teacher, an extremely large woman and apparently just as big brained (though of very little tact), she began to question me about the number of children in our family. I was embarrassed and hemmed and hawed, and finally said there were twelve (my mother had often told people she had twelve children); and Miss Parker quickly rejoined "and you make thirteen." I thought she must have known in advance. Maybe she wanted to "cow" me and keep me timid. I nearly always wanted to fall out with people who asked such questions; but here I was in a situation where I had to put up with it. She said there were twelve children in her family. One day one of the girls told me that Miss Parker had told them that there were thirteen children in Gertrude Beasley's family. I was indignant. I had been betrayed. I finally wormed it out of the girl why she had told them, and she explained that Miss P. was telling some of the antics which she and her brothers used to perform. She had said there were twelve children in her family.

Two things happened when I was fourteen. I had nervous prostrations, and I joined the church. Perhaps no one would agree with me
as to the former, as I was apparently not ill and missed no time at
school. But at night after the chores were done, I had prepared my
lessons and gone to bed, my body would quiver and jerk sometimes
for two hours. Sometimes I woke my sister and she was cross and
struck me; but once she was alarmed and took me into my mother's
room and told her how I shook and shook, making the whole bed
vibrate every night. Every one of them took it seriously for a little;
they looked on me with alarm and pity. Their concern relieved me
somewhat. Then Corrie looked as though she thought I was "putting
on" or said something which made me think she believed I was feign-
ing illness; but Mother and Emma spoke in a sympathetic way to
me and Mother thought I was "studying too hard." I do not remember that this trouble lasted much after this occasion; perhaps drawing attention to myself helped to allay it. But there were many brief
moments when something seemed to be cramping my whole nervous organism; I was in an attitude of holding my breath; many ideas
flocked to my brain at once, and I was counting the seconds or frac-
tion of seconds when I should drop dead. There was always a tinge of
horrible and penetrating fear, regret, and sorrow. Regret, in the sense
of something indefinable which I wanted and had never had.

One Sunday night I walked down the aisle (without quite

knowing I was going to do it) and offered myself for membership in the church. I was agitated inside me a little like the nervous prostrations I had experienced; I felt tongue-tied at the first question. But the pastor understood children and put his question in words which I could understand. He asked when I was saved; and I believe other questions much more intimate and embarrassing which I had difficulty in answering: like, had I given my heart to God? how did I do it? did I pray? etc. And how the women in the choir craned their necks trying to hear what I was saying! When I had finished the preacher blessed and congratulated me. The choir loge seemed to have sunk down lower or else the floor raised itself when the organ began to play. At last I had done it. My Sunday School teacher had often asked me to do it; and I had thought of it many times myself, but was too shy or too afraid. I think I did it out of duty—whatever that vague word means. I felt that it was a thing, church joining, which would get me sooner or later and I might as well do it now and finish with it. Other times I thought it a good thing to do. Undoubtedly, the fact that my mother and sisters had joined the church had something to do with it. The women of the mission society and the businesspeople had finally answered (apparently) all my mother's arguments against joining and now she was in the fold. She told them that she was raised a Methodist, but since she married, she'd seen so many hypocrites in the church that she had been disgusted and stayed out. But when she talked to us children, she'd give cases; why that old Doctor Beasley (my grandfather) would hold Sunday School and talk and pray and then go home and beat his wife. He slept with other women, he even slept with his own sister-in-law that ole Alice Anderson, who was smart enough but an awful sorry woman. She was a schoolteacher. "Even yer Daddy used to talk about what hypocrites they wuz in the church."

One evening before I was baptized, Corrie took me aside and questioned me, in what I considered an offensive way, about having joined the church. Had I been regenerated? She had never heard of it, she went on in the same breath. I thought she was accusing me of insincerity or of having lied to the preacher. "Two years ago," I said. I felt pale and shy and she quit talking and looked sort of "sheepish"… Terror and wonder seized me when Brother Lee Scarborough, the pastor of the First Baptist Church of Abilene, Texas, led me out of the huddle of little girls standing in water waist deep, in the baptistry, to where the choir and congregation could see. I believe he asked me some more questions about when I had given my heart to God, and if I felt at peace with the Savior; then he placed one hand at the back of my neck and raised the other in the air (I suppose a sort of baptismal salute) and went through a formula something like this: "I baptize thee my sister, Gertrude Beasley, in the name of the Father, the Son, and the Holy Ghost." But just before he began this, he whispered to me to tell him my name. I remember distinctly that I was offended, hurt that he did not know. After the baptismal statement, he placed the other hand over my two hands which clasped at my breast and told me to close my eyes and hold my breath; then he put me under the water and brought me up again while the choir began softly, "Just as I am without one plea." My name being inserted in the church book, baptism and congratulations over, the strain was somewhat relieved, although I began to be afraid that the Sunday School teacher would ask me to pray in public, before the class, and that would have been just as embarrassing as when she (the same woman missionary, wife of the banker, Mr. P.) once came to me, the tears rolling down her cheeks when her brother-in-law, Brother Scarborough was calling the sinners to come forward and said, "Little girl, why not give your heart to Jesus? Why not follow Christ *now?*" I hope I shall learn to explain how this hurt my pride and the sense of degradation it gave me.

—⟵✶

My father upset all of us by "coming around" two or three times, when we lived on Butternut Street. I think one of his visits had something to do with what I have described as my nervous breakdown. I say visit, he would come up the alley to the back gate and try to see or talk with some of us. I did not want anyone to know about him, that is my parents' trouble and separation. The years went by, but nothing seemed to be able to ameliorate my feelings about such things. I was just as nervous and frightened as ever at the thought of his coming. Then my mother would turn to recounting how he would beat his children; how he had "run her off from home when she had six children"; he would come home drunk and threaten to kill her; he had mistreated her time and again when she was hardly able to put one foot before the other one; and now sometimes she just thought that if he ever came around and bothered us in any way that she ought to take a shot at him. Often I was kept from my lessons on account of her preachings and accounts of family quarrels and difficulties of twenty years standing. No one thought of showing by countenance or word that he disapproved of her scolding. Sometimes as the years went by some one of us girls would whisper to the others, "I wish Mother would shut up; I'll bet I've heard that story a thousand times."

My mother went away to visit her people in the spring in the hopes of getting a loan of money as times were very hard and it looked as though she might have to sell the property or else lose it on account of failing to make the monthly payments. She came home miffed. She knew she would get no money, though her brothers had talked in a very friendly way. Her sister had hurt her feelings. Anyway, "yer Aunt Maggie" had always despised the Beasleys and hated her children; acted as though she didn't want the children to play together... At this time the school closed with eighth grade and high school graduation exercises. Although my class had finished only half of the eighth grade work, we were called into the exercises and I required a new white dress. Four or five yards of white embroidery and some narrow white lace were purchased, out of which I made the dress. It was very simple. Two ruffles of embroidery made the skirt; a piece with the scallops turned toward the waistline formed the waist and then elbow sleeves with the embroidered edge as finishing; this completed it except for the lace which was whipped in at the neck. Everything went well in spite of the absence of my mother. I remember hating a girl, a couple of years older than myself, whose father was a rich cattle owner; I imagined her attitude was one of condescension towards me. I wore very, very plain clothes, perhaps the plainest in the class and she was always well dressed. But this did not always matter, as I remarked early in life.

From time to time the neighbors called to see us. One day old Mrs. Warren called (a rich woman who lived across the street) and during the course of conversation on raising children or how they were all going to the devil in those days, summed it all up by saying, "But if children go astray their parents are to blame, it's the way they are raised." "The way they are raised" would determine the life they would live. My mother was offended and talked about it many, many times. She guessed the ole lady had heard about Willie and just wanted to hurt her. Perhaps this grandson of hers, who was so wild, was going to give her some trouble yet. Sometimes she felt and declared to herself that she would never put her foot in that woman's house. Ole Warren and ole Mrs. Warren from time to time occupied her attention and her scorn.

⤙✦

A country woman who knew my mother and second sister very well, spoke to my mother about giving me a scholarship to an academy, which was just being built and equipped at Abilene. She, Mrs. Powers, was the owner of a great wheat farm to the north of town and had five children whom she wanted to educate. The youngest had completed the country school, and they had found attempts at riding to school at Abilene a failure. So the woman bought a few acres away out on the west side of town, built a fine looking two-story house in walking distance of the school, and prepared for starting the Powers family to school. At first my mother would have nothing to do with the idea of accepting the scholarship, for, as she told her, it would place her under some obligation to the woman; and as she wanted to be independent in raising and educating her children, and as the public school was a very good one, she declined. But the woman explained to her that there was absolutely no obligation; there was some reduction in fees for a family of six children; she would be compelled to pay the same price for five children; besides the school was well equipped and the professors were all college-bred men.

Finally, my mother gave in; there would be no obligations to live up to and perhaps no more expense than going to the public school; besides the school and the account of the professors attracted all of us. She had early, I believe, placed a great deal of hope in me. None of the others made any effort to improve themselves and I acted as though it would kill me to miss a day at school. For one thing I didn't look as though I was going to be crazy about the men, and maybe I was going to help her make a living. Nearly all the professors I liked, and they took a great interest in me; I completed Latin grammar, read exercises and a few fables, and did some work in Latin composition; and towards the end of the year was admitted to a charming course in elementary philology. We called it word study; I liked being in the class, because I felt that it gave me some superiority over the rest of the students. Anyway, I was delighted with the professor, his discussions of old English words, the tracing of root words from Latin sometimes through French to English, and the study of common Greek roots pleased me. Besides it was a very small quiet class and two of the cleverest young men in the academy were in it. One of them was about twenty-four years old; he was studying for the ministry and knew elementary Greek, and the other was the best Latin student in the school.

The daughter of the professor of religious literature, a girl about a year younger than myself, and I were the only girls. Sometimes these young fellows teased and joked with us and I think we were attracted by them, too, but we were both secretly in love with the professor. He was about thirty years of age, sensitive and highly strung, and I imagined everyone considered him handsome… Adelaide Klingman, my girl friend, and I were talking as we walked up the railway track one day. Prof. Robinson had recently been at their house for dinner and her father had asked her to say grace. Dr. Klingman had known the Professor for several years; he knew the young wife whom Robinson married and who had died. They were very much in love and she was going to have a baby. Adelaide said she knew a lot of things or maybe everything, perhaps I did not know. She knew what her parents were doing when they were lying very close in bed; they didn't think she knew, but she knew anyway. She giggled and ran away from me and began walking the rails, falling off the iron rail from the side she carried her books on. I ran along doing the same thing.

She mentioned the professor again, as her body toppled off perfectly limp on one side and then the other of the rail. "Sometimes I wish he would stick his thing in me," she said. I laughed a little and then became quiet. I don't believe I made any reply; she seemed hurt, as though I had not received this confidence as she had expected… Though I often dreamed of him, I think I had never formed the wish in my mind as clearly as Adelaide. If he touched my hand in giving me a book I would feel a physical sensation just as when I stood very near him. Mentally, I concocted a vague story of his making love to me: I was beautiful, or was going to astound him with my beauty, and I think I dreamed out the marriage ceremony even to the white dress and veil. Many times in my early teens I came very near Adelaide's wish, but usually beat it down with mental blows like those of my father's sledgehammer against the anvil, or like the lashes of the whip on a boy's back for some sexual crime. I see now that I was good at checking my own feelings; I could call myself to law as well as any. Then too the professor once talked very loudly and scolded me in the algebra class. I was frightened, hurt, and in awe of him; besides I imagined every girl in school was dreaming about being in love with him… Once I had daydreams about a boy in the seventh grade; I was getting into bed with him, and then I began to nag and scold myself like an old woman, until the image disappeared. I resisted such a dream with clinched fists and with all the force of my will…

Mrs. Klingman was a clever little woman. She had been trained to be an expression teacher, but her marriage had prevented her teaching except privately. She already had eight children, her fourteen-year-old Adelaide being the oldest; and looked young enough to have eight more. All of this brood appeared bright; each one had a box of tricks. Adelaide played "classical" music; she had studied at the conservatory in Detroit where they had lived before coming to Texas; and the rest of them could play or sing or recite. They were all happy in spite of their numbers; and Klingman and his wife were still in love. At least I imagined they were.

Once I stopped at their house with Adelaide when the father had just come from school. He told us very seriously there was something crawling over there on the wall; we looked and looked, at least I did, and when we turned heads he and his wife were kissing and laughed at us. I felt stupid in my seriousness and yet it seemed jolly to me; Adelaide also thought it was jolly and said they were always like that. He would explain that he had to wait for his wife four years, until he finished college, never kissed her until they rode home in the carriage from the church; and now they were making up for lost time. I think I would have felt some deep shame if I had ever seen the pastor of the First Baptist Church kissing his wife; but perhaps it was only because my mother used to sniff and turn her mouth down in scorn at his "keeping his wife in Mother Hubbards all the time." And

I suppose I would have dropped, dead, if I had ever seen my father kiss my mother.

Times grew harder and harder. My sisters never increased their salaries and they seemed to be compelled to spend most of it for clothing. My mother continued taking in boarders and sewing; my younger brother had afternoon and Saturday jobs, but with it all enough money could not be scraped together to pay the notes; in fact, they had lapsed for several months. Eugene Wood, the land agent, found a buyer and my mother sold the Butternut Street place at a profit of two hundred dollars, squared off with Wood and put the remainder into a house on Chestnut Street, which was known as Main Street farther down towards town. The house had five large rooms and was easily accessible to the city. She would be sure to get boarders here. At least twenty-five dollars a month would accrue from the two outer rooms; and the sums which the children would give her and her gardening and sewing would undoubtedly pay expenses. The two rooms were furnished for boarders and we occupied the other three rooms, folding beds being placed in the sitting room and the dining room and a bed or two in the kitchen. This was easily managed as all the rooms were good sized.

Then my mother set herself about a plan of advertising for boarders. She would put an ad in the paper, erect a sign at the corner of the yard, and then have an advertisement painted on one of the benches near the station. How I dreaded all this. The "sign board" did really go up. It was a small, bright, green plank on which was painted in sharp black letters something like this: Mrs. J. Beasley's Boarding House, Meals served: Dinners 50 c; Suppers 35 c; Breakfasts 25 c. The place was near enough town, surely some extra money would come in from "giving meals." She worked out an elaborate scheme of advertising; she would ask permission to have the name and something about the meals painted on one of them seats at the station; also would mention about the meals; and she supposed she ought to write the address too, so they would know where to come. Then people getting off the train or passing through town would see the sign and come up to the house for their meals. "We have just got to quit being so proud, we're going to starve to death if we don't." Then she would say "these three little ones have got to be fed and clothed and kept in school and you've got to finish your schoolin'. You've just got to keep all your irons to the fire. I guess there'll be *some* way." Then she would go on saying how she stayed awake at night thinking how she could feed the children and pay for the place. "Poor little Roger, he gives me every cent. There never was a better boy ever lived than Roger." She'd go on in her usual tears, "Only one of the boys who has ever cared for me... These other boys don't care whether I starve or what becomes of me." The conversation would last two hours or so at a time. "Here I'm the mother of seven sons, five of them grown men, and I'm continually harassed to death for fear of not making a living. If these boys was married it might be different; but not a one of them has a soul to take care of except hisself. I declare to God, it don't look as though a one of them had a drop of human blood in their body. Just as ignorant as they can be; have to go out and work in somebody's field; I tried to get them to go to school, tried to force Ruel and Sumpter to go and they all talked and treated me as though I was the meanest old woman that ever lived.

"Tried to get Emmer to go to the business college; she just reared and pitched, said she was not going to work all day and go to school at night; had to have some pleasure, you only live once, she and Corrie are always saying, 'you only live once.' Looks like the girls ain't doing much better'n the boys; seems like Emmer will have to have every cent of her money for her clothes; couldn't give me a cent last month. And Corrie has went and bought this piano. Tried to get her to wait at least until we could get the notes caught up on this place. That organ is a good instrument; no, she's got to have a piano, and hasn't never paid Miss S. for all them music lessons. The woman was awful good to her; said she didn't have to pay for them; she sympathized with anyone who was trying to learn; said she had had a hard time herself." So she would go on. I rarely missed a gesture, a facial expression or a word. Sometimes it seemed to do her so much good to talk, but sometimes I felt compelled to listen.

At school (C's Christian Institute or the C.C.I.) life was always jolly. But the school was generally referred to as the Christian College, as it was supported by members of the non-progressive Christian (Campbellite) denomination. Naughty boys gave the interpretation of C.C.I. as Christian College Idiots, this having originated at the ball games. Though the people of this denomination were as great fanatics as any, they were much less emotional, that is, they did not believe in any miracle of conversion; their religion lay in "works" and service, and although my mother scorned them as followers of ole Alexander Campbell, she often repeated their slogan that "faith without works is dead." The non-progressives believed that an instrument in the church was in some way irreligious. But they usually sang more heartily than the choirs of other churches. The young Campbellite preacher, whom I have mentioned in the philology class, used to lead the singing. He had a tuning fork which he tapped to get the correct pitch "Do, sol, mi, do," he would send out sonorous and round. And once when his quartette sang, "Though your sins be as scarlet, they shall be as white as snow...though they be red like crimson, they shall be as wool," I saw people, especially old women, wiping tears away. This was the way they did at the Baptist Church, people were always weeping there. The words and music of this song soothed me very much, "though they be *reeeed* like *crimmmson*, they shall beee as woollll," with a startlingly low bass note on wool made me emotional too; though the usual lack of emotion in the Campbellite churches pleased me; perhaps it was not so much the emotion I wished to be free from as the sense of degradation I felt in being coaxed to ask the Lord to forgive my sins.

Mrs. Klingman decided that I had ability as a dramatic speaker and inveigled me into taking expression lessons of her. At first she offered to give me lessons free, but my mother and I were both unwilling to accept them gratis. I told her I could sew and showed her some of my own clothes which I had made; afterwards she gave me several plain garments to make for her children in exchange for the lessons. I learned a number of pieces which I used to recite to her for instruction as to expression. I adored having the audience look at me and listen to my speaking, especially if they seemed pleased, and so I usually chose recitations which would amuse them. Such pieces were sure to leave them laughing and cheering. Once I gave a long story at a joint meeting of our school societies, a humorous thing in dialect, of a country woman going up in an elevator for the first time; she thought perhaps she had drunk something which had gone to her head. The audience was convulsed for fifteen or twenty minutes. And how it pleased Mrs. Powers (my benefactress)! I shall never forget how radiant was the face of this old farmeress and wheat grower. And once I read what we called a pen picture of Prof. Hoover, the Latin teacher. He had been very severe with the class about learning the declensions of Latin pronouns and had kept us after school. So that in the picture which I had written I quoted a part of the exercise, folding my hands just as he did and using his gestures and queer emphasis with his fingers.

There were four societies for the school, two for the boys and two for the girls. This was to create competition in debate. The young men used to have heated debates, sometimes on political questions and sometimes I wished I had been admitted. But my forte was the recitation, and usually someone or myself spoke a piece while the judges were rendering their decision. Once I gave a long recitation in poetry; I do not remember the title or the author. But it was the story of lovers in a wood, who having kissed one another a number of times, were startled by a little bird which called out, "Do it, do it, do it again...do it again." This time I left the platform feeling hurt or angry or serious; my eyes felt a little as though I wanted to cry; perhaps if I had not called up some such feeling I would have laughed, for when every ear was turned towards my voice in imitation of a little bird crying, "doo eet," I saw the expression on the face of the youngest Powers boys and I thought they thought that the bird had reference to something more intimate than kissing. Anyway, I had seen these boys give their sister a very knowing glance when "it" and "thing" were used in their presence. These words had been connected in some way with sex since I could remember.

United States History also was taught by Hoover. He jarred my credulity with reference to the authenticity of History. There were two histories prescribed as textbooks for the class; we could take our choice. One of them was written by a Yankee and the point of view was different. So men wrote history like they wanted it to sound. I cannot recall cases in point. But this aroused my wonder and astonishment. A little later I was admitted to Dr. Klingman's class of the General History of Europe. I seem to recall nothing which he ever taught me, but my impression is that I thought him a very wise man. How serious we were in that class!... But in the Physical Geography class, it was different. The geography teacher who had charge of the upper grades, (the C.C.I. carried classes from the primary to College) was a woman of no particular cleverness, on the contrary plain and a little giddy. There was a boy in the class whom we considered a great humorist; he could make the teacher laugh until the tears rolled down her cheeks. The custom was to read the geography lesson and then to discuss it. And almost invariably when our humorist was called on to read, we were sure to be entertained. Once when he was reading some dry thing about geological structures, he put in, "and they looked around and found a lot of brass monkeys." And another time when we were reading about the San Francisco earthquake, he read several lines in serious voice and then went on with the same expression saying, that the people were startled: "they acted like a lot of kill-dees with frozen feet dancing on a hot rock." (The kill-dee is a slender-legged bird known to the prairies of Texas.) Other times he would read the text correctly, but in the tone of voice of a negro preacher.

The year's course in English consisted of advanced grammar, composition, rhetoric, and American literature. I recall the name Washington Irving but little more; have a vague image in mind of an old stagecoach; of Ichabod Crane; a slow, ratty, old horse; of Rip Van Winkle and his twenty years of sleep; and of Sleepy Hollow. We had to memorize poetry too; I think it was Thanatopsis, though I cannot be sure; I cannot remember who wrote it; I guess either Bryant or Lowell. Is it William Cullen Bryant or William Cullen Bryan? I would have to look in the book to be sure. At any rate, then, the teacher had a good opinion of my work, for he used to give me extremely high marks on almost all my papers. Adelaide and I were pretty near the top of the list; a few times I received a hundred percent on tests and examinations.

There were a few very "rough" young people who came to this school; one young fellow about twenty years of age was beaten by the president, Dr. Barrett, and then expelled. We all stood around and listened and watched after the two came out of the president's office. Barrett had his coat off and looked as though he'd been having a knock-down-and-drag-out fight. He was "puffing and blowing" and remarked that he had given him what he deserved. The young man, a disgustingly offensive person, started off towards town, down the railway track, cursing and threatening the teacher. A story was circulated about him and one of the Scarborough girls, (a distant relative of the Baptist pastor); she had told someone about their lovemaking; he had put his hands all over her. I believe this girl was expelled from school also…I never liked being among the coarse and vulgar; I preferred the Professor's daughter and the brightest and most serious young men in school. It is true that I often welcomed attention from the dudes and well-dressed, as I have always liked form in other people. I see now that nearly everyone realized that I did not care for the obscene and the vulgar; and the commonest youths, whom I came into contact with, respected my views, and held their tongues in my presence.

The question of cheating in school occurs to me. I believe I am a little afraid I shall not tell the truth about this. Perhaps I am making a fetish of being honest or of coming so near the truth. I cannot recall that the idea ever occurred to me during this year even to write a word on a convenient scrap of paper, though it may be only a failure of memory. In the sixth, seventh, and eighth grades at the public school, I remember having written words on the top of my desk, or the answers to problems, or perhaps names in geography. But this was only on the border of dishonesty; a very different thing, as I considered, from keeping one's book open inside the desk and sliding it back and forth in search of the answer when the teacher was asking her questions.

My mother was pleased with the Christian College. She visited the school exercises and met the professors, several of whom were Yankees. In speaking of the Klingman family my mother would remark, "Aw, all Yankees are well-educated." Then she would go on to explain that the men too, were better to their women; not so much double life, not so deceitful; more open. Some of the supporters of this school had awful queer ideas, as for example believing the body slept after death until the Second Coming, and then they didn't believe in no regeneration; but some of them was awful fine people. "There is good people in all churches." She and Mrs. Powers could not get along. They sympathized with one another in their afflictions, but there was not much love lost between them. My mother would talk and gossip about the Powerses. She had heard that Mr. Powers, her husband, was an awful good man, but Mrs. Powers had just hagged and quarreled and fussed and harassed him about religion, until he had killed hisself. They said it was an accident, but some people said he shot hisself. "Ah, all that story about his being hunting in the pasture and climbing through the bob (barbed) wire fence and the gun going off... Ah," she would turn the corners of her mouth down, "And Mrs. Powers is shore worried... Shore trying to find the true way now..." And if I looked as though I felt too sorry or too disgusted, or too hurt, (I say hurt, though perhaps I was only saying "but it's none of your business," while in the same "hurt" expression I was wearing both curiosity and interest) she would remark, "Sometimes I feel so sorry for her." At other times she would gossip about Nora, a girl a year older than myself. Why had she needed that operation; a big, healthy girl like her; "said it was a tumor, pooh. Bet some feller has ruined her, you know how wild she's al'ays been; wouldn't be surprised that some of them boys (her brothers) done it; that old James looks an awful sneak." The Powers family understood her pretty well; most of all they knew she was in possession of a sharp tongue. They did not visit us too often; if they did, she was apt to use it on them.

During holidays and summers, however, after Nora had succeeded in petting her up or smoothing her down, my mother would let me go to visit them on the farm... In fact, we had known them for several years, Corrie having met them the first year she worked at Minter Dry Goods Co. She had made or sold them hats. One time when I was perhaps thirteen or fourteen, Nora and her younger brother and myself were driving into the country and they began telling stories and asking riddles. Then she began pulling my hair and kept at it until she got out of me something like this, words which she evidently was waiting to hear, "Stop pulling my hair." She and her brother snorted and giggled. Then she went on to ask loud enough so that her brother in the front seat could hear, "Who says that?" or "When does one say that?" And when I didn't know, or had some suspicion of what they were thinking and wanted me to say and wanted to hide it, and would not guess at it, Nora finally ventured, "That is what a girl says when she gets married...on her wedding night." I laughed, I did not want to appear to think their talk was too funny or too obscene... Then they knew another story much funnier than that one; they urged one another through smirks and giggles to tell it. "But maybe, aw, well, you, I can't; maybe she won't...aw you, Zene." Finally one of them started it. The riddle was this: "Mother has a big, black, hairy thing; father has a long, slick thing; father takes his long slick thing and puts it into mother's big, black, hairy thing; what is it?" Then they tried to keep their faces serious and kept demanding an answer. Their giggles had obscured the statement of the riddle somewhat, and I asked them to repeat part of it because I wanted to hear it and feel a barbaric sexual impulse again, or because I couldn't think of anything else to do, or because I really had not heard all. They finally explained, that the mother was holding a pig and the father was sticking a knife into it to kill it!

I did not care a straw for any of the Powerses; sometimes I felt sorry for their mother in much the same way as I pitied my own. I was almost as ashamed of them, when we were in the presence of intelligent, or what I considered superior, people as I was of my own family. But they used to do everything possible to make me happy when I went there. There was always plenty of good things to eat; fried chicken and gravy, homemade bread, milk, butter, honey, preserves, cakes, and pies; and I was always supplied with an old gentle horse to ride, or was carted about in a rubber-tired buggy. The land about there was fertile and the crops were often abundant; but the girls never thought of working in the fields or picking cotton as my sisters used to do; they were well-to-do and could hire help if the three boys were unable to do it. How beautiful the country was there in field, pasture, or ravine! There were cotton fields in which young children worked, often being in the fields for hours alone. I thought of myself and the family when we lived in the country. The pastures were full of flowers; there was a pecan grove near the little ravine; and July saw the cotton fields a mass of green leaves and white and pink blossoms. Nora used to go in swimming in the stream when her sickness was on her. My mother said it would kill ennybody in the world except a horse.

Once during the first year that I knew them, Nora and I drove through the country to see a girl friend of hers. The girl was very gay and talked and joked a lot; she had a small frame with exceedingly small feet. I was amused and fascinated with her chatter. They had lived in Tennessee before coming to Texas and she had a repertory of startling and amusing tales of the grand life they lived there; her tales were of adventure in which only an act of God could have saved her. Others were gruesome such as: a woman once locked a child in the range stove for crying and the negro cook built a fire in the stove and after a couple of hours found she had baked the child. In the evening when we were going to bed, as she came home with us, she told a story of playing once with a little girl in their barn. Having seen the stock in their sex acts, they began to play likewise; her two brothers saw them and called out that they would come and do it for them if they liked. Nora seemed sorry that she had told this story in my presence and the subject was changed. They talked about the "boys" and told about flirtations and love affairs. On such occasions I was always interested to get as much as I could out of the other person, but rarely, almost never, told how I felt, what I thought, and what my experiences were. I had learned very young that people's confidences were betrayed; that sometimes when I had done or told a thing in the best spirit it was used against me. I had no desire to tell anyone my heartaches or even my aspirations. Anyone who had two eyes could see how ambitious I was. I believed Nora was proud of having so nice a girl as myself as a friend.

⤙✶

One day, during the year I attended the Christian College, my mother returned from town where she had been talking with the land agent about the house. I could see her for a block before she reached the steps; she was walking fast and I could see that she was weeping, her face was extraordinarily red. She threw her bag on top of the sewing machine when she entered the dining room and began crying convulsively. "I'd cut my throat this minute, if it wasn't for these three children," she said. "What in the world is the matter, Mother?" I asked. She was choking and crying and cursing. Eugene Wood was going to take the place away from her, she said. "I told these children they'd have to hep me meet the notes. W'y the few boarders I have don't much more'n pay the grocery bill. Corrie's gone and bought that piano and has to pay $5 a month on that when she ain't got a roof for her head. Sumpter worked when he first come back; but now he's just lying around and eating up and as mad as the devil, if I want him to turn his hand or try to find work. Emmer 'as gone off up there (a small town telephone office) and hardly ever sends me a cent. And Roger has got to the point that he wants to dress lak a'll the dudes in town… Poor boy, he was awful good for a while, but now he sees the rest of them eating it up."

I felt that she wanted me to volunteer to quit school and take a job, but I am not sure that I did. She would go through the whole rigmarole of how she had worked since we came to Abilene to try to make a living for "these devilish children," and not a one of them cared a damn about her or wanted to stick by her. All acted as though she wanted it all for herself, as though it wouldn't be a shelter for them too. "Ah declare to God, there never was such a set of devils ever born." She knew that they could all do better than they did. There, she had rented the five acres when we first came and worked lak' a dawg and a nigger to try and sell enough vegetables to pay expenses;

"them oldest boys" lay around or wanted to boss everything, and because she wouldn't put up with it, they had left and wouldn't help. "Rush didn't want to do anything except lie around and eat and sleep; and now when he comes around here his clothes are so nasty that he's a disgrace to civilized human beings. Reuben wanted to boss everything, wanted everything under his control (she used to insinuate that Reuben wanted the property put in his name); looked upon me as a fool, just like his damned ole Daddy. And Wiley was no better… And these younger boys is coming on just like them."

She and Corrie used to quarrel and be in the outs for days and weeks. My sister would sniff, snub as we said, in anger or tears, "Well, I turned over ever' cent to her until I was twenty-one years old, and now that I want a little something for myself she can't talk too mean to me… Ah, God, I *knew* it would be like that… The way I've worked and tried!" Corrie wanted my mother to rent one of the small hotels down the street or one of the boarding houses. Then she could afford to hire help and could make an easy living. I believe she suggested too that my mother should go out as a nurse, at least my mother used to say she wanted her to and "let Corrie stay home and try to get a few music pupils and be the lady."

I finished the year at the Christian College; my marks were among the highest, an average of 95 or 96. Adelaide said her father had mentioned me as being eligible for the prize; but I knew her average was a few points higher than mine. Then she told me how hard a certain girl was working, a very gross country girl who had worked as a maid in someone's house to earn her board; the professors thought she was nearly sure to get it as she had an average of 98. Perhaps I was a little jealous; if so, it was alleviated by Adelaide's attitude in assuming that prizes were not for people such as ourselves. Maybe they were giving it to this girl because they felt sorry for her; I hated people who pitied me. At the close of school, Mrs. Klingman had wanted me to be in the declamation contest, but it was decided that this exercise was for boys only. I was disappointed. During the year when the rules were suspended and some boy had asked me, I was permitted to go to the Lyceum entertainments and to parties with them. And now at the close of school a boy in one of my classes had asked to accompany me to the graduation exercises. I accepted because it looked as though no one else was going to ask me. And when the evening arrived to go, I was "rearing and caving" because I had to go with him. I had always to go with fools and idiots. At first my mother laughed; and then she began, good-naturedly, to scold me.

I was beginning to think that everyone was a fool or an idiot except myself; I must get that out of my head; it would ruin me. What a terrible and disgusting state one must arrive at to be able to make use of the words "fool" and "crazy idiot" as much as I did. But I went on saying that this boy was crazy and that he looked like an idiot. As I think of him now, I believe he must have been very similar to myself. He was serious, not too well-dressed, and had not too many words on his tongue. Fortunately, my mother and sister had come to the exercises, for I fell ill that evening almost before the program began, and they had to send for the Doctor to take me home and prescribe medicine for me. At first I felt my face very hot, and then I didn't know anything until I was put in the Doctor's buggy. I had been delirious, as they said, "talking out of my head." The old family Doctor left pills and calomel for me to take; there was nothing much wrong with me; I was bilious and overworked. How glad I was that all my examinations were finished; suppose it had happened two weeks before; I should have had no grades, no credits. In a few days a long letter came from this boy, saying how sorry he was, and mentioning that since I had gone to the exercises with him, he would like to be permitted to pay the Doctor's charges for taking me home; he thought he ought to. No one but an idiot would ever think of writing to a girl and asking to pay the doctor's bill when she was sick. I had never heard of such a fool. My mother and sister were highly entertained. It seems to me that I once saw this boy afterwards and I didn't speak to him. The little boy whom I liked to go about with was a cigarette fiend and had heart trouble and died a couple of years later.

Barrett and his faculty were planning to establish a school at Denison, Texas for the following year as there were not sufficient funds to be had at the C.C.I., and it was planned that I should go there with them. Enough work was to be given me to pay my board, and the tuition I could pay when I began to teach school. I required one more year to complete what was commonly called the high school course; besides one must be sixteen years old before she was eligible for the State teachers' examination. Of course, my mother was pleased that Dr. Barrett and his teachers were taking so much interest in me. Just one more year. She told this plan to the pastor of the little South Side Baptist Church and he began immediately to try to change her mind about the matter. It was a great pity that a nice, bright girl like myself should "go leave" Abilene to attend school, especially as there was a good Baptist College right there at home, a school of my own denomination. Why did she want me to go off to a Campbellite school? Well, Barrett and his crowd of instructors were awful fine people, well educated, some of them Yankees; and then they were going to let me pay the tuition, $50 or so, the following year when I would begin teaching school. But Brother Druery did not rest until he convinced my mother of the desirability of sending me to Simmons College, the Baptist school at Abilene. He would secure a scholarship for me at Simmons. But my mother was not asking for charity; she wanted to be independent and wanted her children to be likewise; we were all able to work and there was no reason why anything should be given to us. But a scholarship was not a thing which one gave out as charity; it was given as an honor. Everybody knew I was a smart girl; they were all proud of me and wanted to see me get along. Of course, my mother said, I could go back to the public school, but Barrett was going to give a special course for teachers; and they were all college-bred men. Well, if that was what she wanted, she couldn't find a better educated man nowhere than Dr. Cooper, the president of Simmons; he was one of the best educated men in the whole State; a graduate of Yale, and was known (he was a known man) in educational circles in England and Germany where he'd studied. And there wouldn't be any obligation attached to this scholarship; he would arrange and see to it himself. (Most of what I repeat here are fragments of what was told me later.) My mother finally acquiesced, and I went to Simmons instead of to Barrett's school.

—⋆—

During the summer my mother found work for me. Again it was at a soda fountain, but this time in the best drug store in town, the Corner Drug Store at the crossing of Pine and First Streets. I felt as though I'd rather face the gallows than stand behind the counter at the soda fountain; and yet we needed the three or four dollars a week which I was to receive, as much as I can conceive of any family ever needing so small a sum. It was a thousand times worse than passing plates of hot biscuits to the boarders; the entire front of the store was plate glass and one could see you clear across the street. I knew it, for I had often seen the girl in there handing out ice cream, when I was passing on the streetcar, or even when I was walking on the opposite sidewalk… But I was going to Simmons in the fall and would require a whole set of new books. And so I tried to succeed once more as a soda jerker. But how it hurt me! And when men smiled at me as they bought their cigars and lit them and tried to be talkative, I almost died of embarrassment. Maybe they thought I was an idiot. If they teased me or ignored me or snubbed me or tried to flirt with me, I called them idiots for thinking I was one. "They act like I'm a fool," was continually on my lips in those days, concerning whomever offended or embarrassed me. But the crazy fools hadn't any sense anyway.

After a few days or a couple of weeks at the most, my mother informed me that I was not to work at the Drug Store anymore, ole Doctor McGee had said (and she hemmed and hawed, trying to make it sound as insignificant as possible) that I could not do the work; I could see that my mother was suppressing it, if she were angry with me for having lost my job; and in some way I almost knew that she was not mad at me at all. But "all the same," I wept and wailed for a couple of days. This old Doctor and his boys simply did not like me; I used to know the McGee boy at school, maybe he—idiots, fools. Nobody did. My mother said she was promised some sewing and I could do that. Then I got jobs in dry goods stores for a week or two at a time, during sales; once, I believe, in the same shop with my sister.

Already I was teaching a Sunday School class at the Oak Street Baptist Church where we went after moving to Main Street. I think I liked biblical stories and the literature in general; liked the little children who would listen to me (and hated or wanted to pinch or shake those who wiggled and talked out); but in my heart of hearts I never liked the people of the Baptist church and held the best of them in suspicion. I believe my attitude was a little like my mother's attitude towards the Beasley family. I could find a flaw in a facial expression, the way they prayed, their method of shaking hands, the way they

153

treated me, their tone of voice in reading the Bible or whatnot. I had arrived at the point that each meeting accentuated more and more my love of criticizing and poking fun at people. I would cock my hat on the back of my head, or at some other angle, and imitate some man, woman, or child in entering the church. I often reported all the sayings and doings; this person did not speak to me and that one did not like me; this one had hurt my feelings and that one was jealous of me; the preacher was friendly and I did not like him, or else he ignored me altogether and I hated him. The church people said one thing, even taught it in Sunday School, and lived another. A lot of idiots, fools and hypocrites. I was going to quit going to Sunday School and Young People's meetings.

About this time of my life I recall having a terrific quarrel with my mother. She was now about forty-seven years old, and was continually reminding us that the change of life "was working on her," that we ought to try to make life lighter for her, because she might prove to be a very useful old lady and maybe live to be seventy-five years old. As a consequence, when she was "rampaging" we used to keep pretty quiet. Of course, there was always plenty of quarreling and jawing, but nothing so drastic as this. She would throw things around, "I swear to God, I can't stand this," box the ears of someone for having been lazy or "talking back," and carry on until we were all nearly crazy. We were the laziest set of young uns she ever knew (maybe the whole household had slept late on Sunday morning, hadn't gone to church at all that day); every last doggone one of us were just like the Beasleys and there never was a sorrier set of people ever went unhung; "just your ole daddy right over again."

Sometimes these things sounded a little comical and my older sisters and I would exchange glances and suppress our smiles. But this time I was angry enough to have struck her; she had made a remark indicating clearly that she never wanted us "not a damned one of us." "We are not to blame if we look like him (my father)," I snorted, the tears rolling down my cheeks… "We can't help being born…why did you have us?" I railed. My mother grew pale and started towards me, "Shut up, shut up, young lady…I've a notion to beat you in an inch of your life…if you ever talk that way to me again I'm going to use the poker or a stick of wood or anything I can put my hands on you…you just mark my word!" Then she went on saying how she had worked and struggled; "I've gone down to the grave for you children; God in Heaven knows how I've suffered and this is the thanks I get for it!" I felt proud of myself for having mustered the courage to say a thing which I had wanted so often to say; and yet she gave me a sense of having said something degrading; I believe I was extremely sorry I had said it; still, her threat to beat me, it mattered not what I said, rankled in my brain. At such times I used to be limp with disgust and sadness. One did get tired of being nagged and hounded and cursed for no better reason than that one was like one's father.

Once Rush, my third brother, a young man about twenty-four years old, came home. He had been farming and butchering cattle and was wearing the filthiest clothes, it seemed to me, I had ever seen. He said that it was like that slaughtering cows. My mother was disgusted with him, but I think she cried over him too. I remember his coming not only for his greasy and grimy overalls and jacket, and because I was ashamed of him, but also for something he said. He gave me a new word and an idea tremendously arresting. He said that he had seen or been working with the McGuire boys, a family whom we knew when I was six or seven years old. All the McGuire boys had turned out socialists. Had my mother ever heard about socialism? She reminded him of an old snuff-dipping woman whom we once met when we were travelling about the country in wagons like a lot of tramps, "yer daddy wanted to bring us down to the lowest level he could," and of what she had said. The woman and her family were cotton pickers and "just drug around from year to year" picking cotton and getting a living any way they could. They looked like about the nastiest and sorriest people she had ever met; the woman told her with the snuff dripping off the end of the stick that she didn't want no property; didn't want no houses and land for her children to be fighting over when she was dead. She was a socialist. They were people who wanted to set down and have the world make a livin' for them.

My brother said something else; he used the word justice; I believe he said there was "no justice in the world"; the socialists wanted to divide up the land and just give a man as much as he could work. I had never felt that I had ever had an idea or feeling in common with Rush before; my mother often said that sometimes she didn't believe he had more'n half sense. Once, when he had been there and she was disgusted with him, my mother whispered a story which Emma had confided in her about Rush's having tried to arouse her sexually, after she was a great big girl, thirteen years old. Sometimes she was afraid of "these boys." And I felt the same way about them; I would not have liked to sleep in the same room with one of them overnight, alone. Perhaps any highly sexed girl feels that way about an older brother. I disliked having them around on account of that feeling; I was afraid of them. I was afraid of my own wish too, and found all sorts of reasons for hating them and being glad when they left home. They were dirty, vulgar-tongued and ignorant; they knew none of the correct forms of speech; I would have dropped dead had I been forced to introduce them as my brothers to my professors. Perhaps I would have liked them if they had washed up, had taken a job, stuck to it, gone to night school, become serious and given their money to my mother. In short, if they had become as I was going to be. But I think I would have liked it better always if they had *lived* away from home. Well, if they had made themselves over after my prescription, I would have talked socialism with them; it fell on my ears with more poignance and more softly and beautifully than Christianity did (I mean *my first* impressions of religion).

↞❋

September arrived and Brother Druery came in his buggy to take me to Simmons College. I was sure to have to answer embarrassing questions. They would ask about my father; and I would tell them he was dead; no, I wouldn't; yes, I would. Perhaps the girls would make fun of me; maybe they would feel sorry for me; maybe they would all look upon me as belonging to the charity list. I dreaded it; it was like pulling teeth, to use my mother's expression. I felt the scholarship would jeopardize me in some way; my mother's doubts, when Druery had mentioned the subject first, had sunk in. If I recall correctly, I performed my old childish trick when the Bursar asked about my father; my father was not living; "not with my mother" I kept to myself. And how old was I; and what subjects did I wish to take; and where were my credentials. I went through the usual red tape and I believe bought most of the books I required the first day.

At that time (1908) there were no street cars in Abilene and the preacher made arrangements for me to go to school in the college hack which went about picking up children and young people who were furnished with no other means of transportation. The girls whom I remember most distinctly in this hack were Virginia Guitar, whose father was more than a millionaire, and Mary Paxton, oldest daughter of the president of the Citizens National Bank of Abilene. They were gay and full of chatter and wore pretty clothes; besides they had everything one required in the way of book cases and lunch baskets. Mary and I were in one or two of the same classes and sometimes we talked about the lessons; we may even have exchanged answers in Algebra or talked about theorems in geometry. But what interested me was their chatter; they rarely chatted and joked with me, but with one another they were like so many magpies. Their tongues would go, as my mother often described us when we talked too much or too rapidly, "like the clatter bone of a goose's ass (arse)"; and the stream of conversation was just what one would expect. Flirtations, sweethearting, small talk, make-believing; who was elegant, who was clever; Prof. Mullins was the most polite gentleman they had ever known; Virginia remarked every facial expression and every gesture of his hands. This girl wore a necklace of real diamonds. She acted as though it didn't trouble her at all. Mary wore two small glittering stones in rings.

They were both studying French and sometimes tried to speak to one another in this curious language. The teacher was a French woman who scarcely spoke English; but she knew German and Spanish. I should have liked to enter one of the modern language classes, but Latin was required in the academy (as the high school course attached to this school was called) and I had to confine myself to subjects which the teachers' examinations called for, and to courses required for graduation from the academy. That year I studied physics, geometry, algebra, Latin composition (translations from English to Latin), read Caesar and Cicero; Ancient History (Greece and Rome), a part of Modern History of Europe; English and American Poetry; and it seems to me a special course of Shelley and Keats, though it is likely that I only sat in the room where Shelley and Keats were being recited; more rhetoric and composition. The young people of the cream of society rarely talked or joked or played with me. Many times I spent the noon hour studying, as there was always work to do at home, and all lessons required preparation in advance. There were papers to write, problems to solve, history to learn, and Latin to translate. I read on the hack in the morning and sometimes in the afternoon. The theorems in geometry troubled me because I tried to memorize them; and the Latin lesson often required two hours to prepare. This entailed staying up in the evening, burning the midnight oil. Besides I had to throw in one or two courses in Bible that year; in a Christian Institution one had to know something about the Scriptures. But on the whole the work went comparatively well; I had high marks in Latin and good grades in almost everything else. I failed one exam in geometry and had to take it over; never told my mother about this; and at the end of school when my report showed another failure in physics, I was chagrined and hid the letter from my mother.

Dr. Cooper liked my work in Latin; when he was called away for a few days he gave the class into my hands for one day and to a young man for the other day. He announced to the class that both this young fellow and myself were going to be teachers. How I trembled! The president of the school was going to let me teach one of his classes. Perhaps my tongue would stick up in the roof of my mouth and wouldn't come down; perhaps I would forget; perhaps I was not clever anyway. I knew I was not learning as I used to before I began worrying about things; such little things crushed or distracted me then. The day came and I stepped up on the little square rostrum in the corner of the room; and sat in Dr. Cooper's chair; we would begin the lesson; I looked down the list and called on members of the class to translate. After a little, I was able to raise my eyes from Caesar; they all wore serious faces, but my cheeks were burning like fire. There were men in the class, preachers past forty; one of them was about as ugly a man as I have ever seen; but before the class was over, I had found in him an admirable character. One of the girls looked as though she was going to laugh; the flesh around her eyes showed it; and he looked at her in just the right way and at just the right time to suppress her.

The pastor of the First Baptist Church, Brother Lee Scarborough, used to hold the chapel exercises very often. Some of the people had already started calling him Dr. Scarborough. According to the tale which some feller handed on to my mother, the preacher was first known as Lee Scarborough, then he got to be a pretty big preacher and everybody called him Brother Scarborough; and after he'd been off travelling around in the Holy Lands or some place, people called him Dr. Scarborough. She would pooh-pooh; she once heard that he said he went down to the Willow Street Mission on Sunday afternoons (that was when we were living down there) to preach to the washerwomen and the prairie dogs. He kept his wife in mother-hubbards all the time; and then some of the old women cried and snorted around him too much at church to suit her; Mrs. Paxton would cry and snort around him until, "Ah declare to God, I thought she was crazy." There was something in my mother's expression or suggestions which made me think she believed there was a love affair, or some sexual relation, existing between the preacher and Mrs. Paxton. Of course, she did not say so straight out, but her words were sufficient to destroy my confidence. Besides she whispered that a lot of people had heard that, when Scarborough was a boy, he and his father were connected in some way with cattle thieving.

This was a part of my preface to the preacher who was giving some three or four hundred students an evangelical discourse that morning. Then was something inside me that looked just like my mother; perhaps it was a shadowy thing just inside the skin of my face; maybe it even showed at times; one might see it in my eyes or in the flesh around them. The skin around and the lids of my mother's eyes told me so many things. One ought to suppress this thing in the presence of others. While I was sometimes interested watching my mother when we were alone, I should not have liked to have anyone hear her talk or see her expression, especially her eyes; I had a feeling that there was something almost obscene about it. Brother Scarborough pleaded with us to give our hearts and lives to Christ. He told a story of his early life as a cowboy. He had once tied a rope around a bull-yearling's neck; tied the other end around his own waist, and then let the calf out of the pen. "Did you ever run faster than you can!" he cried, while students chuckled. He had run much faster, on that occasion, than he had ever thought it possible. "Tie your life to Christ," he went on, changed, and almost tearful (many times the tears rolled away), "and then you can run faster than you can."

I was disgusted and almost nauseated…I told my stories some-times at home, but life was too hard, too sorrowful, too full of hate to talk much. Besides if I told too much it might be used against me, when my mother or some one of them was angry with me, or wanted to hurt me, or to laugh at me. I picked and chose most of my stories I related to them. My mother and sister had grown to hate one another. This had been brewing for a long time and now since Corrie had had the typhoid fever, their quarreling was like an open sore all the time. My mother was on a tirade when Corrie came down with the fever. Here, we couldn't pay the grocery bill, much less a doctor's bill and one of the family down with a long spell of sickness. And how she had cautioned Corrie to take medicine (she would never see to herself); keep her bowels open; and see that the water she drank at that store was boiled. She boiled water for the whole family at home and stood over the stove and worked and sweat until she felt as though she'd drop dead; but "these children tore down everything she built up." Besides the doctor said she had typhoid fever and it was catching. It was a disgrace: everybody knew it came from filth and neglect. "Ole Doctor said so hisself." She would go on with this conversation interspersing it with curses, tears, and slamming things around, perfectly conscious that the sick girl was hearing every word of it. I always imagined my sister never forgave her for this; perhaps it was only something to tie her hate to; many things had stored up in the past. How ugly and dreary and sad!

At odd times for a few years my mother used to go out as a

sort of nurse, or second to the doctor (I never understood just how they looked upon her) in obstetrics cases. This was when we had few boarders, or no boarders, and the children's money seemed all taken up before the end of the month arrived, and notes on the place were falling in arrears. She invariably came home in a temper and made me feel that we were the lowest people that God ever let breathe for permitting her to go out and work in any such way. Ah, God! One could only wring one's hands, grit one's teeth, shed a few tears, and put it out of one's mind.

⟵✦

In May of that year the county teachers' examinations were held. I had prepared for them a little as a sort of sideline to the work I was carrying at Simmons. I told Dr. Cooper that I wanted to take the exams for a second grade certificate, and asked permission to remain away from school for a week; I wanted a few days in which to cram for them. This was granted and I sat all day and away into the evening in one of our unoccupied rooms going through question and answer books, looking up rules in arithmetic which I perhaps had forgotten, skimming through histories and books on methods and management. There were fourteen subjects: reading, writing, spelling, arithmetic, grammar, composition, geography, Texas History, U.S. History, agriculture, methods and management, School laws, physiology, and another which I do not recall now. All of these papers were to be written in two or three days. There were a few older girls whom I knew at the Christian College and several country teachers taking the tests. On the last day when the averages were made up, the teacher who was helping to mark the papers informed me that I had failed in composition. And then as though to divert a scene, she told me I was still eligible for the third grade county certificate, as composition belonged to the second grade subjects. This threw me into a sort of hysteria internally, but I tried to control myself with the thought that the Superintendent might change his mind after he saw all my papers. I heard them say the tests were difficult this year; this was because they didn't need many teachers; "a lot of people took the exams last summer and passed."

But when the County Superintendent, Mr. E.V. White, wrote out a third grade county certificate and gave it to me, I put my head down on the top of the files near his desk and sobbed like a child. He talked a little as though he were scolding: I must study the subject I was weak in and take the examination again; there was plenty of time; I was only sixteen, the youngest in the crowd; besides a third grade certificate was as good as any for me, because they would not let me teach any but the primary grades; there were people in the county who were teaching on third grade certificates. I took the roll of paper and went home trying to choke back the tears. He had asked me about my father the first day. White knew my father; in fact I had gone to Old Man White's in a wagon with my father when I was nine or ten years old; we went there to pick cotton after we had finished our own; E.V. was a young man then; his sister, an old maid, a woman perhaps twenty-five years of age, had given me a hat; it was a child's hat which just fit my age. And I had liked it very, very much in spite of the fact that someone had given it to me. I showed it to my father and he let me take it home. Maybe White thought I was a fool. I had talked severely about my father and said we never had anything to do with him. On such occasions I always felt that I looked like my mother. My father was a very bad man and you had to be strong, when you couldn't lie to people, and stand up and say he was a bad man; righteousness was the greatest thing in the whole world. Maybe White had just thought he could; that's the reason he had failed me.

I tried to look more cheerful to my mother and to show her that this was a real certificate, a teacher's permit or diploma or whatever she might want to call it; but she saw my tears. "But what are you crying about?" I explained and she supposed there was plenty of time. There would be a teachers' "normal" held in the summer where one could take the state examinations; one's papers were sent to the State Department at Austin and graded there; it was a good thing to take the grading out of the hands of the local people.

Emma did not come home so very often and when she did, seemed to be glad to get out of the quarrels, messes, and fusses as soon as she could. She said so herself. Though she humored my mother more than Corrie, she was not able to do much else, as she required most of her wage to pay her board, and then she always had (she just had to have) clothes. Sometimes she sewed for people at night in order to earn more money. And so Corrie and I were together much more; and we got along very well together. Occasionally, she would take me down a notch or two about the way I looked, or about what I had said.

One evening when we were walking after supper, just after I received my certificate, Corrie began, "Why don't you quit school now and get some work?" And this, when school was nearly out, and it was my last year. I wanted my credits from Simmons; why should I quit now when there were only five weeks more? It was all foolishness, my wanting to do so much. "Aw, we cayn't be nobody nohow," she sighed. I thought she was referring to my oldest sister, or to my father. "But I ain't to blame for what someone else has done," I told her. It wasn't so much that, she said, it was the fact that we had such sorry blood in our veins; you've got to have the right kind of parents to be anything in this world; sometimes she thought she had just about as soon have dawg blood. I had heard remarks as crude as that from her before; but this time I was incensed. "What do you mean?" I demanded. I was angry, as one is after receiving an unexpected blow or a dash of cold water. "Don't you know?" she mocked. I didn't know; I wanted her to tell me. "We've got Indian blood," she stated coolly, as though the fact were sufficient for conviction of crime. I thought so too; I felt convicted, and tried to defend myself. "But, Mother says it ain't so." "Ah," she scorned, "she says a lot of things that ain't so." I went on arguing with her; the Old Man showed no traces of it at all, his eyes were as blue as indigo. "Except in his cheek bones," she put in; but I thought they were not unlike other men's. He looked

Irish; I once heard him say laughingly, "I am Irish." And Mother had known ole grandpa Beasley and surely if there had been anything wrong with him she would have mentioned it; and she even knew great grandpa Beasley. I was getting more angry with her as I talked and she finally admitted that she or no one of the family seemed to know where the Indian blood came in, but she still held her point that it was there. She wasn't going to try to be anything except to just get along, what was the use? She had tried but she saw now; everything was against you.

She repeated that we had Indian blood all right; and I swelled up and railed: "But I don't care if we have!" She tried to laugh about it before I left her as though she had not meant it so seriously as I had taken it. I believe this conversation broke a small lance between us. She had attacked me when I was weak. Everybody was dying to have me quit school and go to work.

I put "my nose in the air" and finished my work at Simmons, and continued to wash and iron and sew and cook and scrub and do anything about the house I could. My young sisters did a lot of work too after school. We all carried on. I did not have a very lively time at Simmons that year; I got excused from the girls' society meetings on Friday as often as I could, first because it bored me, secondly I was embarrassed when called on, and thirdly I had no time for it. And the programs held during the evenings, I seldom attended. I had had a much better social time at the Christian College. I knew some of the lesser lights at Simmons and sometimes we jollied and talked and laughed, but I almost never attended their parties and witnessed no ball games. I always felt embarrassed, perhaps I was ashamed; it was on account of my clothes, or the fact that I was aware of beings superior to myself, or because someone had suspected that I was going to be a missionary. At the Oak Street Church several people had asked different members of the family if I were going to be a missionary; all poor girls who attended that school went for that purpose. They had not noticed that I was especially religious; Brother Druery had made up the scholarship and asked some of the people of that church to subscribe to it; it had leaked out. I felt hurt and timid about it. There was not a particle of this feeling in the plan to go to Barrett's school; it was a simple business loan a little like buying furniture on credit; I could pay for it the following year. I complained to my mother about some of the silly idiots asking if I was going to be a missionary. She said to ignore them; they were only jealous that I was so much smarter in my books than they were. "You're knocking the shine off o' them...you are shore putting some of them in the shade."

—✦

One day I was startled by a lonesome and sad voice. I listened. Hall-o-o-o, hall-o-o-o, it said. I looked out and a man was holding to the small iron gate and fence as though to steady himself. "The Old Man is out there, Mother," I said in my usual agitation. The voice had pierced me like a sharp needle, except it was more tremulous and racked me with some indescribable anguish or sorrow. "Lock that door," she said, while she hurried into the next room and latched the screen; and then we lowered the shades. We peeked out when we did not hear the voice; and my father had turned to go across the street to the lumberyard; he was wiping his eyes and I thought I saw the tears fall. She saw that I was sorry, and changed the expression of her face. "Yes, he's awful sorry, now," she said. My younger sisters, Martha and Alta, seemed to have developed the same attitude that I had always had; they looked faint from fright. There was a blacksmith shop next door to our place on the right; my father secured work there for a while; but so far as I know not a soul of the family ever spoke to him; we even avoided that side of the yard when we thought he was there.

During those years when my father was always "bothering" us, I used to pray that he would die. And then I would be startled at the idea of having asked God to kill somebody; I excused myself on the ground that I wanted Him to take my father away. My mother was angry; she said he was spying; he wanted to see how we were living; he had accused her of taking "these girls and getting into some bad trouble." I always thought she meant to leave the idea that my father had said she would take the girls into a house of prostitution. But I think she was merely referring to the time when they were getting ready to separate; I remembered it; he had trembled and wept and preached, "You are ruined, you are ruined, you mark my word, all of you…if you take these children and go off, you are a ruined family," or something of that nature. Once, though, when he had been at our gate and stumbled away as though he were about to fall, brushing the tears away, some of the children jeered; it seems to me I laughed or smirked or mocked too. My mother acted shocked and scolded us, "Ain't you ashamed, he's your father."

Once he told Mr. Scott, the keeper of the lumberyard that it looked as though I was the only member of the family my mother was trying to educate. Scott had told her. How in the name o' God did he think she could keep the whole family in school, she wondered. She thought she was doing awful well to keep the little children and myself at school. Them older boys never gave her a cent... Sometimes she was mad enough to kill him. After a while he quit coming to the shop and disappeared; we all gave a sigh of relief as though just out of prison.

Emma came home after a surprise letter or two, as a joke, to my mother, saying she was married or was going to get married. She was really fixing to get married. And how many men had asked her to marry them during the last four or five years! Maybe a dozen; maybe twenty, she would have to count them. She told me one day when we were washing and hanging up the clothes that she had six men on the string and every last one of them had asked her to marry him. She often read their letters to my mother. One of them my mother had apparently picked out; he was the son of a wealthy ranchman near Midland, Texas, where Emma had been working in the telephone office. After humming and hawing and poking fun at him (she said he looked like a kill-dee, the slender-legged bird I have mentioned before), she finally decided to marry him; she knew he was crazy about her; after all he was the best bargain. They owned or were renting twenty sections of land, nearly a whole county and had a thousand or more head of fine Hereford cattle and horses.

And what a fine family they were—old Virginians...been in Texas ten years. Charles and his brother went to military school and his mother was a graduate of Mary Baldwin Seminary. She would brag about him in this manner for a while, and then turn to satire and ridicule. He was about as fat as a match. She supposed she'd have a lot of little wheat birds or kill-dees travelling around after her before very long. No, she was not going to have any children; that was going to be strictly understood. Sometimes my mother would laugh and say, "Well, I don't want any of your nasty, shitty little young uns to wash for...I've had thirteen...I guess that'll do me." Then my sister would become riled and say that she need not worry, they were not going to put upon her, then she'd insinuate that we were not going to be permitted to lie around on them either. Often their vulgarity stung me through and through, yet I listened with the greatest eagerness.

Charles McClintic had been to see Emma several times during the past year and knew and liked my mother. They were all old-fashioned Southerners. They talked Emma's plans over with Brother Druery, at least they discussed marriage. Druery said you should marry for love and then character and money if you could. But I think that my mother or my sister mentioned that love went out the window when people were poor, or too poor. She had promised Charles she would let him know when she made up her mind. She telegraphed and he came immediately. But she had been sick and had gone to the hospital. She said right out that Charles would have to pay the bill after they were married. For three or four years she had suffered during her menstrual flow, ever since she fell out of the carriage that time, after which incident the doctor had said she required treatment; this ought to be done before she married. Then too, she had gastritis, caused from eating too much candy. The old family doctor helped to attend her. A curious stool, perhaps an inch or so long, passed from her and the doctor put it in a bottle as a specimen. It looked like a piece of hard excrement covered with mucous. The doctor had left the bottle at the house. My mother picked the bottle up and looked at it. "I wonder if that could be a miscarriage...it could be," she said. I was startled, and yet I was not, she would say anything that came into her head. Many times I accepted her point of view; but I believe she thought I agreed with her more often than I did. I was sickened. Sometimes I looked upon my sister as a coarse, ignorant fool; other times I imagined her beautiful, at least she was pretty and full of wit. Charles did make arrangements to pay the bill; and my mother took just the right attitude; he always looked upon her as an awful fine woman.

I remember the night she went away to marry Charles; my mother had wanted her to be married at home but she had resisted; they were to be married, as the old lady McClintic called it, European fashion. They and his parents were going out to El Paso to the very tip end of the Rio Grande River where a friend of theirs had a great mansion; this was the point where three states met, Texas, New Mexico, and Mexico; they would be married in romantic style there. Afterwards they would go to Juarez. She was going to Midland by the eleven o'clock train. How beautiful and how sad she was! She had been crying for hours before she left; my mother was away nursing; anyway they had quarreled. She was wearing a lacy sort of green hat, just the right kind to make her skin appear more soft and white. Her light-colored, almost golden, hair showed under the drapery of her veil. Her eye lids were thick like those of a beautiful wax doll, and she closed them almost as slowly as an old-fashioned puppet would. She talked to me for a few minutes just before she left; I think the rest of them were asleep or had gone out. She had tried to help Mother but it seemed she could hardly make a living for herself; how she hated the quarreling at home. "I'm doing this mostly for Mother," she sobbed. "Maybe it won't be so hard for you all after a while." I was sad and offended at the same time. I already had a certificate and would likely have another one by the end of the summer. I was sure she needn't bother about me. Some of the little children came in and she kissed us all and told us to be good.

⟵✻

I was fond of being noticed by the best people in town. One day when I was coming home from school (the streetcars were out of commission and the hack didn't run anymore) young Weakley, who was in some of my classes, called to me to ride with him. He belonged to the smart set; and went with the well-to-do and the clever. I accepted and he drove me home in his mother's phaeton. I think we talked about the teacher of geometry on the way home. I tried to suppress whatever pleasure or pride or embarrassment arose in me. When we drove into sight of our block he asked, "Which house is it? Is it this one or that one?" "Yes, stop here," I said, climbing out at the wrong house. It was a well-built and newly painted little house and I wanted him to think it was ours. He turned and went the other way, and I ran across the street to our plain boxed house with slats running down to hide the cracks. It needed weatherboarding and paint to make it a habitable place for a clever person like myself, who had been asked to ride with a member of the first set in town.

Wiley came home and brought my mother news about Willie, my oldest sister. We had not heard for years. My mother would repeat what he had told her in an attitude of profound relief. Well, she had married; the fellow's name was Scrimpshire or something similar to that. She met and married him when the first baby (the bastard) was about a year old. Since then she had had two or three more children. The man was a good man; cared very much for her and gave her everything she needed. He was a German, at least my mother thought the name was German, and a bookkeeper; he made plenty of money. She and her husband had fallen out with the Old Man too; Scrimpshire had kicked him out; he wasn't going to have him lying around on him. So Willie had kicked him out too; she had allowed as much as the Old Man came to Abilene in those days alone... Now she was married; had been married for several years. Germans were always good to their wives, better than most other men; she had noticed it all her life.

The teachers' Summer Normal began the same week I finished my first year at Simmons College; and I entered the course for the second grade State certificate. After the papers were sent away and I thought it all over, I knew I had passed. But then one didn't know how fair those examinations were conducted. After a few weeks a letter and the certificate reached me from the State Department. My mother was 'most as proud as I was.' The vegetable man rang his bell just after I had read the report and showed my mother the certificate. She went out and I could hear her talking: "I'll tell you! that's mighty fine for a little ole seventeen-year-old girl; she was just seventeen in June; now she can go anywhere in this State to teach; got a hundred in three subjects." When she came in the house, I scolded her for telling the peddler about me and my affairs; why did she want to tell *him?*...

Now, the next thing of importance was to find a school. A preacher at Simmons who had had a church in Mulberry Canyon told me of the school there and promised to take me to see the trustees; he knew all of them. We went. Mulberry Canyon is about thirty miles from Abilene and one is able to go part way by train. We carried the contract forms and secured their signatures. I had a look at the schoolhouse; it had been there thirty years and was little better than an old ramshackle barn. The benches were whittled and scarred. We finally got their signatures, only two being required; and then drove over to ole man Snow's to try and find a boarding place. Theirs was a well-appearing almost prosperous-looking house located at the foot of a hill. The children were all grown and out of school; it was a good thing to live in a family where there were no children attending your school. Besides they had plenty of room and had boarded the teacher the year before… Well, had I been successful? Old lady Snow wanted to know. The preacher told her that the president of the board said I looked as though I had vinegar enough to do it. And afterwards he told me the trustee said he knew from the shade of my eyes that I wouldn't put up with no foolishness. Their names were already on the paper… After it was all agreed and we got in the buggy, it was suggested that they might as well sign the contract now, and these rustics had propped their feet up on the hub of the wheel, spread the contract form over the knee and written in their names… The agreement was made. Could I arrange to board with them? As we drove away, everything settled, I looked at the contract again; the names were there; the salary was written in; $65 per month. I was afraid they would want to cut it down, because women teachers were usually not paid as much as men and they had employed a man the year before.

When I reached home they were all interested to know if anyone had asked my age. No, the preacher had kept them off the subject; we all guessed it was because I was wearing a long skirt and shirt waist, both belonging to my sister. I had borrowed my mother's white lawn bonnet…

This was the first of August and school would not begin before November, not before the cotton was picked. I must find some work. This time I got a job as a clerk in the Five and Ten Cent Store. The job paid three dollars and a half per week to begin with and then it was raised to four. This work did not hurt me so much. For one thing, men seldom came in and ogled you. The customers were mostly women. And then there was a girl in the store twenty-three years old, Miss Kate, who understood some things as I understood them and had a sense of humor. She made fun of people and mimicked them in much the same way as I did. Instead of being embarrassed, she would come back to the cash register repeating their conversations and imitating their voices and facial expressions, showing up some of the idiots and fools in town; and we'd have a good laugh. Miss Kate had to help her grandmother make a living and they had it hard too. My mother always said she had consumption, and cautioned me not to stand too near her.

One day the head of the nickel stores of Texas came to see how his shop at Abilene was getting along. He was called the Nickel Store King and had made nearly a million dollars. "Brother So and So is here," said Miss Kate, curling up her nose. She supposed he was going to challenge the Lord again. There was a story that he once said he challenged the Lord; that is, he told the Lord that if He would let him make $10,000, he would give Him a thousand of it; if He would let him make $100,000 he would give Him $10,000; and if He ever let him make a million, he would give the Lord $100,000. "Here,

I've been working in this store three years and I'm getting $4.50 a week. He makes money and gives it to the Lord and pays the girls who work for him starvation wages. Do you call that Christianity? I call that slavery. Do you call that serving God? I call it thievery," said Miss Kate. I applauded; I loved hearing her say such things; I said them myself. Many times I went home from church swearing I would never go again. They were all hypocrites; no, perhaps merely fools. Sometimes it was some petty offense which threw me into this state of mind; I had not been flattered or noticed; but we had a real case against the Nickel Store King.

—<

I went back to the Snow farm about the first week in November, preparing to begin school on the following Monday. The Snow girls and myself swept out the schoolhouse, and then the word came that I must wait three weeks; for only two children or so in the whole community were ready to start.

On arriving at home, I walked in seriously and announced to my mother that I was "fired the first thing." She looked as though she was about to believe it, "I had allowed as much," she said. She looked serious and I was amused and then offended, the latter I suppressed. "No," I said gaily, "I must wait three weeks until they've finished picking the cotton." She thought, she observed, that if I had been turned off, I was certainly taking it lightly. She looked such a good earnest woman; so like a mother. There wasn't a thing about her that annoyed me then; I told her everything the Snows had said. Ole lady Snow said, "Thar goes a man person." Had she ever heard the expression "man person"? The kitchen was in a separate house; just like my mother's old home in Alabama. The dining table was a sort of two-story affair; a small table revolved in the center of it and carried the victuals. In this way, no one ever had to pass anything to anyone. If you wanted butter or honey or meat or whatnot, you turned the revolving table until you came to it, and helped yourself. I was going to have plenty to eat; I would look like a butter ball myself before the year was out.

The baby of the family was a girl of nineteen, two years older than myself, I emphasized; she was a little stupid, I did not like her. There were two boys, Deck and Dillard, who carried on a lot of comic conversation, and two ole maids; Miss Hester was about twenty-five, and the other one, I could not imagine her age; she had cataracts which seemed to be growing over both eyes. The ole man and the ole lady, I guessed, were awful good people. The ole man was a little bit comical too; he said someone gave him some advice twenty years ago, when he first came to Texas, which he always tried to follow (it was about the weather) and that was: when you go out in Texas you should take your umbrella, fan, and overcoat.

I had a talk with the County Superintendent; he told me I ought to urge them to build a new schoolhouse; the bonds had already been voted. I did write them a letter and told them that I had been advised by the County Superintendent that they had money at hand with which to build a new schoolhouse. I wanted to urge them for the sake of the community to complete the house as soon as possible; both they and the Superintendent knew what a bad condition the old house was in; and as for myself I regarded it as a disgrace to civilization. White told me later that they thought my statement pretty strong; I must be a very bold person.

The time came and I went back to take charge of my school. Monday morning found me with a rather large black oilcloth bag under my arm, making my way to the little schoolhouse. For weeks I had thought seriously and with some trepidation about this first morning. The thought seized me that I had been walking for a very long time; I did not see the schoolhouse; I turned back for a little and then decided I was wrong. At last, I faced a barbed wire fence and sank down on my knees to crawl under it; I felt myself the same size and aspect as in the seventh grade; I began to whimper and cry like a child. I could not remember how those girls went the other day. Fear and loneliness made me think to pray; I began the formula which I had gone through for weeks before with reference to my school, my teaching—asking for protection, wisdom, strength, and guidance…

I surveyed the country again and began to walk; I was sure the house in the distance was the right one now. At the door, two school children were waiting; I gave them a serious good morning and went in. The bag contained books, a pencil, a small clock, two bells—a small call bell and a hand bell. I took them out and placed them on the table. A man came in with his little girl; he asked if I were the teacher; I thought he must be a little silly; he irritated me; anyone could see I was the teacher. After he told me about his little girl, he stood around for a few minutes and I was afraid he was going to wait until I opened school. This would have made it more embarrassing, as I was going to open with a special and serious exercise. Maybe I would drop the book if an older person watched me read. At nine o'clock, I rang the bell and about a dozen boys and girls, mostly young children, entered the room. I took their names and set them to work and waited. If any were late for the opening exercises, those present would tell them about it. I drew out the Bible, asked them to put their pencils down and give attention. The selection was: "And though I speak with the tongues of men and of angels and have not charity I am become as sounding brass or a tinkling cymbal…and though I have the gift of prophecy and understand all knowledge… and though I give my goods to the poor, etc., etc…and have not charity…I am nothing… Faith, Hope, Love, these three, but the greatest of these is Love." Something like that. I asked them to bow their heads, and I repeated the Lord's prayer. If I felt emotion when I began, I was bored before I finished. I noticed a few smirks from some of the children, but I went on in explanation of the rules and work of the school. We would have a devotional exercise on Monday mornings, and they were to learn the Lord's prayer so they could repeat it with me. I had made a list of general principles defining what they could or could not do in the classroom or on the playground.

Before the day was over, I got tangled up in an arithmetic problem, but it was only because I was embarrassed. A sixteen-year-old boy in the fourth grade asked me to solve a problem of finding the area of a field; I found the distance around the field instead. He told me it was not the answer and looked as though he thought he had caught me: "Oh," said I, "it's the area you want, then you must multiply the length by the breadth." After I had seen the answer, I was sure then; and I took the attitude that it was inconceivable that I should be wrong. The first few days were bliss; I recall nothing to mar them, not even anything similar to the arithmetic incident which I believe, now that I think again, must have happened several days later. I was not going to be a scold or a cross person like my teacher of the sixth grade; I would be one of the lambs and we would all play always.

But the wind howled and whistled through the cracks one day; the children had become well acquainted with one another, and seemed no longer to fear the accentuation or raising of my voice. They whispered and giggled and some of the older boys even talked out loud. I kept a small boy in, as an example to the rest, showing them they would be punished if they whispered or disobeyed my commands. The boy protested saying the large boy had talked much more than he had. I stayed awake at night; thought, prayed, and dreamed about school. Almost every night during the first three weeks, I dreamed of having to whip someone. Finally, a small boy furnished me an excellent opportunity of demonstrating the beginning of my reign of terror. Someone reported the little boy had said damn on the playground. He confessed; and I went out and cut a "limb" from a bush and switched him. Then I began writing down the names of pupils who whispered or disobeyed the rules and kept them after school. A boy a half a head taller than myself refused to stay one recess; walked out of the schoolhouse and said he didn't have to obey me. I was in a frenzy; the nerves almost broke in the back of my head. I sent his brother for a good-sized limb and told him to come in the house, that he would have to take a whipping. He refused to come in, and I stamped and roared and told him, "All right, you are expelled from school!" The school laws stated that repeated insolence and refusal to carry out school regulations were punishable by expulsion.

The boy finally left the grounds, and I went on with the work. He was a nephew of the Snows, who reported that he did not like school anyway; that I should not worry, as they were going to move at Christmas. But I prepared for his return on Monday just the same; I put a leather strap about two and a half feet long in my bag, also a copy of the school laws. After the exercises, I made a long talk on discipline, obedience, and respect for others. I said the school had witnessed the conduct of one of its members on Friday, and that I was reading passages of the school law on his case. Before that boy could return to school, he had to take the most severe punishment that could be meted out to him; if he refused then the law expelled him, for I had the support of the trustees. Then I went on to say (I stood up very tall and my skirt grew even longer) that it did not matter one iota to me who the offender was; whether he was the oldest boy or the youngest boy in school, was of no consequence, that insolence and disobedience would be punished with the utmost severity. I warned against whispering and wasting time in school, the lack of preparation of lessons, and bad conduct on the playground. And by the time the first month closed for the Christmas recess I had formulated a code of regulations as rigid and tyrannous as those of my old sixth grade teacher, and had instilled almost as much fear in their hearts as Zora Shackleford used to create. The boy never returned to school; the first inning was in my favor. I had come in like a lamb and was going out like a lion.

The Snows often questioned me about my school, but I was as closemouthed concerning it as I was about the affairs of my family. It was difficult enough without having people use my own words against me. I mistrusted almost everyone and was almost as clever at keeping a silent tongue, on subjects which concerned me, as a woman of fifty.

I presented my first voucher at Christmas and received the sum of $65, which was enough to pay off two notes on the place, if there had not been so many other debts to pay. It was gobbled up, and I was given $10 to pay my board and a dollar or two which I required to go and come on the train. Emma and Charles came home for Christmas. They had given my mother $15 or so, but as she said, they always ate up more than the amount they gave. It was just a little "hush" money to keep her in a good humor while they were there. They were going to do so much, and they did nothing to help her. I think my mother watched my attitude in handing over the money to her and I believe she was not disappointed. Anyway, at that Christmas, she was sad and angry and quarrelsome. I remember telling Emma very seriously that I was going to try to make Mother happy and she cried about it.

Sumpter had come home and my mother said she wanted me to be good to him and not to argue with him; she had never seen a boy cry as he cried when he came back; he certainly was sorry and pleaded with her to forgive him; maybe he was going to settle down and help now. I think she remembered the terrific quarrel I had with him just before he left home. He was quarreling with my mother, because she wanted him to look for work, or to help do the washing, or something which he did not want to do. The older boys would do nothing about the house. For example, if they were out of work for days and weeks and had absolutely nothing to do, they would not turn their hands to help me with the washing, even though there was enough labor connected with it each week to kill a horse—not even to build fires or bring water. Oh, God, how I hated my brothers! Sumpter was calling out to my mother as they quarreled: "It is a lie or you are a liar!" and I drew the shovel from under the stove and screamed: "You've got to shut up!" He laughed in a diabolical way and said he would not leave a greasy spot of me if I struck him with that shovel. Then he turned on me: "Why in the devil don't you git out and go to work." "My God," said my mother, "just look at her wrists, sometimes it looks as though the bones are coming through the skin." All the trouble with my wrists, she said, came of washing his ole heavy underwear and the sheets; I washed as much as any nigger in town; talk about work, I earned my living at washing. "And she's not going to wash your clothes anymore when you are lying around here doing nothing," she said.

Well, after a year or two, he was back and we must be friendly. If he asked me to go to the show with him, as he had apparently told my mother he was going to, I must go. A young man, whom I met during the summer normal, asked me to go, but I turned him down and went with my brother. Anyway I was not at all interested in any special man; I suspected them all, but in spite of it all I dreamed and hoped. We went to see *Saint Elmo*. I had just read it the month before at the Snows'; it was the first love novel I ever read. I wept copiously and was afraid some of the Snows would come in and catch me... As we were going in the opera house (the theater was always referred to as the "opera house") I met one of the young men who was graduating from Simmons College that year; he was to receive the AB degree. How I hated introducing my brother to him! Fancy, my brother was in the first or second grade when he left school and now he was nineteen and had received little improvement; he was unable to speak the simplest sentences correctly. Besides I hated having people I knew see me sitting in second- or third-rate seats. Another thing which irritated me and brought ugly thoughts and pictures to my mind was what Sumpter said, as we were going down; yet I felt he was trying to confide in me. "When a feller is tryin' to live right, there is al'ays some nigger on every corner." I was startled and disgusted and made no answer. I was fidgety and troubled and tried to suppress it all. In the end I was compensated a little; the heroine's name was Edna; that is my first name.

I was glad to leave for my school work again; for at the Snows' I was often alone in my room; anyway, if they asked questions which I did not want to answer, or which embarrassed me, I changed the subject, or simply did not reply. I had ordered the *Normal Instructor*, a teacher's journal; the Superintendent had recommended that all teachers read William James's *Talks to Teachers* that year; and then there was other reading material at the Snows which found a warm place in my heart. It was the *Appeal to Reason* edited by Eugene V. Debs. Oh Lord, here was a paper which discussed women's rights! I do not believe that it had occurred to me that there were people in the world who were thinking and writing seriously about this question. Equal rights for women was one of the planks in the socialist platform. Of course, the whole socialist program stirred me deeply, but I had in some way sworn allegiance to women first. I believe I read the socialist ideas in the *Appeal to Reason* with perhaps more fervor and hope, and I am sure with more intelligence, than I learned the stories of Christ on the colored Sunday School cards, when I was six or seven years old. There were twenty planks in the socialist platform, and I think I once knew what all of them were. And how the criticisms of life in that paper interested me! Old man Snow would say to Deskin, "Did you show Gertrude this?" (sometimes he'd gasp and repeat "Miss Gertrude"), or he would ask me what I thought of some other article. I talked socialism with the boys, especially Deskin, quite a lot. He explained the socialist land system; all land would belong to the state and each man would be given what he could work; the system of taxation was often discussed too.

I kept a firm grip on my school after Christmas. The strap I had with me always; and I was exacting and severe. But I read my William James religiously also; perhaps I thought it appeared clever to say I was studying psychology; or maybe the suggestion came from some one of the Snows. Once when I read aloud (we all sat around the stove in the evening) what James said about old fogyism, the old woman seemed miffed and said all young people in those days looked upon their parents as old fogies. Much of the book was not clear to me, but I did derive the doctrine of interest; and while I was severe and perhaps punished too often, I planned all sorts of work which I considered of interest to the child mind, in drawing, map work in geography, and made special plans and required definite work from all in each subject. We moved into the new schoolhouse before very long and all children started to school. Once two families of boys had a great quarrel and fight on their way to school; and it was reported to me. I discovered just who they were and kept them after school and tanned the last one of them; I would teach them how to quarrel and fight and use profane language when they were coming to my school. The strap was a heavy one, and I had worked myself up to a high pitch; as a consequence it was said that nearly all these boys carried black and blue rings on their legs which they showed their parents. One man even reported the affair to the County Superintendent, and came to me in a great fit of anger. The Superintendent and trustees applauded me; they said that community had been running wild for a long time; they needed a good tight rein; and I think they did not object to my using a heavy whip. The trustees visited, the Superintendent visited, and others came in to look on. Once I heard a whisper that someone had said I kept the best school they had had in that community. The kids were scared to death of me; I could squelch them with a look. The punishments which I meted out were usually for misconduct outside the classroom.

—✦

I met a young man that year who called on me about twice a week. I knew his parents and sister, and two of his young brothers came to school to me. I had licked both of them. We used to go to prayer meeting almost every Wednesday night. Not that we went there to pray, for I usually did my praying in private. He had a new rubber-tired buggy and a fine horse; and then he was jolly; he could amuse me; we laughed a lot. He had sense enough to know that I considered myself a woman of intelligence and he egged me on. How one saw and felt my superiority in the presence of those country girls! We became friendly and he made love to me; and we used to hold hands almost always when we drove home at night. One moonlit night when the horse had fairly crawled home and was walking in at the Snows' gate, he asked me to marry him. I began laughing, as though something extremely humorous had just burst in my mind. He asked why I laughed, and I said because I knew exactly what he was going to say. When the buggy stopped at the Snows' yard fence, he tried to kiss me before we got out. I pushed him away. The moonlight was streaming through the mesquite and oak trees in the yard, where we walked through, almost like day.

He kissed my hand. I drew away from him and began to talk to him as though I were his aunt. All the trouble in the world came through kissing. People did not stop at kissing and presently they had lost everything. But he could kiss me, he said, without going any farther. He told of a love affair with a girl whom he used to kiss; when they parted, nothing more ever happened. His parents both knew he was in love with me; he cared; and he wanted me to care. We shook hands and I tripped up to my room. I looked out of my window on the still, sweet night and I wished we had done everything. A sexual emotion swept me; but I composed myself and bradded down the head of the demon within me. Had the ole lady Snow seen him kiss my hand! I was startled... Now I was able to criticize him. He was a fool or maybe he thought I was one; but I was not fool enough to let a man kiss me. He kept coming and went on holding my hand, but never tried to kiss me again. Many times he talked to me about marriage, which I laughed off or made a joke of. I was the strangest person he had ever met, sometimes he thought there was absolutely no emotion in me; perhaps it was only because I did not care for him; he knew I did not care, but he wished I would try. When he put his hand over mine he felt no response; only once had my hand ever moved in his. He told when it was. He had wanted to cry. Everyone knew he was inclined to be a little wild, but he would be an excellent man if he married a good woman.

I dreamed of Vernon Trout a good deal that year, but always with the result that I saw it would prevent my going on. Anyway he once said jokingly that $65 a month would support both of us, if we got married; I could make the living. Of course we both laughed heartily at such wit, but just the same, I was no fool.

—

Emma came from Midland two or three times that year to see my mother who was still working at odd times as a nurse. Emma was not getting along with her mother-in-law; both women wanted to run everything. The old lady McClintic used to write my mother about their difficulties; Mrs. Mc and my mother were apparently great friends for the simple reason that they were both of Scotch ancestry and both old-fashioned Southerners. One letter stated that Emma must be like her father; she had scolded Charles for spending so much money for dresses for his wife, a girl who had come out of the cotton patch... My sister had apparently told her husband and mother-in-law everything and they were both using it as a lever to place her in any position convenient to themselves. Yes, this was love; this was marriage. No one but a fool would ever think of going into a thing like that. My mother was disgusted too. She was sick and quarrelsome: "These children don't care how I have to work; I saw blood in my bowel movement this morning; I'm blowing out great knots of blood and matter from my nose; I'm coughing up great hunks from my bronchial tubes; I have these hot flashes all the time now; it just looks like I will go crazy when my sickness is on me, I'm so depressed." Emma would stay two or three weeks (and later two or three months) with us, "helping Mother," just to be away from her mother-in-law and the ranch.

I made a trip home every month to cash my voucher. But was usually glad to get back to the Snow farm. There were many attractions; the socialist papers, and people of my own age or older to talk to. I found out the socialist position with reference to capital punishment; I held it as my position too. They wanted to abolish the United States Senate; Senators were usually rich men and plutocrats who were of no use in our government; I agreed. Then I met the son and daughter (both several years my senior) of an atheist. The terms atheist, infidel, and agnostic were all applied to him. The Snows told me the old man was a Greek scholar, but his son informed me that his father had forgotten most of his Greek and Latin. But the fact that he did not believe in God aroused my curiosity more. It seems to me, the son said his father was an atheist, but the daughter said he was an agnostic; he merely said he did not know whether there was a God or not. Deskin Snow asked if I knew the difference between those three words and then went on to explain... The son asked if

I had a diploma from Simmons; how much Latin had I read? I had had beginning, Caesar and Cicero, and would finish reading Virgil and stand my exams at Simmons when school was out. I only lacked a little being through and would finish that June. The atheist's son had read more; Horace and Pliny. The daughter had taught school and had been to Europe. She said I would go to Europe too, after I had taught a few years; one must; one owed it to oneself. I will not say that the ideas I gained that year were new to me; I thought I knew them already, but it required books and conversation to give them form. It was like dropping seeds in a fertile garden.

I received the *Normal Instructor* regularly. I think it was published in Illinois and one number contained a large photograph of Ella Flagg Young, who was then (1910) superintendent or was going to be superintendent of the Chicago Schools. An article told of her life and work. She had been a teacher, principal, or superintendent in Chicago for more than forty years, and now she was the head and receiving $10,000 a year. The account stirred me; I looked at her portrait; I thought my mouth was firm like hers and my forehead almost as high. I read on; she was only seventeen years old when she began teaching school.

School closed with exercises and I sent for my mother to come. She helped me to become more prejudiced against the Snows; I told her Deskin once said to me that I had better marry him while I could get him; she said the devil wouldn't have those ole Snow boys for soap grease. It tickled me. He once asked me the names of my sisters.

I gave him four names, but he said there were five, someone had told him about my oldest sister. Once when we were riding to Merkel, he said he could make me angry; he had made Vernon Trout's sister angry; I said he couldn't; I was not so silly as to be angry when people planned it. He poked his arm in a very stupid and awkward way around my shoulders. I gave him a look like those I sometimes gave school children, and he took it away and sat up straight. Sometimes when we sat around the store and talked socialism, I thought him handsome; other times when he filled his lower lip full of snuff and smirked about people and showed me up as not being as clever as I thought I was, I hated him. His brother was even more disgusting to me at times. This notwithstanding the fact that they had been very kind to me and we had had many jolly times together.

Once after school was out, I quoted something from the *Ripsaw*, a vulgar socialist paper; I was going to subscribe for it, or for the *Appeal to Reason*. My mother said she believed I was crazy.

I went back to Simmons. I entered the physics class for a review before the examination and was surprised to find how easy it appeared. I excused myself for having failed the last exam on the ground that I was sad or sick or overworked or worried. I read Virgil to Prof. Tolman and received my mark after an oral examination. There was a history examination to pass and I would be ready for the diploma from the academy of Simmons College. The expression teacher asked me to enter the play *As You Like It* in the role of Audrey. At first I was a little offended at being offered this part, but when I saw I could be amusing in it, I was pleased. The play was given at the opera house, and the *Abilene Daily Reporter* stated I had been very witty and amused the audience greatly. I was charmed when I saw I had pleased my physics teacher. I got a glance at his face when the audience was roaring, and he liked it too. Dr. Olson was a scientist and a serious man. He was religious but he would have nothing to do with the foolishness of the church. At least I supposed him religious, I had heard him pray at chapel. And up until this time I had been frightened almost to death of him. He was a PhD graduate of Yale and had studied in Germany. Many times I complained at home and said he thought I was little better than an idiot. He was frightfully severe in both class work and examination. I felt better when he liked my acting.

I made my graduation dress of plain white embroidery, and my mother and I went to the graduation exercises. I had told her that I did not want any flowers; we were too poor. There were greetings and congratulations and I met and talked with one of the AB graduates, a young man whom I knew was engaged but who attracted me immensely, I was almost in love with him. He told me that Eugene Wood, the land agent, had told him what a noble girl I was; I was paying for my mother's home. It did not worry me to have him mention it; but it would have been an offense from another. There was invocation and speaking and the president made his charge to the class. Diplomas were handed around and flowers and presents brought in. My name was called; you could hear it all over the auditorium and a girl came with a large bouquet of white and pink roses and flowers. When we got home, my mother said, "I thought you would look conspicuous without no flowers." She had sent to an ole German woman who had beautiful flowers and took in washing and purchased them for fifty cents. She looked shy and I said they were pretty and we changed the subject.

This happened the first week of June, 1910 and I began to count my blessings. I had a second grade state certificate; I had taught school one year and earned $325, besides learning a lot of things; I had paid off several notes on our place; I was a graduate of the academy of Simmons College and still I was only seventeen years old. But I would be eighteen on the twentieth; I was going to go on and on and on.

⟵✸

During one of these years Reuben, my second brother, came home. He had been all over the southwest and west and I think as far north as Montana. The best we could make out he had ridden the bumpers. He was full of socialist talk and the right of man to the fruits of his labor. And when my mother mentioned something about God, he said the socialists were atheists and that the only God there was was within man himself; he was a socialist; he was an atheist, he said. My mother told him that she did not believe in no such doctrine and that anybody who come preaching such ideas around her could not stay in her house. I was on the side of my brother's ideas, though I had no use for him. I had no desire to talk to him beyond the commonplaces and kept quiet. Anyway it seems to me I was in the midst of another examination. He said I was not smart at all; that I had to study too hard. He learned everything in a flash without studying; he was the clever member of the family. While I did not like to have him say it, I was sometimes afraid it was true. Often the subjects I studied were mixed up and intangible like fog. I would have liked to have talked with him but sooner or later he would have showed me up a fool; or he would have shouted out, "God Amighty, you little fool, you don't know that and you think you are smart!" Or if I had chanced to get the better of him in an argument, he would have cursed me or threatened to strike me; and if I had laughed and jeered at him a bit perhaps he *would* have struck me. I always imagined my older brothers wanted to impress upon me to keep me in my place and not to think I was so "Goddamn smart." And this infuriated me so that the few times I saw them during those years I never wanted to talk with them. Perhaps I wanted to use their methods against them. I wanted to say: you low-down scoundrel, why don't you take a decent job, go to night school, and send money home to the family. But such talk was confined to male members of the family more nearly my own age... I liked what he said; but I didn't like what my mother said to him. I was not sure about atheism, although it interested me immensely, but I was pretty certain in my heart of hearts that I was a socialist.

In the summer I attended the normal again and stood the examination for a first grade state certificate. I passed. One incident of that summer occurs to me. A teacher, a woman of some thirty-five years passed me on the campus, "Are you Miss Gertrude Beasley?" she inquired. I was a little taken back. "The first time I ever saw you," she went on, "I thought you were the ugliest girl I ever saw in my life." I was astonished and a little angry as one is when water is thrown in the face. Then she explained that since she had known me she had changed her mind: President Sandefer (of Simmons) had said I was a very bright girl; he had talked about me in one of his classes.

The following year I took a one-teacher school five miles from town and came home every weekend. I received $65 a month and paid $10 each month for board. But it lasted six months and I received payment for institute attendance which made the amount for the year a little over $400. I still wore old clothes in the country and exceedingly plain and severe ones. It was just as well as they made me look even more serious and much older. Sometimes I imagined I looked twenty-five years old. I tried out all the new methods I had read of, or as many as I could, and instituted work which I considered adaptable to the children. Mothers came and told me how grateful they were that their children had fallen under my instruction.

But I was severe and cross with all forms of nonsense and I had difficulties enough. Once I whipped a seventeen-year-old boy, who was a head taller than myself. He had distracted the attention of the class by making obscene pictures while a book agent was speaking to them. He had committed other small offenses. After school I took out my leather strap and told him to come forward and take off his coat. I made a second demand and he shed his coat, and stood there in his shirt sleeves for me to lash his back and shoulders. It seems to me he was one of those fellows who would show no emotion; he merely relaxed his muscles when the stroke came. I was boarding at his house across the road at the time. As far as I could make out, he did not relate his story to his parents. Perhaps he did and they brought about his changed attitude. For after a few days, he began to act as though I had conferred some special favor on him. He didn't annoy me again and the school settled down for a long time. He was a little dull in his books… Once I asked an older boy to take off his coat; he didn't want to and I took hold of the collar and helped him. I felt something tingling in my nerves a little like what I have described as nervous prostrations for a day or so afterwards. The trustee told my mother that I was an extremely high-strung woman; "She can fight her weight in wildcat." But he thought I would give up some of my fractiousness and high temper as I grew older.

In the fall before my second school began, I worked at the Nickel Store again and received about $4 a week, but "every little bit helped." Then I made arrangements to take twenty-five music lessons and went there three times a week at seven o'clock in the morning for musical instruction. The teacher loaned me a history of music and talked to me about some of the great masters. I talked with the professor at the Business College about taking out a scholarship for shorthand or bookkeeping, saying that if I did not make use of it for the time allotted perhaps he would let me transfer it to my brother, Roger. Roger only hissed and supposed I was going to "run the place now," when I mentioned it to him. I started the course, but I do not recall what arrangements I made; I remember glancing at a shorthand book at odd times in the store. Perhaps I merely bought a book and studied alone. A Mexican girl twelve or fourteen years of age used to come in the store. She carried a Spanish primer. I was interested. I bought a primer and she sometimes stopped at the counter and read sentences to me. Now I did not mind the Nickel Store work; weighing and handing out bags of candy. I was extremely active and serious. My mother said she thought I had gone crazy; I was trying to kill myself, studying.

At Pleasant Hill, my second school, some of the mothers asked me to help their small daughters in music. I knew very little about it, but I could teach the notes and first exercise. A few children came to me after school and I was paid a small fee. I played the organ at school and sometimes at Sunday School. A man thirty or thirty-five years old who used to plough in the garden next to the schoolhouse and whom I had met at "singing" once sent a note up to our house to ask if I would go to the show with him. I hastened to turn him down; I didn't like the way he looked at me; he was a divorced man. No one sparked me that year. I can't remember a single beau. I studied some that winter at odd times as I intended going back to school for the spring quarter. I remember working problems in College Algebra.

School let out in April and I entered the classes at Simmons. There was a new teacher of English, who could say satirical and ironical things to the class, a cross person, a great scold. She found the scholarship in English exceedingly low, unbelievably low. After I had passed the examination with something above eighty, she did not want to give me credit because she said I had not been there full time; I should take a year off for study; I could not finish my education piecemeal like that. I would never be through. I told her I couldn't, but I did not explain why; I was irritated and hurt. I earned ten college credits; and I counted my score again. I had added on a first grade state certificate and ten college credits. I was still only eighteen; wouldn't be nineteen until the twentieth of the month.

⤎❋

During one of these years when I was at the height of my seriousness, my mother called me to look at something she had found in the doctor's book, a treatise on sex such as I imagine a midwife might possess. The name of the book was in a foreign language; my mother explained that it meant life. "Gertrude," she began, putting her finger under certain phrases of the book, "it says here that if a girl is in love, maybe she is not of the right age; maybe he's awful poor…it tells about a poor violinist and a girl… Says it's much better for the baby when they are in love." She talked on almost like a seventeen-year-old girl who was just beginning to wonder at love. Then she turned to the name and the portrait of the woman at the front of the book, the author. It was a "for-i-gen" name, she said; she put her finger under it and spelled it out: How did I pronounce it? She looked at the portrait: "Just look at that face; she looks like you; how ugly she is! But, God, I'll bet she's smart." She said she believed I was going to be just like the author of that book; I was thinking I was sure to have degrees after my name like those of the woman in the portrait. She talked on of what the writer said about sex and lovemaking and I saw her lips tremble. She got up to leave the room. I had never noticed that her hands and wrists were so small; and how softly her feet moved! "Ah, God," said she, "what a different woman I would-a been if ennybody had ever cared for me." I wanted to throw myself at her feet and clutch at her skirts. "But, Mother, I'm here: don't forget; I'm here," I wanted to cry out. Once when she talked like that I made a vow: "I will do something about it, I will tell, Mother; I will tell; I swear I will tell your story." I read some of this book, and one day she called my attention to a photographic plate of the fetus in the uterus: "I'm just going to tell you children everything and then if you go astray it ain't my fault." I thought she was not afraid I would ever go astray; she only wanted someone to talk to.

That summer I began the study of German and kept on with Spanish. I also did trigonometry and chemistry. And in the fall, I borrowed fifty dollars from the Citizen's National Bank and went back to Simmons College until my school opened in November. I read history books, Bryce's *Commonwealth*, German, Economics. That year I became a principal; it was the two-teacher school at Colony Hill, five miles south of Abilene. I received $75 a month for six months, and the institute fee made the yearly salary something more than $450. The fourth year I taught at Potosi, Texas, a village with stores and blacksmith shops, for five months at the same salary, as principal, having one assistant. And the fifth year a tobacco-chewing, whiskey-drinking, old codger (he was one of the hard sinners who had been regenerated) who made the benches for the new house at Potosi and who watched me teach, informed the people of the community, and they came and told me, that he would give "Miz Beasley a *hunderd* dollars a month" to come and teach their school. I had many offers those last three years.

One day during the first years, or it may have been before I began to teach, my mother brought a letter to me. She sat down on the piano stool and propped her elbow on the piano to listen. "Gertrude, you read this letter to me," she said, "what does it say?" I looked at the name; it was from my father. I read, "Oh, my darling wife, oh, my little children," and the tears streamed out of my eyes. "But, I read that," she went on perfectly composed, "What does it say farther down?" She kept on talking; it looked like anybody on earth would have sense enough to go on off now to some other part of the country, or even to a strange country, and let us alone; it looked like he wanted to harass and devil us all to death; after all these years he was still bothering us; keeping us cramped or else stirred up; it looked like he was about the meanest man that God ever let live. I tried two or three times to read, but my throat hurt and I wiped away tears. "Aw, give me that letter," she demanded, "I'm going to burn it up; no, I won't, I'm going to seal it up and put it back in the post office just like it was; and don't you tell a soul about this." She was placid and dry and a little quarrelsome.

⤙✷

I made a lot of acquaintances during the five years I taught and studied for the bachelor's degree. They were mostly young schoolteachers and students, plain girls, who had sense enough to humor me a little and not to try to get under my skin or become too familiar. But the young men I met were nearly all awkward and stupid; perhaps it was only because I could not have the one I wanted. I remember dreaming about a round-faced, brown-eyed, young fellow (just the kind you see in advertisements and in American Express offices throughout the world) who gave me no attention, and then another one who belonged to Abilene's smart set. I fancied them writing me beautiful and poignant love letters but that was as far as it ever went. Then there was another young fellow whom I liked; he was going to be a scientist; in fact was a star pupil of the science Professor's. He didn't believe he would ever be a Christian, he told me, his thoughts were too black. I wondered. One day he was handing out books at the library and gave me the wrong one. "This isn't the book I want, honey," I said. He exploded with laughter and told several students who knew me about it. I had said it absentmindedly, accidentally. After that he used to talk and joke with me. What did I intend to do after I finished the bachelor's degree?

Once I gave him a long story, saying I was going to study law and go in to one of the Western suffragette states and become a senator or governor. He said all lawyers were crooks; and often when I passed through the library, he would crook his fore finger and hold it up, this being sign language for "crook," a scoundrel, which he maintained all lawyers were. Another time I told him seriously about my intention of going to Columbia; I said jokingly to study for a doctor's degree. He made a jest of it, and he and his friends called me Doctor Beasley after that, or "Doc" for short. Sometimes he joked about a student whom he declared was in love with me, and who had "eyes like fried eggs and feet like shovels." He would hold up his hands in silent raillery, if I looked at him in the library, and gradually separate them until the space was two feet; this was to indicate the length of my admirer's feet! I encouraged his childish antics, much to the surprise of some of the students, and furthered this absurdity by signaling to him the size of the freckles on his girl's cheeks... But we were often serious and critical too in conversation, and sometimes lapsed into cynicism and contumely. He once had a falling out with the Head of the School and called me a diplomat because I would not criticize "Prexy." The President, he considered, was a narrow-minded man; he stood up in chapel and censured cigarette smoking as though immorality resided in tobacco.

My friend was attending Simmons for exactly what he could get out of it; some of the professors he considered first rate, especially the science teacher; but there was "an awful lot of bunk being handed out at school." He knew a little about socialism and I imagined him a sympathizer; although he thought the people in the country were ignorant of socialist principles and often didn't know what they were talking about... I told my mother about our jokes and conversation; she said she believed I was in love with this student. I liked him immensely...

Sometimes in the summer during those years, young men called on me, but they were almost invariably people whom I did not like. Their feet were too big; their hands were too thick; they had nothing to say of any importance or interest; they were nearly all fools. Every idiot in town had asked for an engagement. Many times they came to the threshold of making love but they never crossed. I used to complain to my mother and sometimes she was greatly amused at my criticism. "Men don't want a smart woman."

—◆

My two brothers just older than myself, Ruel and Sumpter, got married. Both were under twenty-one years of age, and my mother called on me to write the letters granting them permission to buy the licenses. In each instance she would remark that she had thought it all over and she guessed it was the best; she didn't know what trouble these boys might get into; maybe they would settle down and become steady men; maybe they were never going to help her. Ruel married a poor cotton-picking, snuff-dipping girl; but Sumpter wed one of the music students of Simmons College who had been giving private music lessons at Abilene. She was at least eight years older than my brother, she could have been more though; sometimes in certain clothes she looked extremely young and pretty. I could not understand it, I, who was so ambitious, and who cared so little for men. Why, my brother had quit school in the first grade, and could scarcely write his name. Moreover he had always refused to improve himself. Here was a capable woman, much older, well educated (she was a Yankee and much better educated than the average Southern girl) who was going to marry an ignorant boy. My brother was con-verted during their courtship; secured a job as engineer at the largest hotel in town (I always felt that his position was little better than that of a janitor); negotiated with a land company to build them a house about the size of a match box; and got married.

A young preacher at Simmons, a handsome young man whom everyone knew to be highly sexed and a great emotional flirt, offici-ated. I played a few bars of Mendelssohn's Wedding March as they entered the room. Well, two more fools had met, and I helped as much as I could in getting them joined together, both under their direction and that of my mother. There was another example to add to my skepticism... My mother began whispering about Pansy, Sumpter's wife. She had told both my mother and Sumpter about an accident which she had a year or so before she met my brother. She had sat down on a long chinaheaded pin, which was sticking in her clothes, on getting out of the bathtub, and had to be taken to the Hollis Sanitorium to have it removed from the vaginal passage. My mother would sniff up her little short nose; the young preacher used to go with Pansy. She guessed that the young evangelist, whom everybody thought was such a glorious Christian, had ruined her. "I'll bet anything she was fooling with herself trying to make herself come unwell," she brought out. Interest, disgust, curiosity, anger.

Sometimes I thought I hated my mother more bitterly than anyone in the world. "Now look here, Mother, who told you about this?" I demanded. Pansy was the only person who had told her about it; "she told herself," she went on as though that were sufficient proof of the pudding. Oh Lord, I do not say that I was ever conscious of wanting to lay hands on my mother; I think it was a greater hate than one has in a physical fight. It seems to me I wanted to hide my face, to run away, to curse. What right had she to say that Pansy had been ruined and was trying to commit an abortion? It could have been true that the thing happened as Pansy said, many girls in those days used pins like that to pin up their skirts with; she could have sat down on it, just as she described. Afterwards they had babies and heartaches and trouble; they couldn't find work; they quarreled and talked of separating and my mother egged it on. Oh God, those awful days! Sometimes I complained that there was no one to help us and mentioned that both these fool boys had married before they were twenty-one. My mother would fly into a temper, "Who's to blame for it? Who wrote out the letters for them? You done it yourself!" What an impossible old fool! Other times, she would say the same thing I had said, as though she had discovered a new idea.

⤙✶

In the summer after I finished my third school and the summer quarter at Simmons, I took my mother on a few days' trip to Galveston. I borrowed $50 from old man Paxton at the bank, and gave the usual note with my mother's signature and my own, which was to be paid back in four months at ten percent interest. The interest was always computed at ten percent. Return tickets were very cheap as we did not take a sleeper; and the whole journey for two cost a little less than $25. We took food from the delicatessens and prepared our own feasts in the room; went bathing twice a day and sightseeing.

One day we visited the military posts to see the big guns and so on. A polite, young sub officer met us; showed and explained the whole thing. He was from Michigan, a Yankee and big and attractive. He stood up like an arrow, wore his uniform well. My mother mentioned having noticed so many "ole Cath'lic churches" in Galveston and he opined bravely that they were a monumental fraud. I liked hearing monumental; he couldn't be a very ignorant man and use a word like that, even though he was only a corporal... It's a curious thing, though I've noticed it all my life, how the currents in some bodies tend to reach out to certain others. It seemed to me that almost everything he said was correct; he was even amusing. He had met the approval of my mother who had read *Thirty Years in Hell*, and believed that the cellars of Catholic churches were planted with babies' graves, illegitimate children whom "theym ole priests" had given the nuns. Once when I was a child, we passed a Catholic priest and she warned me not to get too near him.

I liked his eyes, of the soldier, best of all; they were just the right shade of brown; I couldn't make them out quite. And the corners of his mouth turned up more than any person's I had ever seen. His hair grew in graceful curves about his temple. We started to go. He said he was on leave the following day and asked if he could come out to show us the city. I made no engagement, but left my telephone number; and when he called the next morning I said he could come; of course my mother was going also. He was delighted. What a lot of longing looks we gave one another that day; my mother said she could not let us get out of her sight for fear we would run away. We walked on the sea wall and he talked sentimentally about the sea. Once when I put my hand in the water, he drew out his handkerchief to dry it. Our hands touched; it was something like an electric shock. We promised to write. He brought flowers to the train which was already moving when he arrived; my mother declared she saw him kiss my hand, when I reached out to take them. He sent me music and wrote love letters for about a year; we exchanged photographs of ourselves. He asked me to marry him and once more I assumed the role of aunt or mother superior, and laid down the law about quick marriages; one ought to know a person eight or ten years before marriage.

I would like to see that letter now. I was twenty years old. It was the fourth year of my teaching; but how much and how often I dreamed of him! I held imaginary, sentimental conversations with him by the hour. The first mental picture of having a baby, that is the first image which impressed itself sufficiently so that I remember it, came to me that year. It was a picture of a woman and a tiny baby in bed, and a man kneeling at the bedside kissing the woman's hand. I think he was overcome with the wonder and beauty of mother-hood. This image was so clear to me that sometimes I felt as though I could reach out and touch my sweetheart, who was five hundred miles away at Galveston. Sometimes when I sang, "Say, darling, say, when I'm far away, Sometimes you may think of me dear," and other ditties like, "How can I bear to leave thee, one parting kiss I give thee, etc." someone in the family would remind me of whom I sang. They laughed about it and I began to laugh too. I would amuse the whole household by pretending or mimicking, "Say, darling, say." And rid-icule, a sharp instrument, cut short a romance. Anyway, it seemed to me that a degree from Simmons College was the most important thing in my life. Then I could go on. There was no end to my wants. My mother once said, "I wouldn't think of him too much, child, he's probably got the syphilis; nearly all soldiers have."

The land agent made a discovery about my mother's property. Back taxes had been accumulating for years, and before she could get a warranty deed to the place, these taxes had to be paid. I believe the remaining notes which we owed on the place amounted to $500 after I had finished my second school. And the last three years I taught there in Texas, the money nearly all went to pay up the back taxes and the interest on the notes. It was just like pouring water in a hole, my mother would say. And if I seemed sad or overworked or too quiet, she would begin scolding and talking about the others. "They have all jes' set down and left you the bag to hold," she would observe. "Ah declare to God I think it's the meanest thing I ever heard of; as though you could make a living for this *whole* family." Corrie had never paid her board; Roger was trying to compete with all the millionaires in town; she couldn't take these little children out of school. Then she would go into a tirade about "yer devilish ole daddy"; every damn one of the children were just like him. She tried to tell him that they couldn't make a living for so many children. Once when she had ten children and we were living down there in Coleman County, she went out to the lots where he was harnessing horses and where "none of the children couldn't hear them"; she had said, "Bill, we've got to quit having so many children, I want us to quit." And he had cursed her and talked as though he wanted to cut her throat. "There'll be more wimmen in hell for trying to keep from having babies than for any other one thing," he railed. "And that, after we had *ten* children. I don't care what you say, there ain't no sorrier man ever lived than yer daddy."

One summer morning as I was going out to Simmons by street-car, some young teachers began telling me compliments which they had heard of my work as a teacher. The President of Simmons had given a lecture at Colorado at a teachers' institute on the personality of the teacher. "He told about you," one said, "I knew it was you he was talking about…he said you could make people do anything you wanted them to do…he said you weighed about ninety pounds." There was a silence. "How much do you weigh, Gertrude?" another asked. I told them about 115; and I thought they all looked as though they thought the whole story of my work had been exaggerated accordingly. I used to organize community gatherings, programs, and lectures on education in all my schools; and several times the President or members of his faculty came and spoke to the people on community work or education. He said and did many magnificent things. His was a great heart. Sometimes when he spoke, I sat back and thought: my dear man, you are a socialist. He was a good friend of mine. One day when I was talking about him, my mother said, "Yes, but that man's got nigger blood, just as sure as you are living, child, he's got colored blood; I've seen too many mixtures." Sometimes I was afraid people might hear her insinuations and her whispers. It took all the starch out of me.

When I was twenty and Roger was eighteen, I tried once more to get him to go to the Business College. I offered to buy the scholarship. He was irritated. "Don't you get smart," he said, "I educated you." He was trembling with anger. It ignited me; the idea of him or any of my brothers talking about having helped me was a hideous untruth. "You lie, you low-down dawg; it's a lie, it's a damn lie," I cried. He began weeping, "Mother took me out of school, when I was twelve years old, and sent me out to pick cotton; why didn't she take you out of school and make you earn money at picking cotton!" My mother intervened and told Roger that he had failed in his work at school, didn't seem to be doing any good, and so she thought she would put him to work. Anyway, it looked as though we were going to starve. But he thought it was only an excuse. She meant to take him out anyway. I had forgotten how he had gone out in the cold and picked cotton and brought the money home. My mother had said that she tried to get him to go to school again after the cotton season, but he refused. I tried to point out that I worked and then went back to school; it was all nonsense to refuse to go to school only because you were not up with your class. I had studied at night and worked hard to keep in school. "It's because you are so stupid," he said, "I never had to study as you study; before I'll go around looking as you do, keeping my nose in a book all the time, I'll be ignorant the rest of my life. Take that old maid…"

My mother once said that Roger told her that when he met me coming down the sidewalk (he was driving the wagon for Minter Dry

Goods Company), he looked the other way, because he was afraid I would speak to him and someone would see or hear. He said that I took such long steps, my neck stuck out so far and my clothes were so dowdy that he was ashamed of me; "he said he believed you was the ugliest girl he had ever seen." The tables were being turned; I disliked introducing any member of the family to people I considered intelligent; because I knew that as soon as he opened his mouth he would put his foot in it; now they were getting ashamed of me. I was always ashamed of their speech. For example, my mother would use words like "needcesity" for necessity; "hope" for helped (i.e., "he came in and hope me"); "remlent" for remnant, and the like. None of them was ever capable of carrying on an intelligent conversation. My home life was in every way a retrogression: there was no soul, no love, no intelligence.

—⤙✦

In early life, I used to fancy myself as a sort of Joseph for the family. I was going to be great and famous and rich and good. They were going to bow down to me and I would give gifts which would make them happy. Perhaps I dreamed of friendship and mutual intelligence, for a great emotion swept me, and I saw that we embraced and were kissing each other. For some years this dream occurred to me. I was going to lead my seven brothers and five sisters to happiness and intelligence. I suppose it was only a desire to make them conform to my wishes, to give them souls and minds like my own. There was a theory in those days (I don't know whether it grew in my own mind or in someone else's), that every child should pay for his raising. For example, I had been living without earning money regularly for sixteen years; I owed my mother $1,600; $100 for each year since you were born was the very least one could offer. (I am pretty sure this was my mother's theory.) In my blunt way, I accepted it; I was willing to pay it. But I almost fell out with my mother for her suggestion about buying five suits of clothes, one for each of my older brothers. She thought that when I began to teach I ought to present each one of them with a new suit of clothes. They would cost only about twenty dollars apiece. One time a suit for Wiley, another time one for Reuben, one for Rush, one for Ruel, and then one for Sumpter. She guessed they'd tried to help at first; anyway, "Fias you I'd do it just to show em." Recalling this has amused me very much. I was disgusted with the suggestion at the time.

Once President Sandefer met Corrie when she was teaching music at some small country village, making about the same amount which she had made in the shop. He asked her to come to Simmons. I tried to get her to take up school teaching as the second grade certificate was not difficult to obtain; and as a primary teacher she would earn twice as much as she then received and then have time for music lessons. The country people often asked me to teach their children music; she said the subjects were too difficult for her, then she turned on me, "You are not to blame that the Lord gave you a better brain than He gave the rest of us." It was not through my own efforts that

I had been able to learn; it was a gift from God. Anyway you had to have good parents to be anything in this world. "I know what I wish, I wish I had never been born!" How many times have I heard her say that! One was just as bad as the other; she did not say that the Old Man was a good man, but she knew that Mother was absolutely no better than he was. "If anything, the Old Man has a better heart than she has. Then Mother is art awful liar; Mother is a terrible liar. I know what's the matter with us; I know why we hate one another so much; it's because there never was a speck of love in our family!" She was too hurt to try to do anything; she knew how she had tried and how Mother had talked to her, "Someday you will be sick and out of work and you'll see how she'll talk to you, too... You are all right now as long as you turn over your money to her." Then she repeated how my mother had talked when she had the fever and how she had prayed to die; it would have been a thousand times better. Then she became furious and told what the proprietor of the shop had said; Corrie considered it a gross insult and wanted to leave immediately, but my mother did not want her to give up the money. There was no use to try; one could do nothing having been born of such parents.

She told how another had stirred up the terrible mess when she left my father. Did I know why she did it? It was only because she didn't want to have any more children. She explained to me that Mother need not have had so many children; it was all laziness; the thing was very simple; she had heard; you had to get up and wash yourself. Once when she said we could never be anybody, I thought she was referring to Willie. No, she didn't think of Willie anymore; she had been that way all her life; Willie used to act like that with Reuben. She told of having come upon Willie and Reuben "carrying on like that" in the cotton patch, when Willie was sixteen years old or past. Then, "they said," she had more than one man, when she got in the family way there at Roscoe; didn't know to whom the child belonged; that was the trouble. No, she had put Willie out of her mind altogether. This last was new information to me, and her use of "they say" made me angry; I had found out how much harm stories which began with "they say" were doing... I remembered how my mother once sneered (I was then nine or ten years old and Willie was past twenty) when Willie was taking turpentine, apparently to make her menstruate; and later how she had observed that after Reuben had seen Willie "in a fix" in that prostitute house that he could not "face the music any more" and left the country. She thought his conscience was hurting him; he knew he was to blame.

After such conversations, I would drive the thoughts from my mind and settle down to trigonometry, geology, or some other subject which required all my attention to understand. But sometimes, when I was tired or had made a low mark, I said it was due to the fact that I had been thinking about our old mess. Often I scolded them severely at home for talking in my presence; it didn't help matters any, and I had something else to do. I studied astronomy too at Simmons, and I remember a deep wish for more time to really learn something about it, to enjoy it. But I galloped on. I did the required courses in

English, Shakespeare, English poetry, general literature and whatnot; advanced American History, the Reformation, and others; I read Freytag's *Soll und Haben* (I think that was the name; I have no idea what it was about); Schiller's *William Tell* (it seems to me I gathered the impression from my teacher that there was sociology and even revolution in the background of this play); Goethe's *Faust* ("Some say and sometimes I think it is true, that it is the greatest soul drama that has ever been written," said my teacher, with tears in her eyes). I read courses in first, second, and third year Spanish. (I remember something about a princess in a tower, and "I killed seven with one stroke.") My specialty was psychology, sociology, and school management. I felt I knew almost everything I read in sociology before I read it; much of the elementary psychology was only common sense sayings; and many people regarded me almost as a specialist on educational questions. All these subjects were very easy and I usually got high marks.

I became very interested in the study of German under Mrs. Millar, a teacher whom I considered one of the brightest people I had ever known. She was a master's graduate of Vanderbilt University... I used to go to a German girl and her mother in the evenings; they could get the meaning out of *Faust* for me. I could look up words for hours and still get nothing from my study; but my German friends helped me a great deal. I went to German Sunday School sometimes, in order to read elementary German and hear it spoken. In my *Faust* class there were only four or five girls, all twenty or past. How frankly Mrs. Millar talked to us about love affairs! She thought love had a great power over the souls of men: that when one loved, one gave oneself sometimes without knowing it. She told us she had had three young women friends, who had given themselves somewhat as Goethe had described it; and only one of them had married the man whom she was in love with. One of these women had had a baby and everyone had given her up, but she had remained loyal to her. One of the girls used to criticize her; she was terribly mushy.

I told my mother and Corrie about our *Faust* class conversations. Both turned the corners of their mouths down, pooh-poohed and said, "There is something wrong with that woman." Corrie remarked with an obscene smirk that she ought to get married; she guessed that was what she was wanting. There was no one at home with whom you could discuss anything in literature, science, or history. And I was a great talker. We never got above the commonplaces and vulgarities of life in the home circle; and often I declared to myself that there was not a damn one of them who wanted anything different. Our humor was always coarse or stupid and sometimes obscene. It was an impossible outfit. Once when I was studying geology, I tried to explain to my mother the Professor's interpretation of Genesis and the scientist's idea of evolution. Perhaps the days mentioned in the Bible were cycles; man had developed from the lowest forms of life, at least there were many evidences. She curled up her lip before I had finished and said, "Ennybody who comes preaching that ole fool doctrine to me, about men springin' from monkeys, can't stay in my house." I grew quiet; there was no use to argue with her, she could not argue, she only laid down the law. But I was angry and would have liked to quarrel with her; that was a good thing to separate on; she believed one thing and I believed another; I had a right to stick to my opinion. Besides then I would be free and I would have all of my own money. But I thought again; she had about the hardest life I had ever heard of. Besides it would be making an excuse to leave. The boys always quarreled with her and then left. Sometimes I thought she was a person of great character and strength to talk like that. I never disputed with her and threatened to leave and never come back as the rest of them did. Comparatively speaking, we had very few words, and the others thought she was partial to me. I thought so too.

—✦

I went down to Bethel to teach the fifth year. They promised a new schoolhouse, but it was still under construction and the school occupied the old building for several weeks, a boxed house which had been the scene of cursing and fighting, tobacco chewing and bench whittling for many a year, not to mention the camp meetings in the summer. The boys both of this district and the neighboring district, Potosi, all referred to Bethel as "Buzzard Roost." Many people came to me with stories of how the preceding schools had behaved. There was a family of C's who always tried to break up the school, they drew knives and sticks of wood on the teacher, and the year before a fourteen-year-old had threatened the teacher's life with the wood ax; he chased the old man around the building with the ax drawn on him. There were eight or nine boys in this family and six of them came to school to me. I met the oldest one who married that summer before he was seventeen. He spit his tobacco juice out the window and told me what bad boys his brothers were; but the men teachers had not known how to manage them. I had studied sociology; I had lost some of my belief in the efficacy of the stick, and had become an advocate of the juvenile court and delinquency homes.

I went to see the boys' mother, to invite her to a gathering at the school. She was one of the saddest women I have ever seen; she seemed to me gentle and tender in her ignorance. The Christmas before she had tried to commit suicide, when her husband and sons had gone away to a dance. The father was a fiddler. I went away serious and sad. My father was a fiddler too. My mother had seven sons and though they never gave a teacher any trouble, at the core of life they were much the same. From what I could find out about these boys, they were steeped in bestiality and crime. The school went on for three months in comparative peace and serenity, but as I watched the fourteen-year-old boy, I felt that sooner or later he was going to give me trouble. One day, after I had used up all my talk and methodology on him, he raised a row on the ball ground and began cursing at the top of his voice. I went out and called to him in my lowest and most serious tones to come in the house. Meantime, I had placed a tree root, from one to three inches in diameter, where I could place my hand on it conveniently. This was to reinforce me in case my strap was insufficient. I reminded him of other misdemeanors and misconduct, and said I was going to whip him. "No you ain't," said he; "don't touch me," he threatened.

I began lashing him across the back and shoulders with the strap, and he struck me a heavy blow under one eye. (I carried a black ring for three weeks.) How many things flashed through my mind as I raised the root! I thought of the hardness of my club and how angry I was; I did not want to kill him. I struck and he dropped on the bench and cried out, "You have killed me." I had raised a good-sized bump on the side of his head. I was astonished and looked on, I think, for a moment, then he started towards me again. I struck him several heavy blows across the arm and wrist and he sank down weeping; "You have broken my arm." I went on lashing him, and four brothers younger than himself rushed in with knives drawn. I picked up the root and started towards them, "Close your knives or I strike, put that shovel down," I thundered. The little boys (they were twelve, eleven, nine, and seven about) grew pale, their knives clicked, and they put their weapons away. Then I turned on them one at a time and lashed them for interfering. As one beats a horse I called a boy whom I could depend on and sent for the trustees. One of them was working on the house nearby. The fourteen-year-old boy told the trustees I had broken his arm. They examined it and felt the bump on his head. His arm was not broken. I told the trustees the boy must be expelled from school. They agreed and I warned him in their presence that he should not put his foot on the school ground again during that session.

Ole Man Bondurant, who employed me, walked around on his heels and flapped his feet down that afternoon after school. "It's the first time that boy has ever been conquered," he said. But it didn't stop with that; the father took it up; if I had-a been a man he would-a beat nine kinds of hell out o' me; it was whispered that I was to be tarred and feathered. And the wife of one of the trustees informed me they said more than that, they were going to pour tar in my other end.

I telephoned my mother and told her I was having trouble with some of the heathens in the community, and that I had to have something to protect myself with. She understood and hired a "rig" from the livery stable; she and Corrie came the same afternoon bringing two pistols; one to leave with me and the other for themselves, as they had to leave after dark. I remember what I said to myself when I found they had brought me the gun. I thought I was entirely in the right. I thought of what I had come to that school for—righteousness; I made a Wilsonian speech to myself. I had come with schoolbooks and the olive branch under my arm. "And now… and now…if anybody crosses my path, I will shoot and I will shoot to kill!" I made this vow many times during the following weeks. I told the trustees I was not going to be a fool; I would do whatever was necessary to protect myself. I talked for blood and for bluff at the same time; I thought: if I can't bluff you, I shall kill you, that is whomever was fool enough to try to attack me. People in both communities applauded and cheered me on. My young sister came out mainly to help keep an eye on the gun; she was sent by my mother who was more nervous about this affair than I was, though I suffered and had trouble enough. I went on with educational programs and had what some of them called big to-dos at the school. I invited President Sandefer who had spoken to my people before in other communities to come and make a speech. George Paxton, head of the Citizens' National Bank of Abilene came in his automobile bringing Sandefer, Smith, the comity Superintendent of Taylor County, and Anderson the editor of the *Abilene Daily Reporter*. The Editor wrote a column article about my school; he mentioned that this school was paying me a hundred dollars a month; he said it indicated the value they placed on my services.

I received higher salaries than almost any young country schoolteacher, I think, in Texas. I always got money out of them...I think now of the material which I worked with there. At one house the father had been sent to the penitentiary as a cattle thief; at another, one brother had killed a brother over property, and one of the girls had an illegitimate child of whom a "nole snuff-dipping woman" whispered that "they said" her brother had given it to her; another was the house of a manslaughterer who killed his neighbor; there was a baby case in court too for many months. There were others. One day I was talking to one of the boys about the number of tenant farmers in the district. More than half my pupils came from poor renters' homes. Some of the people talked a little about socialism. I was keeping a chart of school attendance among such people, as I intended to write my thesis on some phase of the rural question. I felt full of fire and emotion when I finished talking to some of the older pupils about living conditions; and as I entered the house with fists clenched, I felt much as I felt when I resolved to "shoot to kill" the tar and feather mongers. But this time, the vow was something like this: "Someday I will strike the land system of this country, and I will strike to hurt." I found that boys of tenant farmers, often others too, fourteen years old and past, attended school only about three weeks during the year.

⤛✳

The spring quarter of 1914 found me back at Simmons. I finished with the class of 1914; the faculty having pronounced me a titled graduate of Simmons College, Abilene, Texas, I became a Bachelor of Arts. This happened on the third of June, 1914; and once more I counted up what I had accomplished over the past five years. The degree was supposed to give me a life certificate to teach in Texas; I had had five years of teaching experience, having earned something over $2,100, $1,200 odd of which I had given to my family. I was being offered positions; one school thought they could pay $125 a month but we made no agreement. And still I was only twenty-one years old; I wouldn't be twenty-two until the twentieth of the month.

I went to the McClintic ranch to visit Emma and to get a rest. I took along a volume of Common Law loaned me by Mr. Wagstaff, the leading lawyer of Abilene, who attended to my mother's business affairs. He believed generally speaking that women were no good at law, but he thought I had a lip firm enough, and a jaw steady enough to do it. He encouraged me.

I came home, borrowed two hundred dollars of Paxton and went to the summer school at the University of Chicago. Ole Man McClintic had said it was just like going to hell to go to Chicago. I had a picture in mind of myself staying in some hotel or place and someone trying to enter when I did not want them to. Almost invariably those who had never been there thought it was a dangerous place for a young woman to go to alone. I secured a revolver and packed it in my trunk. Then I wired the YWCA of Chicago to send their Aid to meet me. I was going to take no chances of being kidnapped. But I met a woman and her daughter on the train, who were bound for the same place, and the three of us stopped at the Y together the first night in Chicago. Nothing happened to us. The Y's Aid escorted me to the Campus, and they recommended a place to stay; I said I wanted a place of reasonable price and I was directed to the Elinor Club, a working girls' home, conveniently located near the University... At the University, a negro student, a mulatto, gave me the surprise of my life; he was almost intellectual; although I said in secret that he was only aping his master; they were all apes. I can't remember that I had ever read an unprejudiced discussion of the negro question. They served only one purpose in the South, exploitation. When I went to the swimming pool I found negro girls floating about in the water. The first impulse was to refuse to go in; then I remembered

I was in Yankee land and when in Rome—I slid off into the water. One day a girl at the Elinor Club read a telegram in the paper to me; it was of a negro lynching in Texas. "What do you mean, Beasley," she asked, "ain't your people civilized yet?" I defended my people. I said sometimes it was necessary. I told the most gruesome horrors I could remember, of negroes raping white women and cutting off their breasts. But didn't we have legislation and courts in the South? I held on in the argument; I kept my point. Afterwards I moved into a room with a mild, sweet-voiced girl, Lucy Hoffman, whom my opponents in the argument nicknamed "Love"; we were known as "Love" and "Lyncher." Happily, this appellation did not last long, for there was a wave of appendages according to one's profession or according to what one imagined one wanted to become. They decided to call me "Judge" because of my interest in law; but, they said, I was a country person and downstate they always said "Jedge." So I became "Judge Beasley" or plain "Jedge" to those who knew me best.

I began to see how little I was getting out of the Summer School and to wish I could stay in Chicago or near the city in order to study at the University during my spare time. I read an advertisement in the paper of a teacher's agency. I called and told them of my training and experience; of course, they could find me a position… The Cook County teachers' examinations were being given the last of August and I decided to try them. I read a history of the State of Illinois and other subjects new to me in preparation. An Elinor Club girl asked if I were Irish, when she heard I was to stand the examinations; my round face and eyes looked Irish. The girl seriously advised me to wear a Cross, as she said the Superintendent was Irish and that eighty percent of the teachers in Chicago and Illinois were Cath'lics; they had the schools under their thumbs; Cath'lics controlled the government of the State. I appeared for examination and was called before the Irish Superintendent for a test in oral reading. He didn't speak English much better than my mother; I was much more able as a superintendent than he was. I had good marks and was granted the Cook County (the county in which Chicago is located) teacher's certificate.

I was employed at Highland Park to teach the fifth grade and elementary German in the sixth, seventh, and eighth grades, and received $80 a month. Having registered for courses at the University extension classes, I attended Thursday afternoons and Saturdays. One was a class in German, Contemporary German Literature, I believe it was called; we read the works of Hauptmann and Sudermann in English and German. But the Professor lectured in German and one was compelled to speak German in class. I stayed after the class and talked with the teacher; I told him of my elementary classes in German at Highland Park and read my simple tales to him for correction in pronunciation. He said I did fairly well; he was kind and interested. Sometimes I imagined he was delighted with me; I dreamed about being in love with him and spun tales by the yard about his coming to Highland Park to see me. But the vision never got beyond holding my hand or trying to kiss me; maybe it was going to be a strong thing, like *Faust*, if it had developed. I was like that, I remember, at Simmons sometimes too, though I think my professors would be very surprised to learn it. On a spring day when the heavens were so clear that one could almost see the atmosphere moving, and there were shapes and fancies moving out of a distant mirage, I kindly disposed of my professor's wife, and became myself his adorable spouse, holding long and intimate conversations—jocular, witty, amorous, or tender. Once in an Economics class, an automobile came out of my fancy and sped along not too fast towards the Girls' Dormitory; a happy couple sat in the motor and the woman held a young baby. By some hook or crook, the woman had become exceedingly beautiful; she was myself. I scolded the thing in me which created this, and the circuit was interrupted when I found that the man in the picture was President Sandefer whose daughter I was graduating with.

←❧

I did not like Mr. Smith, the Principal at Highland Park, for although he was only a little silly, he catered to the well-to-do too much to suit me. He was afraid my pronunciation was low German; I told him the Professor said I was doing fairly well and he never bothered me again… Wealthy parents sometimes invited us to visit them, to spend the night or weekend. Once I went with another teacher to visit a family who lived in an adorable bungalow summerhouse near the lakeshore. Its size and proportions and color just fit the fall of the year. There were friends and relatives visiting including a brother-in-law, Sir Charles. I did not know before that men stood in a formal way, when women entered the room; and I think I should have been much more amazed had this custom not been mentioned to me in advance. Down home the men folk might compete in offering a girl a chair, but I had never seen men rise and remain standing like that. During the afternoon they asked what I was studying at the University; I told something which Professor Judd had written or said in his lectures. I imagined they thought I had spoken interestingly or cleverly; and that the teacher who accompanied me was jealous, although I was perfectly sure she was ashamed of my appearance, and nearly always faintly amused at my talk.

I opened accounts at all the big department stores in Chicago and by Thanksgiving had secured the clothes I required. One of my patrons invited me to Thanksgiving dinner and in the afternoon I danced with her husband; it was the first time a man ever had his arm around my waist. I was getting jollier and jollier and going to the devil as fast as I could go. Another time when I was there and the parents came up in the evening to show me the dainty little blue room, the wife remarked that perhaps I would want her to unhook my dress at the back. "I came up to do that myself!" protested her husband.

As I would be free and alone for several days during Christmas, I wrote a letter to Jane Addams to ask if I might visit and learn something about Hull House. I had read about her and her work. How lubricating pleasure is to the human ego! She wrote me a friendly letter inviting me to come. My feet sprang as I walked and my head went up almost to the clouds. I felt a little like that when I visited the home of Frances Willard at Evanston, too. I told the secretary there of the prohibition campaigns in Texas. The Willards could go on, but people like myself would continue to carry on. Besides she was the only American woman whose bust was in the Hall of Fame. Women like Willard, Addams, and myself would go on and on and on. I stood the Chicago teachers' examination, instead of visiting Hull House that Christmas, and passed; I could teach all grades to the high school.

Another thing which happened at Highland Park and which I have found a common occurrence among a large mass of the youth of America and, I believe, throughout the world, comes to mind. One day a little girl in my room was writing notes. I compelled her to hand one of them to me. It was a childish discussion of sexual intercourse and, I believe, it was illustrated. I asked her mother to come to see me, and I showed her the note. She said she knew already. We walked home partway together, and the mother told me that she believed her little girl, who was only ten years old, knew as much about sex matters as she did. She wiped tears away and said the father was no help to her in raising her children; she had had a son several years the girl's senior who was drowned in Lake Michigan. She knew something ought to be done, but she didn't know what to do. She thanked me for my interest in her daughter and asked me to keep her informed as to the girl's conduct. The child was what America calls a "roughneck," extremely frank, and good-hearted, though not overly sensitive or clever. I thought: here is a woman who has had only two children, lives in luxury and is apparently well-educated, and this thing happens just the same.

At home my mother had moved into a rooming house, the transaction was completed before I left. But she was angry and hurt at having to do it; although it was perfectly clear that she would never get a living in the other house. Corrie persuaded her to make the change; she had known the woman who had this rooming house before, pronounced her a nice woman, and said she had made a lot of money there. Roger, who was then eighteen or nineteen, had joined the Navy with Hale Kirby, the Mayor's son; Martha was sixteen; Alta, fourteen and Major about twelve; the last three being in school, but could be of considerable help in a rooming house. The notes on the place ($500) were being carried by E.N. Kirby, the Mayor; and if I recall correctly, we were only able to pay the interest on this money as most every cent during the past three years had gone to pay the back taxes and dry goods and grocery bills.

It appalls me when I think of how much I wanted to help and yet how little I accomplished; for although I paid the family enough money to buy a modest house and lot (not perhaps on Main Street), it looked as though we were nearer the poorhouse, when I finished my last year in the country schools, than we were at the beginning. Well,

"Gertrude couldn't make a living for the whole family"; Roger sent some money home but not nearly as much as my mother expected; Corrie's contributions amounted to a few dollars a month or nothing; and Major, although a child, earned money at selling papers. Boarders at the old place scarcely paid the grocer's. We had to do something… My mother said she was sure to be insulted going to a public rooming house downtown with four daughters (if I had remained at home). She reminded us of a scrape she had a few years past. A man had rapped at the door asking for a room and when my mother let him in, he asked her if she didn't have some girls there; "his face looked like the devil's in hell." My mother described once more how she had levelled her six-shooter on him, and told him she'd teach him how to come in her house asking such questions; "I'll have you know I'm a respectable woman"; she told him who she was and said everybody in town knew her and her children. The man dropped on his knees, asking God to forgive him, and told my mother his name. He had known us twenty years before; he kept the store at Cross Plains, near where I was born and where my parents used to go to buy groceries. "Of course I know you, Mrs. Beasley, there never was a better woman ever lived," my mother repeated that the man had said to her. He begged forgiveness. Then she would turn her mouth down and say, "But I know yer damned old Daddy sent 'em there; he wanted to find out how we was living." Sometimes she thought that if anybody like that ever came again she ought to kill him.

But my mother never contemplated killing anyone; she was *just talking,* like most her conversation. At the time I left for Chicago, my mother was having a terrific quarrel with Corrie and seemed angry with all of us. Perhaps she was angry with me for having borrowed $200; if so, I do not recall that she mentioned it. And when I kissed her goodbye, she would not kiss me. I did not receive a letter from her for a long time—October—though I wrote her a number of letters, one each week. I worried a lot; I thought she was perhaps angry with me for not returning home, besides I could not send any money home for several months as I had to pay back the money I owed. It is impossible to estimate how much the home affairs drained my nervous energy the first four years in Chicago. And when it became almost unbearable, I began to say that they would have to try to get along without me. Anyway old man Clark, the night watchman, was being given a small percent, to bring people to the "Acme House" as my mother called her place; he was a reliable man; knew my mother and all of us well; and everyone in the family was able to work. There were eighteen rooms in the apartment, the second story of a dry goods shop; if there was too much work my mother could always employ a young negro as help. I was sure they could get along, at least until I was firmly established in the Chicago School System.

I was offered a teacher's post in Chicago. One had to substitute for at least four months in the Chicago schools, before one was assigned to a permanent place with a fixed salary; and as I had had five years of experience and a half year at Highland Park I expected to receive several increases over the first year salary. I told Dr. Butler, my Dean at the extension courses, about having come into Chicago to teach and of the required probationary service. He sent me to a friend of his, Mr. Leslie Lewis, who was principal of a magnificent school not very far from the Club where I had come back to live. He required a substitute for his seventh grade for a few days; Mr. Lewis was pleased with my work and sent for me to teach the first division of the eighth grade for three and a half months.

After I had been there a week or so, a girl in my room circulated a petition asking Mr. Lewis to send them a certain other teacher. Seeing a paper being handed around from desk to desk, I naturally took it up to see what was happening. I presented it to Mr. Lewis immediately. Previous to this he had telephoned to Mrs. Young, the late Chicago Superintendent, about me. "Go back to your room," said he, "and if anyone else circulates a paper send him to me, I'm running this school." The Assistant Principal informed me that it was because I was not a Catholic that the petition had been circulated. A primary teacher, a Catholic, who had been teaching under Mr. Lewis and whose room had been closed was being sent out to substitute. She was pulling every wire she could get hold of from the Superintendent down to get the place which had been assigned to me on account of its convenience.

After a few months (I began work in the Chicago Schools in

January 1915) I went to see the Superintendent, Mrs. Young; I wanted to be assigned to a permanent place as quickly as possible and at the highest salary securable. I had to wait two hours; and as the door to her office was open part of the time, I could see the way in which she received men principals and superintendents of schools. It amused me tremendously; big husky men sat on the edge of their chairs and appeared nervous when discussing school affairs with her. It was high time the tables were turned; we had had enough of men's superior leadership. I saw her walk down the hall; she wore a dress very similar to the one of the portrait in the *Normal Instructor* which I had admired so at the age of seventeen; after a little more than five years I saw my woman, my hero; she walked a little from side to side like a virile, middle-western man. My time came to go in. "Mrs. Young, I am Gertrude Beasley," I told her. "Yes, Miss Beasley, I know who you are, sit down," said she, extending her hand. "You have been taking Virginia Lewis' place at Mr. Lewis' school." So the wire-pulling had really reached Mrs. Young. Something flashed through my mind about a telephone conversation which Mr. Lewis once had; I thought it was with her. Other people had been there to pull wires with her for a convenient place, now I was wire-pulling for myself. I told her of my qualifications and experience; when could I expect to be appointed to a regular post? Would she look into my case and help me to secure a place? Something like that. I had a degree. Would it place my salary higher? etc. I cannot be accurate as to her reply to all these questions, but she told me to come to see her in

September. She could or thought she could do something for me. She was friendly, almost warm. I went home encouraged. I told my friends at the Elinor Club how the men who talked with Ella Flagg Young trembled in their boots; it was my idea of a good time to see men afraid of a woman.

At the Elinor Club, I made many friends and got along extremely well. In the first place I never told anyone anything which I had not thought out in advance as all right for her to know. I lied about my father and never mentioned any of the children in the family except my two older sisters and the four children younger than myself. And this was strictly for my most intimate friends. Sometimes people in Chicago told me they thought I was an only child. I always felt grateful for such statements, and wondered why I hadn't told people that. I knew all of the latest slang and used all the little words for God like Gee, Gee-whiz, Golly, Gosh. Other girls said Gad; I liked it and said By Gad, too.

Nearly everybody thought me jolly; some said I was coarse and vulgar, so Lucy informed me. And the person who called me "Lyncher" at first was surprised to find that I was "almost brilliant." We conversed about women and babies. She was a nurse of the Red Cross. She told me how women of the best families often bore syphilitic children; we exchanged views.

That half year from January to June I earned $60 a month, the lowest salary I had ever received. But I was paying only $16 per month for my room and board. I found tutoring to do and went from seven to eight in the morning, to give lessons. Rich Jews paid me $1.50 an hour. By the time the spring quarter of Teachers College commenced, I had already earned nearly a half year's work at the University. But I was still in debt for clothes and owed a Doctor at Highland Park... The March winds from Lake Michigan gave me a continuous cold. I had lost most of my physical strength. Lucy Hoffman thought I had tuberculosis. One morning when I had had hay fever for about a month and was complaining because I had to get up, Lucy climbed out of bed talking to herself, "My Lud, twenty-two years old and her health absolutely gone." She advised me to take care of myself and not to take any more work at the University. She told of one of her sisters who had died of consumption.

I paid back my loan and my debts for my clothes all except $10 or so on a coat suit which I have never paid to this day. Also I never paid the woman osteopath the last $15. These are the only debts which I can think of that I ever failed to pay. All letters from home were sad, quarrelsome, dull, and altogether vulgar. None of the children wanted to help my mother; they were all too good to be chambermaids; Martha and Alta did not earn their salt; she didn't know how in the name o' God she was going to make a living. Maybe she would add that she was kept by the power of God and He would bring her through. I sent money home before school closed.

I noted that for one thing the family was growing smaller and smaller. Corrie met her husband in a boardinghouse in Dallas where she stayed while buying hats for the store in which she worked at

Abilene. He was a contractor, a carpenter, an architect. She wrote me how happy she was; she would show me the wonderful letters he had written if she ever saw me again. She hoped I was going to find someone very soon; I thought she was wishing me harm; perhaps she was adding; you can't be anybody anyway.

—⊷—

I took life easy that summer even though I studied, drank milk or cream two or three times a day, and began to feel my normal strength again. From the first day school opened in September I was called out to substitute. I registered for Saturday courses again; and a Chicago woman principal, a Smith graduate, helped me to get a place in the Evening School, which lasted five months during the year, where I could earn more money. That is, she told me to tell the principal she had sent me to him. He employed me and I received $40 a month extra for this work. My work in the evening school was largely with immigrants, who came because they wanted to learn. Men and women sometimes fifty years old attended the class; it was the most pleasant and consequently the easiest work I ever had in Chicago. I felt my work of importance and service. Then the principal was neither a czar, a hypocrite, nor a fool as many of them were.

This school was located on the north side and I moved to the YWCA on Michigan Avenue, a large hotel which accommodated 400 girls and women, as it was centrally located. That year I was in the day school from 8:30 a.m. to 3:15 p.m.; I attended University classes on Friday afternoons and on Saturdays; and taught evening school four nights a week for five months in the winter. There were many interesting girls at the YWCA who studied at the Art Institute, Musical College, or Dramatic Schools. I made several warm friends there; we went to opera, exhibitions at the Art Institute, theatre, lectures, and visited a fair amount.

I wrote a term paper for Doctor Butler that year which he praised and asked me to read before the class. Encouraged, I decided it was good enough for publication. I called on one of the editors of the *Chicago Daily News*; I was unashamed and unafraid; O, happy state! I told him what I had written about and showed him the paper. "Young lady, you talk interestingly," he said, "leave your manuscript with us." If my mother had been present she would have whispered to me later, "Your tongue was going like the clatter bone..." and I would have interrupted her and gone on thinking how smart I looked; clothes were wonderful things; one ought always to wear a hat as saucy and pretty as mine before going to see an editor. I remember distinctly saying that my hat had won this recognition. After a few weeks I received a letter from the *Chicago Daily News* and a check for $4.19. I looked up the article; they had headlined it differently; it was something about saving time and energy in school. I showed it to the Superintendent of the YWCA, a cunning and sharp-tongued old woman, not because I loved her and wanted her to share a joy with me, but because I had a lot of the "fias-you-I'd-show-'em" attitude of my mother. I remembered what she had said to me when I was called to her office for the first time, when I first arrived in the city. I told her I was going to work for a master's degree at the University of Chicago. She gave me a curious smile and said that a lot of girls came there thinking they were going to take higher degrees. One girl studied there for years, but she never learned that "like as if" was incorrect and the professors would have nothing to do with her; you had to have proper training at the place you came from to take a higher degree from the University of Chicago. I knew that "like as if" had never been one of my mistakes; I thought over the few words I had uttered in her presence, and decided she merely wanted to insult me. But when I showed her the newspaper article, she patted me on the back and told the girls at my table "we have an authoress with us."

There were many interesting things and people to see and hear in Chicago those first two years. I believe it was when I lived at the Elinor Club, I slipped out on a Sunday afternoon and went to hear Margaret Sanger. Although I talked and debated with the girls on nearly all subjects, birth control being one of my favorites, I think I never told them I had really heard Mrs. Sanger discuss the question of contraceptives. It seems to me her two lovely children sat on the platform. Altogether I was immensely pleased with her; she had a beautiful voice and manner, and discussed her subject in a scientific way. She had learned better than to offend the police by giving prescriptions. I bought one of her books, *What Every Mother Should Know*, and hid it away in the lowest drawer among my underclothing.

"A hellva lot of use you'll ever have for such a book." Mrs. Sanger was a woman who would have understood my mother, I was sure.

—◂✦

The second spring in Chicago found me again without strength. The lake winds came and brought me terrific colds and I had a recurrence during the whole winter of the pain in the back of my head and neck. It was a sort of nervous irritation which kept me tired and easily provoked especially when among children. The woman osteopath at Highland Park had helped me the year before, but now I was even worse and suffered severe cramps during my monthly sickness. My last year in the country schools of Texas had almost made a nervous wreck of me... It looked as though I was going to collapse in spite of everything. I had no money to spend on a Doctor; had not paid the last one. Letters from home were crying hard times. What horrified me was the idea of being sick. Maybe I did have consumption. Anyway, I had visualized just what would happen to me if I were ill. I had dreamed many times during the first year or so (it was a sort of nightmare) of finding myself in Texas when I did not want to be there. They would bundle me up and send me home if I were sick. I could almost hear my mother's voice. "Every damn one of these children come back on me for me to make a living for them; there is no use of anybody being sick if they will take care of themselves." Besides what a horrible thing to fail like that. I couldn't stand failure.

Maybe they would all say I wasn't smart (clever) anyway. I was so weak that I turned to God again... I always prayed some in a sort of stereotyped way, but not as I did every morning on my way to school, when I taught the country schools in Texas. I didn't miss a day in Texas that I didn't ask for guidance and strength; and this fervently and in secret. That last year I had been a praying gun toter, who had sworn to shoot to kill; and how I dwelt on the words courage and strength; one needed physical strength for gun playing and sticks.

Now I was a praying atheist. I had heard Emma Goldman several times; I liked particularly her lecture on atheism. I told the girls at my table that I didn't believe there were any men who had brains like hers. She had said that only weak people who required something to lean on believed in God; I quoted her with fluency and enthusiasm. I used to hold forth with a young woman, a music teacher, on our imperialistic policy in Mexico and would quote Scott Nearing. I talked socialism and anarchism almost in the same breath; sometimes I made fun of them and sometimes I argued their position so strongly that my opponent said I was going to become a bomb thrower... If I could only last until the night school closed! I could not give up the night school work on account of the money; besides it would mean defeat. I had to finish the winter courses I had started; I couldn't afford to lose the credits or the money either which I had paid for them. I must keep my place in the day schools. I became emotional and terribly sorry for myself. About this time, I moved into a small single room at the Y. How glad I was to be alone! I began doing something which I had never done before in my life. I sank down every night on my knees at my bed and prayed, it seemed to me, as I had never prayed before. I don't remember what I said, but I think I was asking for strength, strength, and more strength. As far as I recall, I went on talking atheism to the girls and continued prayers while locked in my room. I do not remember when the praying wave left me; but I think about the time the night school closed. Anyway, I went to a nose and throat specialist who cauterized my nose and helped my colds and sneezing. I did not register for courses during the spring quarter and I was better. "Yer ole Daddy al'ays had something wrong with him; he had kidney trouble, bladder trouble, heart failure; didn't think he would live long; al'ays something wrong with 'em." Vague conversations passed through my mind. I dispelled them.

That same spring the Woman's Party with Alice Paul at the head was organizing for the November campaign. I volunteered and organized some meetings for them.

I do not recall that young men visited me more than two or three times during these two years. All except one of them were dull. I met a young man, an art student, at one of the Y parties; we carried on a lively flirtation all evening, schoolchildren fashion; once he threatened to take me in some dark corner and kiss me. I was amused but pretended I was annoyed.

In June, 1916, I received a notice from the Board of Education stating: "You were advanced to the third ($775) year of the elementary teacher's salary schedule." Now I could go home. Besides it was arranged that I should have an upper grade the following year which paid $50 more. And with the night school my salary would amount to a little over a thousand dollars… I packed my trunk, and when the negro porter at the Y came for it he cried out at seeing me, "Ah, you's the little lady what made dat big speech; sho' can make a speech!" He had heard my four-minute speech on the work of the Woman's Party in the auditorium. I swelled up with pride; even the porter knew I had leadership.

On the train I carried on a mild flirtation with some young men, but before I reached Fort Worth an old man came and sat by me. We exchanged cards. He said the name Beasley was well known in Virginia as far back as the Virginia Assembly. A certain Beasley in those early days had been highly esteemed; then there was a Senator Beasley who was a brilliant man and very handsome. He knew the stock and he was perfectly sure that I belonged to them. But I told him that my father's people came from Tennessee and Mississippi. That made no difference; members of the family had moved there from Virginia. He thought the name was English; of course I knew, he went on, that the first families of the country came from the early

English and Scotch-Irish stock of Virginia. He offered to see me safely to a hotel in Fort Worth; I was afraid; I waited in the station until my train came.

The train arrived early in the morning and I hastened to the Acme Rooms. My mother and I wept in one another's arms and she told me how thankful she was to have me back. Martha and Alta slept on and even after they began to wake, they showed no signs of wanting to speak to me. My mother called to them in a cross voice and told them to "get up from there" and speak to me. They acted sulky. She talked about business and home affairs and the children. And after a few hours we went down to the house where Corrie and her husband were living. Corrie had grown stouter; she must have weighed 160 pounds. When she saw me, she curled up her lip and said, "God, look at her, I knew she would be like that; she looks half dead." She went on talking as though she were angry enough to swear. Then my mother put in, "For Heaven sakes, ain't you going to kiss the child?" We walked towards one another and let our cheeks and the corners of our mouths touch. Corrie acted as though I ought to be beaten or kicked out altogether for coming home thin and pale. My jaws were hollow; and I was fool enough to believe that what I was doing was a good thing. I weighed 105 pounds; normally, it should have reached 120 or 125 pounds. The doctor gave me a prescription and I began to take an iron compound. My mother talked about the way in which Corrie had received me; it just beat anything she ever saw; she knew that Corrie could act the biggest fool she had ever heard of. She said Corrie refused to tell her anything about her plans to marry Jack West... My mother whispered that Jack had killed a man; he had a wife and children in Louisiana; she didn't know whether he had been divorced or not; Martha had seen a little instrument in the bathroom which Jack had left there; she was sure he had a "nole bad disease."

I told them about the suffrage campaign in Chicago. My mother adored having me quote the negro porter about my speech. Corrie said that Jack hated all suffragettes and told me not to speak of it in his presence. I knew Jack didn't have much more sense than those people at "Buzzard Roost" who had threatened to waylay me; to tell the truth I was afraid of him; I passed him and kept quiet. Corrie was proud of his being a bully; men were afraid of him and then he sure knew how to talk to "ole fast women." Some boardinghouse woman in Dallas had offended him and he said he cursed her and told her she wouldn't even make a good whore. I was disgusted, even nauseated; my nightmare had come true; I was in Texas without willing it.

After a week or two Corrie and Jack left for Idaho. Jack would not travel unless he could afford first class accommodations, she told me proudly, as though to impress me with the high qualities of her husband. She wasn't doing a thing to keep from having a baby; "I guess I'll have a baby when Jack gets ready for me to," she informed me as though to scorn my idea that women should determine when and under what conditions they would bear children. Then the most appalling of all: she was selling her piano; Jack hated music, he didn't even like to hear her play. She spoke as though it were a manly trait in him. But I never believed, with all the sacrifice that Corrie was willing to make for Jack, that she was in love with him. I thought she was as bitter as gall inside.

I went to visit Emma at Sweetwater. She gave me a special diet of raw eggs and milk and recommended an osteopath doctor whom she and my mother had patronized. The doctor said there was so much constriction at the base of the brain, in the nerves of my neck and shoulders that it could develop into something like epileptic fits, if I did not have something done for it. Of course, his treatments could cure me; I should learn to relax. My nervous system was in a bad way; my neck and spine were stiff and sore to the touch; I saw immediately that I could have a flirtation or a love affair or whatever one chose to call it with the Doctor. We were attracted by each other. I dreamed of him or at least of some composite lover who included some of him. He gave me to understand that he thought I was clever and sweet and beautiful. I had the most beautiful skin he had ever seen; in fact, we were all favored in that respect; my mother and sister were the same. He once mentioned venereal disease, saying a lot of people came to him to be cured as he offered hot mineral baths in connection with the treatments. I talked and gave statistics of this disease as one would in a sociology class. He said I spoke more frankly on the subject than any woman he had ever heard. He treated my body just as the woman did at Highland Park except for massaging my breasts. Why didn't I stop him and say that my thin flat breasts needed no attention? No, I liked it; I let him do it. He acted as though he did it to all women; I mentioned something about it to my sister; she said some doctors did it, but it was not necessary. She told how a "nole fool doctor" at Midland had done everything he could, apparently, to arouse her sexually; he had placed his hands on or near her sexual parts.

I took the treatments of Dr. C. for about three weeks. I could egg him on with a look or a smile and defeat his attempts at caresses or amorous words with other looks and still other smiles or with what he called ironic talk. I had an ironic tongue in my mouth; I was a cynic too, he thought. Another day he would tell me how much sex energy I had and that I was ashamed of it; I wanted to run from the thing in me which made me the gifted woman that I was. All intelligent and brilliant people were extremely passionate; I knew it as well as he did. When he put his hands on my legs or came too near my sexual parts, I nearly burned up with sex energy. One day when he was massaging my head and neck he started to kiss me; I knew he was going to do it and I liked it; but I drew away as though I were horrified and told him to stop. He said I knew we were exactly alike and that we cared for one another. He made me admit it. But I told him I did not want to hurt anyone with my love affairs. (He was about thirty years old and had a wife and two children.) But the lie in this was greater than the truth; I was defending myself, after having had my breasts massaged, from the attacks of such people as my mother, Corrie, and Emma; and against the arrows and slings of public opinion. At times I doubted, too; all men were beasts or fools;

the man could make love at the beginning, but the woman was always let down and was heartbroken. I had seen enough of it and I wasn't going to be a fool. I wouldn't have had my mother and my sisters gossiping about me, as she and myself used to gossip about the others, for anything in the world. We all gossiped about one another...

Dr. C. tried to reason with me; he said I didn't need to think he was a libertine who made love to every girl or old woman who came to him; country women came there at times with cotton in their hair, he poked fun at them; he had lived with two women during the past three years or so; one of them was the wife of a well-known citizen of Sweetwater, and the other was a woman he had cured of a venereal disease; the latter frightened me; perhaps C. had a disease too. One day his talk and behavior amused me; I laughed and laughed, shaking all over. He was angry but I went on talking and laughing; this had been a course in experimental psychology; he was really very interesting under certain stimuli, I told him. I saw him twice afterwards, but he never looked at me. Sometimes I laughed about it; I said it was an experience; I was going to write a story now. But the important thing was that I was not the sort of person my family and most of my friends thought I was.

I secured an extension of my railway ticket through the Doctor's recommendation that I was too ill to travel and stayed at home seven weeks. My mother and I gossiped, talked, and planned. I told her what tremendous salaries high school teachers and principals in Chicago received; $1,500 to $4,000. Superintendent Shoop was then getting $12,000 a year. Of course, it would take time to get into a really big post, but I was already eligible; I had to take examinations and wait my chance. I was sure I could get a position which paid much more than $1,050 outside Chicago, but I had to finish the master's degree and I might as well do it now. She said that some of the tony people in the Baptist Church there at Abilene were terribly afraid I was teaching negro children. I told her there was not a single colored child in the school to which I had been assigned; and there wasn't a solitary one in the school to which I would be transferred. She informed me that a lot of the "scissorbills and razorbacks" there in Abilene were scared to death I was going to climb up. "It done her a lot of good that I didn't pay no attention to them."

—◄✦

Martha and Alta were seventeen and nineteen that summer. They entertained beaux nearly every night and went to swimming pools, driving, and to the movies. They scarcely ever asked me. This did not hurt me as I had nothing of interest to say to them and their sweethearts. But we talked a good deal in private. They said Mother had tried to beat them with sticks of wood, or with anything she could lay her hands on, when she was angry. She had cursed them and threatened to send them away from home: I believed most of what they told. Sometimes they thought she was crazy. Other times they thought it was all pure devil in her. During those years someone of

the family had told my mother that Corrie once said that she ought
to be beaten for cursing the children, for being like the Beasleys and
for her tirades. They ought to get together with a whip or something
and make her shut up. The girls said my mother acted exactly like
a raving maniac, on hearing this. They became really frightened at
the way she talked, screamed, and threatened. Oh God, those awful
days! It was almost unbearable when I left home; and it did seem that
things had grown worse during my two years' absence.

I went to visit Mrs. Powers who gave me the scholarship when
I was fifteen in the country; I was called to the telephone and my
mother in an angry voice said she wanted to tell me what a niggerish
thing had happened in her family; the negroes in the quarter would
not have acted more disgracefully; Alta had run away and married R.
C. Hart. He was twenty and she, seventeen; both a year too young
to obtain licenses; they had lied about their ages. She broke off, her
voice indicating that she was crying. I went home and Alta and R. C.
came back in a few days and begged forgiveness. My mother began to
talk against his mother and a relative of his who had said she was an
ignorant woman. So it went on. Martha was getting ready to marry
Hale Kirby, the son of Abilene's Mayor, whom she had been sweethearting with since they were in the primary grades, and who joined
the Navy with Roger.

I was glad to get away; sometimes I wished I had stayed in
Chicago, although my mother and I remained the warmest of friends
throughout the summer, as we had the majority of the time after I

began to teach school. She had a reason to be friendly; I gave her more money than all the rest of the children put together during a period of nearly ten years. And then I often imagined that she cared more for me than she did for the rest of the children. I cried and thought and fancied, after Corrie told me there never had been a drop of love between our parents, until I dreamed a thing that gave me a lot of satisfaction. And that was that my parents had "made up," had really forgiven one another when I was conceived; my father had said the thing my mother wanted to hear; they did care for one brief moment.

But I believe I must have accepted much of what my mother said, to have got along with her so well. Once when the girls were telling their quarrels and how my mother talked about everybody in the family, I asked them what she said about me: "Oh, she thinks you are perfect; she even threatens to tell you about us, as though we cared," they said. One day when my mother and I were alone and she was talking against my father, repeating the old rigamarole which I had heard since I could remember, I said quietly without knowing I was going to say it, "But, Mother, you have made many mistakes too." She took my words in the best of spirit and said she knew she had; she was only sixteen years old when she married; and she was so ignorant. "Oh God, how ignorant I was! I declare to God I didn't know a bit more than my hand knows." She would put out her hand and look at it as though to say it was totally lacking in intelligence. If she had been older and hadn't been so ignorant, perhaps she would have "known how to handle yer Daddy better." It wasn't all ignorance.

"Then I was such a coward, Oh God, what a coward I was! I knew but I was an awful coward." Once when we were talking about birth control and abortions, she told me she had made three abortions. "That would-a made sixteen children." Of course, she believed that people could keep from getting that way; but after they were once like that, "caught up," they couldn't do anything about it. She said the last time she miscarried a terrible thing appeared to her. The image of a child was clutching at her skirts and pleading with her; it had the saddest face of anyone she had ever seen. She vowed before her God that she would die before she would ever do a thing like that again. After that she had her thirteenth child.

I went back to Chicago in August. I shall never forget the first letter my mother wrote. She said that for hours after the train left I seemed so near to her that she wanted to go on talking. We had both wept nearly all day, the day I left; just like two peasants.

Martha married in October 1916, and my mother and Major were left alone. I began teaching at the Libby School to which I had been transferred in Chicago; registered for courses and went through the same routine at evening school. I drank milk and cream daily, and after one or two months I had gained fifteen pounds. My trip to Texas had certainly repaid me. I wrote the story of the Doctor who gave me osteopath treatments and myself, but most of it was so insincere and consequently so boring that I refrain from giving any of it here.

The name "Edna Ward," the author of the story, was my own first name and the name of the young corporal, whom my mother and myself met at Galveston in the summer of 1912, and whom I imagined I was in love with for about a year. I took the story to the principal of a Cultural Review School to be read, as the man advertised that he was able to help people at short story writing. He received the manuscript and called me for a conference. The story writer booster asked me to read the tale aloud to him; as I did so he made notes and suggestions. It was a horrible ordeal, for although we were alone, I almost burned up with shame, my face blazed as though I had a high temperature. It lasted about two hours. He finished and took a fee of three dollars from me. He believed I could write, he said; what I required was experience; I ought to make a sex story of "Texas and Sexes"; as it stood it sounded as though the wedding bells were going to ring. People didn't want to hear stories of that sort these days; sex stories were in vogue. He sat close to me in the streetcar, and I thought he meant to suggest that he would give me all the experience I required. The incident cured me of story writing for a long, long time.

As I read the story now, I begin to realize the mass of lies upon which I lived. They were half lies, expediency lies, and black lies. I not only lied about my troubles, personal and in the family, but I tried to make people, like Lucy Hoffman and other personal friends of mine, believe that we were a jolly and carefree lot, that I was extremely fond of my family, and felt great affection for my mother who was an adorable, old-fashioned type. And yet I knew that my tongue had slipped once or twice. Sometimes when I talked, it seemed that voices cried in my ears, "liar, liar, liar!" My first story is full of the milk-and-water stupidities which I handed out to Lucy. I wrote as though story writing was not a medium for telling what life had been to me, but a means of picturing life as I imagined people thought it should be. Oh, to be an honest liar.

⤙✦

Many political meetings were held in Chicago in the autumn of 1916. I remember particularly well the meeting of the Woman's Party in the Blackstone Theatre which was addressed by representatives of all the presidential candidates. Dudley Field Malone was the Wilsonian representative, who stated that the Democrats always held suffrage as a question of state's rights; but he pleaded with the women to have patience and put Wilson back in office; he had kept us out of war; Malone was of the opinion that Wilson would eventually support the National Suffrage Amendment. The women hissed him; Malone was almost consumed with anger. Other party representatives appeared, and then Allan Benson, the Socialist candidate, came out to make his speech. He was a plain, small man with a simple and direct method of speaking. I felt moisture in my throat and eyes when he spoke. If I remember rightly, he said he hadn't come there to bargain or make pledges to the members of the Woman's Party. Woman Suffrage, Universal suffrage, was one of the planks in the Socialist Platform. The Socialists had always stood for woman suffrage and would continue to work for the women regardless of whether or not they received a single vote from the Woman's Party. I knew whom I would vote for. I pledged myself while Allan Benson was talking. The vote was a sacred thing. One had to discharge one's duty according to one's conscience. I voted for the Socialist Benson and threw my vote away.

⟶✶

I hated the Chicago School System. The Libby School where I taught was a perfect hell of lies and stupidities. I marvel when I think that a sensitive person, as I consider myself to be, stood five years of the most hideous of all forms of prostitution, the prostitution of the intellect. I have suffered because of it; the Chicago system has sucked my blood and brain; and if I am dead, it has helped to kill me. America is the land of murderous institutions though. To be sure, they do not kill the body, but they leave us like Frankenstein's monster, a being without a soul. The principal tried for nearly two years to break my spirit and to make of me a petticoated soldier such as herself. I think she did not succeed, although sometimes I cry out in my despair that America *has* killed me, and I might as well confess it. I am too sick and too sad to write about the Chicago School System and its donkeyish women. I merely record here that I fell out with the Principal.

But fortunately I had collected a good deal of evidence against her. The Principal could record a low mark against the teacher and give her a devil of a trouble about promotions and the like. But I had a convincing tongue in my head; I often made people see my point. I took my papers and called on the District Superintendent. I showed her class papers from my room which the principal had marked and also a paper from another class. My class had an average of 99 (this was drill work in spelling); the principal had marked the papers in blue pencil Good. And the teacher who had always agreed with the principal, whom I described to the District Superintendent as a combination of a spy and a negro servant, had an average of 97; which the principal marked Excellent plus. The mark E plus stood ten or fifteen points above Good. Then I put a profound question to the District Superintendent: If 97 is Excellent plus for Miss Christy, why should 99 be marked merely Good for Miss Beasley? I said I was always discriminated against in that way; I showed other papers to illustrate my point. The Superintendent said she was not accustomed to talking to teachers about their principals, but this looked very bad on the part of the principal; the head of the school should have the same standard for all. I told her more of how the Libby School was conducted, of hypocrisy, of lies, and of unfair advantage; I said she would excuse me, but all this illustrated that the Principal was either a fool or a crook. I understood what she wanted; but I never wiped up the floor with myself for anyone; I could not kowtow or use the stupid flattery which the other teachers used to curry favors from the head of the school. I could not pretend for the sake of expediency, and I did not intend to try. I was transferred immediately to the Copernicus, which many people thought the best school in the city.

The names of three or four young men occur to me, young men with whom I was friendly or partly in love, or hoped they would be in love with me. One of them, George Hay, who was about twenty-two when I met him first was sensitive, with a good deal of general intelligence, though he was only a stenographer, and had a good opinion of himself. He aspired to be a "colyum writer" like B.L.T. (Bert Leston Taylor) and wrote me many letters, often clever, in imitation of Ring Lardner. Once he wrote a prosaic, almost businesslike letter, asking me to marry him. I never answered it; I never answered any of his letters; but mentioned clever or witty things he had said when I saw him. He said and thought I was a practical person; he was a poet. But practical and poetic people always hit it off awfully well together. I called him an ass and a fool to his back and a nut to his face. One night, George Hay lingered a bit at the steps, "Gertrude, will you marry me?" I put my head back and laughed, "Yes, tomorrow at nine minutes past one!" I said, as I ran up the stairs.

I had much sweeter dreams about Ryon, a Stanford graduate who attended the Law School. I knew he was engaged, at least everyone said so. We talked about women for one thing; sometimes I imagined he almost understood the drama of the woman's movement. His talk pleased me immensely; he looked upon his mother, who was a doctor, as a woman of great intelligence and capabilities; her scientific acumen was even higher than that of his father who was also a physician. "Think, only think, what this war will mean to woman's progress," he once said to me. There would be all sorts of stupidities and crimes on both sides committed in the name of love and patriotism. I said there would be a colossal spread of disease and a lot of babies whom no one wanted. We talked economics, education, psychology. We went out to dance sometimes. He never made love to me, but I believed he thought I was intelligent, sometimes perhaps brilliant, and attractive. When he went home and sent an announcement of his marriage, it cut me deeply, much more than I had imagined it would. The people at Lanahan's boardinghouse noticed I was sad and teased me about it. I denied it bitterly and threatened Lucy that I would quit with them all if they were going to be so stupid.

I met two other fellows the last year at Chicago. One was a young reporter on the *Chicago Daily News* and the other was a PhD of Columbia, a man past forty who had decided to study medicine at the University of Chicago. Whitacre, the reporter, was a bright, clean fellow with a great interest in the social sciences. He read Bertrand Russell's books and used to bring them to me. He had been fortunate in the selection of his mother; she had answered his first questions about sex and explained everything to him. Consequently, when he started to school and the children began whispering their obscene talk in his ears, he was too wise to be particularly shocked or curious and turned away from their common words with an air of superiority. I think he had a decent childhood and youth and I imagined from his talk and behavior that he never had sexual relations with women. He once put his arm around me when we sat on the Midway, but I drew away from him. He had always contended that I was a practical person; I thought he intended to be the brains and let me do the work in our institution.

The appearance of Boyce, the PhD graduate, pleased my vanity almost more than any man I had ever known. He was tall and well built; sometimes I thought him extremely handsome; besides he had studied and travelled, having been a student in Europe for three years. I was flattered. I gave him as much encouragement as I had ever given anyone. But he was often blunt and offensive in his remarks to me. In the first place he guessed me six years older than I was and once he summed up women by saying that about the only thing they could do was to bear children. I went to my room that evening saying: yes, he's another one who believes that the highest service a woman is capable of rendering is that which Marguerite rendered Faust. One day when we sat in the park he tried to kiss me. I pulled away and said dryly that I did not want him to kiss me; it was all right if one wanted but I did not want. He said it was no fun for him either if I didn't want... He had lived with many women since he was twenty-eight, but between the ages of eighteen and twenty-eight he had lived like a woman. I was immensely interested in his talk. He had had all kinds of women from students in Europe, doctors and writers, to Indian squaws in the Northwest; many of them had had a lot of experience in love affairs. In fact, a woman of no sex experience was of no interest to him. He told of a girl who had drawn away from him, as I had, and later had thrown herself into his arms; he not only suggested it, but I seem to remember that he actually said that perhaps I was going to do that. He thought every woman should make her own living, there was no reason why a man should support a woman merely because he had sexual relations with her. I agreed with him. He excited a lot of strong feelings of resentment in me and also vigorous passion, which I subdued in part by calling him an ass and an egotist. I did not like Boyce's philosophy; for although he had a doctor's degree from the department of economy of Columbia University, I thought his ideas on the subject were about as poor as they could be. He hadn't much more sense than a fat-headed, high school boy, especially in his defense of the capitalist system. And when he mentioned birth control, I doubted his sincerity; I thought he merely wanted an excuse to talk about sex, this, in spite of the fact that sex psychology was one of my favorite subjects; I talked family limitation and the like to whomever would listen to me.

—←✴

Letters from home showed we were still in financial straits. My mother sent a letter to me in Chicago from E.N. Kirby which stated that we still owed $715.00, principal and interest, on the old home. I had to put my money into the back taxes, as the tax authorities and land agent threatened loss of the property altogether if it were not paid. Even the money which I sent home from Chicago during the first two and a half years was used to pay other debts with. When I received letters from my mother complaining that no one helped her, I felt my nerves tingle, as I imagined they did when one has an epileptic fit. I used to feel this sometimes during my last years in Texas too. I would be sitting at the table and the futility and sadness of everything would strike me; I would clinch my fists and choke a little, the breath would leave me soon, if not, I should begin screaming like a raving maniac. Oh God, how hard life is! I could hear my mother's quarrelsome voice when I opened the letter; perhaps she was ill, in bed with one of her nervous sick headaches; perhaps she was angry and throwing things about and threatening the children that God would punish them for leaving and not trying to provide a home for her.

In July of the same year, 1917, my mother enclosed another Kirby letter, calling her attention to the matter of the interest due on her notes. "I have carried this matter for a long time, and have only received Fifty Dollars on same, which sum was sent me on April 5th, last, by Miss Gertrude." The letter urged a settlement.

During these years my mother barely made a living out of the rooms; sometimes she wrote that she was afraid she could not pay expenses in this flat of eighteen rooms. Roger had come home from the Navy but as far as I could make out, he earned no money immediately; I seem to remember that my mother wrote of a quarrel they had had; Roger was "too good" to bring people to the rooms from the train.

I used to complain to Lucy Hoffman about the low salary I was getting. During the three years I worked day and evening, I earned only a little over $1,000 a year. That was very little for a teacher with a bachelor's degree, with experience, etc. She would listen to me and agree; but when I bored her, she would turn on me, "Gertrude, you have the most practical mind; you are always talking about money." Then she'd make a speech to the effect that money was not everything; why didn't I try to enjoy my life a little. Lucy told me she sent $10 home each month; but I never told her anything about my affairs; a thing now and then slipped out of me. Once when I suggested that I had given my family money in the past Lucy did not believe it; she thought I had a young bank account of my own; she sometimes told me frankly, when we had our give and take conversations, that I was the tightest person with my money she had ever come across; and sometimes when she told my fortune she pronounced me an exceptionally selfish person. I was a practical person; I wanted to climb up; I wanted to make money; I had a good conceit—my hand, everything about me, indicated it. Nearly all my friends in Chicago felt the same way about me; I could entertain them with my slang and often coarse wit; I was a good sort, a good scout. If they displeased me with their criticism, I handed them one back quite as scorching.

—←❦

I used to visit a friend, a Mrs. Sarah W., who believed in a sort of method of reading one's character, Red Cross, queer people, and whatnot. She used to leave me so miffed with her character study that I hoped I would never go again; but the food was good, the flat was delightful, and we sang and danced and did about as we pleased at her weekend parties. I told Sarah only what I wished her to know; she was not capable of really interesting me, but I pretended a lot.

I met quite a wide range of frivolous, gay, and mediocre people at Sarah's. One evening a young fellow who had written a waltz which he received $500 for was present. How Sarah loved his chatter; he monopolized the whole table, a dozen people or more, with his conversation. I had lost my audience; I could think of nothing to say. I imagined Sarah was saying: here's a university student, studying for a master's degree, but she can't begin to compete with this young fellow; he was brilliant; I was phlegmatic… There was only one girl in all this crowd who took particular pains to try to make me happy. Mary White was a Southern girl four years my senior who studied and graduated at the Chicago Musical College. We met at the Y. Sometimes I realized she saw inside me somewhat, though I never told her anything that mattered, that is about my home affairs, though she told me very frankly. She adored her father but hated her mother. What an open-hearted, lovely person she was! Sometimes when we met at Sarah's or some other mutual friend's, or at my place, she'd kiss me, not once but many times, and say, "Gertrude, you are the purtiest thing I ever saw in my life." She was gentle and warm and sincere, but I never had the courage to tell her about the things which hurt and saddened me.

Sophie, one of my friends, was an adorable little British girl, secretary at the British Consul's Office in Chicago. I liked her immensely, but her snobbery and pro-British sentiment aroused my deep-seated sense of democracy and my resentment. I was full of anti-British feeling; I recall few young Irish people who could begin to pronounce the polemics against England that I could. I seemed to have taken it in with my mother's milk, but I believe the school and press influenced me more. I think I began to hate the British with the study of American history. So when the Great War came and there was talk of German swine, a picture of a pen of hogs, some white some black, similar to those my father or our neighbors owned when I was a young child, often came to my mind. I could see hogs rearing up on their hind legs as the corn or swill was being poured into them. And the white pigs stood up the tallest, tramped the corn more fiercely, and turned over the trough just as often as the black ones did. The white swine were the British and the black swine Britain's enemies. They were all swine, those people at war; you couldn't get around that. This attitude often worked well and gave me much opportunity for argument. When I talked with my British friend, I was sure to be pro-Irish; and with my friend of German extraction I was anti-Kaiser, anti-Prussian.

⤙✢

At Christmas, 1917, I went to Texas again, not because I wanted to, but because I thought I ought to. My mother had been ill and I was worried; she had had a slight paralytic stroke, but had entirely recovered by the time I arrived. I read Bertrand Russell's *Why Men Fight* on the train and after a few days with my mother heard her fervent enunciation, "Ah don't cair what you say, Ah think it's a nawful noble thing for a young man to serve his country." She spoke earnestly; I did not try to change her views...

There were seven of us children gathered at Abilene that Christmas. Wiley, my oldest brother, had come home; I had not seen him for eight or ten years; it looked like a sort of family reunion. Then there were Emma, Roger, Martha, Alta, Major, and myself. The girls each prepared a feast at their respective houses and invited the family. We went to Sweetwater by automobile to attend a dinner at Emma's. My mother rehearsed the whole story of the family quarrels, disappointments, and sorrows; there was no sorrier race of people ever went unhung than the Beasleys. She told how "obscene tongued" they were in their families; and retold what the Old Man once said at the table before the children, a half dozen of whom were men and women or nearly grown. I remembered the occasion; I was about ten years old at the time, it was in Nolan County. The conversation was at the breakfast table; my mother had said the hens were not laying regularly in reply to my father's complaint about an insufficient supply of eggs for breakfast. My father then made some remark, looked at Reuben, and chuckled. My mother left the table in a temper. Now I knew what all this was about: my mother actually saw Reuben (then about twenty years old) trying to use the hens to satisfy himself sexually, or else she had what she called plain proof. She had found some of her hens hardly able to walk and upon examining them, found their rectums torn and bleeding. My mother said that she was afraid she would lose her mind before she had a chance to leave my father; it looked as though some of the older boys were following in his footsteps. I do not recall that my mother ever suggested or insinuated that my father had ever stooped to bestiality, but she insinuated many times that he had, or he wanted to, or he was going to live with Willie, my oldest sister, as his wife.

My mother and Wiley whispered some and talked out loud a good deal about the past. Wiley thought his brothers, Reuben, Rush, Ruel, and Sumpter had all treated him awful sorry. I believe one story was that Reuben once pulled a gun on him and threatened to kill him... One day he sat by the gas stove and spelled out a few words to me from the *Abilene Daily Reporter*, then he put the paper aside and talked. He watched my expression to see if I were receiving what he said gravely enough. "Gertrude, I guess you know who ole Eugene V. Debs is, don't you? Well, I know quite a lot about 'em myself. I've heard some of them Socialists in Oklahoma—an' it's all on account of that, that they've got my name up there in Washington—they keep everything down up there in papers... You laugh but it sa fact. They've got your name too, because you believe in this thing about women keepin' from havin' children." I told him he was crazy, that the authorities in Washington had never heard of me. Yes, all his brothers and sisters had always thought he was crazy, but they were going to find out he was not the fool they imagined... One day he was telling my mother what a great number of women, whom one never suspected, had promiscuous sexual relations with men. My mother began talking as though she were preaching: "You children, hear me, there ain't never been... I swear before God that no man ever laid a finger on me except your father; not even when I'as a child, my brothers nor nobody; w'y, good God, I never heard o' such a thing; it nearly run me crazy when I found out what that ole Alice Beasley had taught my children; that's one reason I wanted to leave yer cussed ole Daddy; I'as afraid we was going to be lower than the niggers in the quarters." Sometimes such speeches left me perfectly cold; I had heard them so often; other times they filled me with horror and I resolved to do something about it.

One day Wiley, Major, Emma, and I were walking in the country. The boys walked several rods in the foreground; Emma began to talk: "Sometimes I feel so sorry for Wiley, that I don't know what to do, and other times I think I hate him." She told me that Wiley and Reuben and Rush, all of them, had nearly killed her, when she was a child, trying to have sexual intercourse with her. They had sometimes tied her hands as though she were an animal and then tried to satisfy themselves... Once she thought she was going to die and thought of telling Mother but she couldn't; she was afraid; it seemed to her she could not have been more than five or six years old. I listened and wept with her; but I did not tell her a word of my own experiences with them.

Once my mother related this story to me. She also told how my father once beat Wiley until she had to beg for the child's life, because he thought "Wiley had been up to something of that sort with Willie." I asked her if she knew that this thing happened to me when I was a child. She said she once found Ruel punching at me with his finger when I was a mere baby; and she nearly spanked the skin off him. I had no notion of telling her my experiences, for I learned many years earlier how she treated such information. Perhaps also I was just as "guilty" as my brothers, at least as two of them, for although the three oldest boys forced this experience upon me against my will; I believe that with the smaller boys more nearly my own size I liked it as much as they did. (It may be due to something I read in Havelock Ellis's books, that I write the last sentence.) But I imagined if I confide this to my mother and then someday she "rears up" and begins calling us the lowest down set she has ever heard of, I shall want to drop dead or else I shall want to strike her dead.

We talked about business affairs and the property. My mother showed me a copy of her will in which I was made the executrix; Roger and Major were the only other children mentioned, we were each to receive a third of the property. The girls had all married; their husbands could take care of them and the other boys had not helped; she had always promised that the property should go to those who worked and helped to pay for it. I did not believe that Roger or Major would ever give her as much money as I had given her. During my eight and a half years of teaching I had given her more than $2,000. I did not believe the will meant anything especially; I thought she had had it drawn up in order to get Roger's promise to help her. She had to coax and beg and promise the boys to get them to turn their hands. Abilene was getting on the boom and my mother thought that after a few months we ought to buy the lot next to our house. If I paid for it, it should be put in my name she suggested. At first I said no; then my mother insisted, saying my health might not always be good, as I had been working so hard. The conversation sounded as though we would make the transaction immediately. I finally said that if we made the deal on the ground that I should pay for the lot that it could be put in my name. Something made me want to cry; I thought I read in my mother's expression that she had not meant a word of what she had said; she was just talking; perhaps she would be angry and say I was trying to get the property in my hands. Nothing ever came of this talk. When I mentioned the sum I had already paid she said she allowed I had paid much more than $2,000, during all the years I had taught school; "God knows I don't know what I would-a done without you; you was my main support for five years; you shore have staid by me; I'm going to stand by the children that stands by me." My mother would say that she was afraid I was working myself to death, teaching day and night and studying too; "You're going to kill yourself; you'll break your health down and then your education won't do you no good; I want you to let this be your last year that you teach night school." It helped a lot when she talked that way; some-one understood that I was working.

Roger had been working in the oil fields or some place with Rush; the Old Man had been there also. They made "big wages" in the oil fields. But Rush and the Old Man drank their money up or spent it on prostitutes as fast as they made it. He related something about a letter which Rush once received from my mother; how he had read it and then passed it over to the Old Man; they both sat around the stove and cried like babies; "Mother, he said you was the best woman that ever lived." We all dried our eyes and my mother sniffed and said, "It's a pity but what he could-a found that out long ago." Reuben and Rush had both married Oklahoma girls; they were sisters, and one quarter or one eighth Indian. Roger said they were exceptionally ignorant, but very good-hearted girls; and the boys seemed to be getting along well with them. My mother and I both opined that we never expected them boys to marry anyone with intelligence; they knew a smart woman would never put up with them.

I think none of us wanted it known that their wives had Indian blood. This put Wiley to talking: "I known why some of this family has al'ays acted so sorry; it's because we've got Indian blood ourselves; that's what's the matter with us." My mother took up the discussion. She had heard some of my father's people say there was an Indian in the family some place, but she could never ascertain where it was. "I knew great grandfather (Beasley) and, if he was a Beasley, you've got to give the devil his dues, there never was a finer man ever lived," my mother opined again for the hundredth time. He was a well-appearing man, looked like he might have been Scotch or German; in fact, some people thought the name Beasley was German. The only thing she ever heard "yer great-gran'-Daddy" say about his nationality was that he was "Turkeyho." (I was never sure about this word "Turkey-ho" perhaps it was like my mother's use of need-cessity.) She backed my brother right off the board and stood up for our great grandfather Beasley, saying he was as straight and as fine a man as she had ever known; he was almost as good a man as her father.

My mother retold a story which I had heard at least a dozen times from her lips; I knew it by heart; I could tell you exactly how it would end. Once when my parents were newly married, great grandfather Beasley came to see them. He was then past seventy but as straight and supple as a young man. My mother was preparing the meal and great grandfather Beasley began to talk about her to my father. He said, "Bill, you don't realize what a fine little wife you've got." My mother would go on lingering over the words, "He al'ays said yer Daddy done better than any of the boys," meaning his choice of a wife had been satisfactory. Then she would tell how quickly she stepped and how easily she got around when she was young, "He said I stepped jest to suit 'em." This incident always closed with the same words: "He said I stepped just to suit him. You couldn't squeeze blood out of a turnip; great grandfather Beasley was sure white all the way through"; then "there was yer gran' Daddy and yer Daddy, both showed no particular signs of Indian blood, yer Daddy had high cheek bones but so did the Scotch." But, Wiley put in, it came from some woman in the line. Then my mother described my father's mother; she had about the fairest skin and lightest colored hair one could find; her name was Anderson and she was of English descent...

Wiley still held on; he said there were strong Indian characteristics in nearly all our faces. It was in the mother of grandpa Beasley; he did not know how much was there, but our great grandmother on the Old Man's side had given us Indian blood. My mother thought the strain must have been weak in her or else "yer grand-pa would-a showed it more." She ended the conversation by saying that she had "just about as soon have nigger blood er dawg blood as Indian blood" in her veins. None of us thought of taking a stand against such a statement at the time it was made though, no doubt, each turned it over in his mind afterwards; we skulked out of the room as a dog does when kicked by his master, with our ears drawn back, our tails between our legs, looking for a place to hide and lick our wounds. There was no use to reason with her; sometimes I felt my mother the most repulsive and ignorant woman I had ever heard of. She was incarnate vulgarity and looked upon it as a mark of superiority.

Once I had a talk with her about the name, Beasley. She often reckoned it German. I pointed out that it couldn't be anything but English; several people in Chicago including professors had remarked it. I went over all the praise I had ever heard of people by our name. Elizabeth Beasley, who is, I was pretty sure, my second cousin, had studied music in Chicago. She was called a clever girl and well thought of. Others told of having known Beasleys in Tennessee or Virginia. A woman, a principal of a fashionable, private school for girls on Michigan Avenue, told me she could see I was an aristocrat. (By the way, this person got a lot of work out of me and never paid me a cent.) Many people thought I was of good stock. I retold the story of the old Virginian who thought it would be a pity, I being of a fine old Southern family, if I should marry a Yankee. My mother sniffed and said that everyone knew the Beasleys were intelligent enough and good-looking enough; but they were such devils.

⤙⚹

The Acme Rooms were in good shape the second time I went home; the rooms which my mother and Major occupied were excellently equipped. She was living much more comfortably than I lived in Chicago; most of the difficult work was sent out and part of the time she had negro help. It was a mind slavery that kept her so unhappy; why, housing people was a sociological problem; it could be intelligent and serviceable. But we were all possessed with the idea that it was a damnable business; it was a degrading thing that one's mother had to keep a rooming house; especially a woman who had borne thirteen children and worked and struggled for them as my mother had. All were healthy, able-bodied people, yet the whole family together had not been able to prepare a home for their mother who was getting old and not as able to work as she once was.

We wept in one another's arms again, said goodbye, and I went back to Chicago. The visit had been satisfactory in a way; but in another sense it left me unmoved. I had spent two weeks discussing and observing appetites, human behavior, and efforts at thinking more repulsive than the most exaggerated examples of animal psychology. But I had been full of pity and resolution too.

—≺✦

By the end of the summer of 1918, I had finished the required courses for the master's degree, Dr. Judd had accepted my thesis, and I passed the final examination in August... From my university courses I received small doses of history and literature, a little larger dose of sociology and economics, and a much larger lump of psychology and philosophy. It was all fed to me from an American silver spoon and calculated by my professors to make me a hundred percent. American first; an educator and a human being second and third. I did not rebel very much; I made a few magnificent private addresses about the damnation which American education wrought, but I think they pleased me more than they pleased my hearers. As a matter of fact, I liked many of these courses; some of them fascinated me... I was fond of my professors, but I played with some of them a little. In a final test Mr. Leavitt, professor of industrial education, once asked what we had liked most about his course. I wrote several paragraphs explaining that the best thing about the course was the professor's method of presentation; he had given us first-rate live material; and there was no limitation as to opinions, discussions, or activity. It sounded a little thick, but I believed nearly everything I wrote myself. I could have been in love with Leavitt without willing it very much, but I was not... I wrote lyrics about some of the professors. Once when I had been to see Dr. Judd I went home and wrote: The Wealth of the Soul... When I presented my marks to Judd, he complained, saying they were low, I should have an average of B or B minus; he didn't like to accept a C. I contended the marking system was at fault; they were compelled to fit their classes to curves, the professor's mind was made up before the class came to him. The marking system might fit the intelligence of people in mass, but it was my opinion that it was unfair in highly specialized classes. I told him that Professor Parker had complained of my entering his class because of my age and experience; I had come out with a C. I said it sometimes happened that people with age and experience who were willing to argue and make trouble about the grading system got the high marks. Something of that sort. He looked at my marks again; it looked as though I was going to average a B minus or a little above that...

One day when I had finished a conference with Dean Gray, a young Professor of the School of Education about my own age, I wrote: Love's Challenge. A small poetry magazine and publishing agency who read my verse sent me a contract form, saying they had secured a Viennese professor at the Chicago Musical College to write the music for my lyric, and if I would only sign on the dotted line and send them $35, the royalty accruing from our song would soon repay me a hundred fold. I hadn't the money to spare as I was planning to go to Columbia University the following summer... I dreamed about Dr. Butler, Dean of the extension school; and Professor Blanchard, head of the department of Public Speaking too. I recall distinctly that I once fancied myself on the portico of Dr. Butler's residence. The figure was aerial and graceful, and wearing flowing white garments. I was in his house as an angel or a fairy or simply as an amorous woman in her nightdress. Professor Blanchard was an exceptionally attractive man; I found it out on the train one night as we came home from the classes; it simply appeared to me instantly as any miracle does.

After much blood and sweat, I found I had passed the master's examinations. I thought two of my professors had me singled out as a flunker. I had relapses to my attitude of about the age of puberty, when I imagined everyone looked upon me as a queer person, almost an idiot. Jernegan and Parker would be sure to say I was not clever. I had something a little like nervous prostrations and wished I could drop dead if I didn't pass; even after the diploma was in my hands and Judd and Angell had made their speeches in Latin over us, as we passed in file at graduation, and the cap and gown procession had filed out, I was still unsatisfied. I wanted to rush home and look at my diploma, perhaps it was a plain white sheet of paper without a single letter or mark on it. I did; it said:

Universitas Chicaginiensis

Omnibus ad quos hae Litterae pervenerint

Salutem:

Ednam Gertrudam Beasley, etc.

Margaret M. and myself were the youngest members of the class of master's graduates from the School of Education. We were both twenty-six; she had taught five years and I had taught nine years. The rest of the class were mainly superintendents of schools and professors of education ranging in age from about thirty to fifty. What a lovely girl Margaret was and how brilliant at mathematics! She taught algebra and geometry in a high school and had credits in courses in higher mathematics. How happy I should have been if we had become warm friends! But we did not; we were merely friendly as the occasion demanded. No one whom I was ever particularly keen about was ever keen about me.

At the time of my graduation there was a young man about twenty-four years old who was taking the doctor's degree. His father was there—an old man with a long beard, I believe they said he was a Pole—to see the son graduate; the father could neither read nor write. Yet son and father went about the campus as the most affectionate comrades. It hurt me deeply, because I was not like that. Not a single friend or relative came to see me graduate; I was sorry and glad too; sorry there was no one to pat me on the back, and glad that none of my family were there, for I should have wanted to drop dead each time one of them opened his mouth. I believe to many this attitude would be inconceivable; it is difficult to explain how one suffers from it. I used to be almost speechless if anyone looked at my mother's writing on the envelope. Once old Mrs. Reel, the woman of the house where I lived, near the Midway, asked if the letter were from my great grandmother. My mother had left off the last "e" in Gertrude; I imagined the writing indicated that it was from the hand of an extraordinarily ignorant person. I snatched up the letters from home, if possible, when no one was looking. Wiley sent me a New Year's card and the same horror struck me... This threw me into conjecturing what I would do if one day Wiley or my father should knock at the door and ask to see me. The scene would be something like this: My father would ask Mrs. Reel if there was a girl by the name of Beasley staying at her house. Then he would say he was my father and that he wanted to see me. Mrs. Reel would come and say, "Gertrude, your father is here and wants to see you." I would reply that the man was crazy, that my father was dead; likewise, I would deny Wiley with his ignorant talk and appearance... Once I received a sad letter from Corrie telling me of her troubles. It looked as though old Mrs. Reel had opened it. When I read it, I was startled and worked myself up into a nervous frenzy. She had told of some prostitutes who lived near them in Idaho who had succeeded in attracting Jack. One sentence in the letter read about like this: "One of these old devils of women told me that it was easier to have intercourse with a dog than it was with a man." If Mrs. Reel had read the letter, she was just the kind of a person who would have gossiped about it. For a minute I was frightened almost to death and I wished the whole damned outfit, my relatives, were all in hell. I wished to be free from them and rid of them altogether... Corrie had written me also that she was going to have a baby; I went out and walked alone at dusk and thought and prayed about her and her child. I hoped she was having the child because she had loved and wanted it; and I prayed she would be happy. It was a terrible thing to bring a human being into the world under any circumstance; a tragedy, yes, a crime to bring one unloved, unwanted.

⤙✦

In the fall of 1918 I was ill with a cold: I thought I had influenza. The children at the Copernicus School had worn me out physically and nervously. Although the Principal was a good teacher, the Chicago System had killed her, too; that is, it tied her hands so often that she became only a tool. During those few days in bed, I saw through everything. It did not matter what position one held in the Chicago Schools, dishonesty, stupidity, futility would swamp one. There was no scope for initiative, for originality, for fair play; there was no such thing as a square deal; the whole thing was a hodgepodge of compromises and lies. Moreover, it was the same in every department of life; the church, press, politics. I knew. I didn't believe there was any way out. What a blessing it would be if I should die now; it would be the best; I had found out what a deceiver life was, and I was perfectly willing to give it all up. I lay there and saw my coffin, a plain funeral. A large portrait of myself semi-life-size in master's cap and gown, stood on my mother's dresser. I was pretty sure my mother was pleased with me; but I would fail her; this stupid, dishonest, ugly life would kill me; I wanted to die.

Things were going much better at home; my mother was making money out of the rooms; I had helped her a good deal, but now I was sad and discouraged; and Oh God, how tired I was! I am not sure that the idea of love occurred to me when I was making believe that I wanted to die. Sophie, a girl who lived in the same boardinghouse came bringing me a present; it was an electric iron. Once I mended a skirt for her and she wrote some verses about it:

Dear Little Gertie
Who tucked up my skirtie
And saved me the agonie... etc.

Yes, the English were all like that; they could not conceive of an American except as a seamstress or a laundress. I wrote verses about her, some of which were serious and beautiful; of course, I made them ridiculous when I was miffed. But the first attempt was:

Dear Little Sophie, with eyes of violet-blue,
Your cheeks are as pale as flowers in the dew;

But your dear eyes send out your light so true,

With a wealth of meaning and loveliness too.

I see a blue flower with leaves of gold,

When your eyes and your hair I behold; etc. etc.

Sophie sent for the doctor. He gave me medicine and said I could return to my class in a few days.

The last year in Chicago I meant to do some writing. For one thing I was going to complete my master's thesis, "Educational Legislation and Administration in Texas 1820–1860" and make a book of it.

In the spring of 1919, the Recommendation Committee of the University of Chicago sent me to interview Normal School Presidents who were in the city looking for supervisors and instructors... I signed a contract as Supervisor in the Upper Grades in the State Normal School at Bellingham, Washington, to begin the following September. This position paid $1,500, but one could live for $30 a month. I had already planned to go to Japan when I completed my year at Bellingham...

I went to New York via Washington, DC in the summer. Having visited the places of interest in the capital, I hurried on to Columbia where I registered for courses in Criminal Law and Advanced Psychology. I was going to climb out of school teaching altogether... I carried on a lot of mild flirtations at Columbia that summer and had a wonderfully good time. I found two warm friends in Marian O.

of Ohio and Elinor K. of Mass., young teachers who were students at the summer school. I talked in a large way to Elinor, saying I was going to vamp this fellow, walk away with that professor or elope with someone else; and both Marian and I tried to impress Elinor with the wild life we led "out West" by piling up in the middle of M's couch in her room at Whittier Hall and smoking cigarettes when we were expecting Elinor to come in. A girl who never used face powder would be sure to be shocked…

I received a check from the Board of Education of Chicago for $72; my salary had been raised; it was retroactive from the past six months. I bought a serge dress, a velvet hat, and new slippers; it was July. All the smartest and best-dressed girls wore serge in summer and georgette in winter. Elinor honored me with the title "Chicago vamp" and many commented on how smartly I dressed. Once when I attended a dancing class in the evening at Teachers College, the instructor remarked that I danced well and asked me to assist her with one of the groups in social dancing.

One evening I met and danced with a young man several times; it was a "pick up," I had not been introduced to him. We went out for ice cream and afterwards he called on me several times. He was just the right size for dancing, and we got along well together, but I liked his jokes better; he was full of stories and nonsensical remarks which kept our crowd roaring; "You have this dance out? Well, I'm going to dance with the girl over there in the green 'shimmy,'" he would remark. Once when everyone was quiet he observed seriously that everything a girl wore began with a "c," "there is camisole, combination…" He told a story of a negro who was tried for having three wives; the Judge pronounced the defendant guilty of bigamy; the niggers in the court room scratched their heads in wonderment; the terminology had puzzled them; finally a colored gentleman in the back of the court room rose and said, "Oh, no, Judge, dat ain't bigamy, dat's trigonometry!" Warner was chock full of such humor… One evening just before the session closed Marian and Elinor's brother, Elinor and a superintendent from Albany, Maine, Warner and myself made the boat trip to Atlantic Highlands; we had three or four hours of dancing on board. I thought I had never had so much attention from men in my life. There were a half dozen of Warner's friends, mostly superintendents, on board. Sometimes I felt all eyes on me at once; they hung on my words and laughed at my silliest comments. Elinor's friend, the Albany Superintendent, insisted on taking the dust from my oxfords with his handkerchief each time I sat down, until I was embarrassed and flabbergasted. Warner never made love to me; he held me much too tight during part of the dances; and once when we stood in the dark, he put his hands over mine; I didn't mind, I liked it.

Leaving the others, we walked two or three blocks to my place alone. "You don't know what meeting you has meant to me this summer." Something like that. We talked on about good times, other sessions perhaps in the future, and so on, and stopping at my door I said: "Well, perhaps I shall see you again." "Do you really think you will?" he asked, in a queer tone while taking a photograph from his inside pocket. I was miffed. "It doesn't matter." It was a snapshot of two little girls. "These are my little girls; they are both lovely children, just like their mother. I couldn't tell you I was married, because I was afraid you wouldn't go out with me. My wife is arriving here day after tomorrow and I want you to meet her." I laughed about it as best I could, said goodnight and ran up to my room.

The next day I met Marian and Elinor; I felt a strange atmosphere immediately and at first took the attitude that the affair was none of their business. Elinor asked if Warner showed me the picture of his kids; "so they are the bachelors Mr. Warner told you he was living with down at Norfolk!" Warner had told me he was living with three bachelors, and I had passed it on to the girls. Elinor explained the whole thing and hoped I was not going to be offended as they were all good friends of mine. "Warner talked about you all the time, both to the men in his class and at the dormitory," she said. The fellows decided he had lost his head and the affair was going to be a tragedy if something wasn't done. So the New England Superintendent had told Warner, and the rest of the fellows had backed him up, that if he didn't come and tell me he was married the Superintendent would. I should know it. Warner was the brightest and wittiest man in his class and a fine fellow too; and I was a nice girl. Their New England consciences wouldn't let them sit by and see the lives of two lovely people spoiled. About the most amorous thing I had ever thought of with regard to Warner was: I hoped he would write to me when I went out to the State of Washington; that the letters would be real love letters; for no one whom I was interested in had ever written me satisfactorily. I tossed the whole thing in the air and laughed about it. Warner had handled me very neatly; Elinor found he had been frightfully clever. Other times I was a little angry with him; also with the others for meddling in my affairs. One evening, Elinor and her brother and I were walking on the campus and met Warner who walked home with us. At the door he put his hand on my shoulder and said he was going to give me some advice: Get married; it was a crime that a girl with a wonderful personality was going about the country teaching school; "Why haven't you married?" "It's because I've never met anyone like yourself," I answered, mocking him... I never told this story to anyone; I'm sure it would have entertained some of my friends, but I kept it to myself.

I visited the wife of Dr. Mullins, my teacher at Simmons; Mullins was then teaching mathematics at Barnard College, Columbia. Mrs. Mullins reminded me of how hard I worked at Simmons; I taught half the year and then did as much work as other students; "and you are just as young and vivacious as you can be." I told her the secret lay in the fact that I had usually liked my work, but I told myself that it was because I had been in love that summer. My mother was coming to Chicago for a visit; she would arrive August twentieth. I wrote to the Gladstone Hotel to reserve a room; it was a good hotel not too far away from my friends, within several minutes of the University. There was no one there who knew me and we could be quite alone... Plenty of time still remained for completing the journey we had planned. Elinor, Marian, and I went to Boston by boat where a friend of Elinor's, a Radcliffe graduate, took great interest in pointing out the places of historic interest; then Marian and I went to Niagara Falls and Buffalo, making the trip by boat on Lake Erie to Cleveland, and to our final destinations, in my case, Chicago, by rail…

—<*

A telegram announced the train and I went to meet my mother. She looked extremely tired and a little helpless when my eyes fell on her first. She had been sitting up in the chair car during the forty-two hours or so from Texas; her feet were swollen. She told how affairs were going at home as we sat in the streetcar and remarked about her clothes; she thought anything was good enough for the train; "I've got good clothes in my grip." We had a private bath attached to our room and she was pleased with my selection of a place to stay. After her bath I knelt down and rubbed cream on her swollen feet; she had kept her shoes on all the way. I was glad of an opportunity to be humble before her like that; maybe one ought to kneel down and pray; we looked a little like the hard-shelled Baptists at foot wash-ing. "I'll do that, Gertrude," she finally pushed me away. She took out her clothes; there were the best of silk stockings, underwear and nightgowns, the latter, my sisters had helped her make; a white linen dress which just fit her and had evidently been laundered by one of the girls, for no one else would have taken so many pains with it; an

Alice-blue silk sweater and other clothes. She required a new hat. She had delayed buying because she thought she would find better ones in Chicago. She must have new slippers too. We went to Marshall Field's the next day and she found exactly what she wanted; the hat was an excellent quality of black velvet; it cost $13.75. When she paid for the hat, she let the shop girl see the large roll of bills in her purse. It was as though one child said to another, "I'll bet you have never had such lovely sweets." I remarked that it didn't matter, meaning that the shop girl was not interested in what was in my mother's purse. "You've got to show some people," she said, and then as though she were apologizing, "I guess all of us have got to be silly sometimes." My mother was good at making funny little remarks. She said something which amused the clerk who went away saying, "She's the cutest thing I ever saw in my life."

An old bachelor, who lived at the same boardinghouse on Blackstone Avenue where I had been during the past year, who had been trying to pay me court, and who had an automobile, made an engagement to show my mother the city. We picked up Lucy Hoffman, whom I had roomed with two years in Chicago; and went on to my boardinghouse where Sophie and two young men, who sat at our table, were awaiting us. One of these fellows had said jokingly that he knew in advance how my mother would talk, everybody in Texas talked like that; he mimicked them and we all laughed. In the automobile that evening he entertained Sophie with his jokes and mimicry. I sat in the front seat with the old bachelor in a perfect hell of wanting to laugh and cry, feeling that everyone knew I was pretending and worst of all that I was insincere with my friends; both of us yelled back to my mother who was about one-third deaf, as we drove through a howling wind. Why had I not told the girls that my mother was an uneducated woman? I could see they were both astonished...

On Sunday we went to Mandell Hall, the University Chapel. I waved her hair; she loved having it done; "you could always do my hair better than anybody else"; it was like the old days in Texas. I felt once more how fine and soft her hair was; it was like silk; no wonder she used to say that Corrie and myself had hair almost as coarse as ole Pete's (an old mule of ours) tail. And her skin, not of her face and hands, for they were tanned; but of her body, her breasts. Her skin was almost milk-white and fine-grained too. Once when I was a child I felt a sexual impulse while observing the baby suckling at her white breast. Sometimes I felt strong attractions in her; there were flashes of something almost exquisite, extremely delicate, inordinately sensitive. She wore the white dress and the blue sweater, the latter exactly suited her eyes. I had never seen them quite so blue. With that outfit and the new hat she looked almost like a big bourgeoise. As the usher seated us in the chapel my mother spied a negro sitting in front of us; she nudged me and whispered, "As black as a coal!" When we walked home she observed that some of "them ole scissor-bills" at the Baptist church in Abilene would curl up their noses at her if she told 'em she had sat in the chapel with a negro. (The term scissor-bill she had taken from an evangelist, who once preached in Abilene, and who reproached the sinners with names such as "razor-backs" and "scissorbills," the former referred to mountain swine and the latter to a nonsinging Texas bird of no particular beauty with a scissors-like tail.)

Afterwards when I met Lucy she began, as though I had lied to her on a colossal scale, "But, Gertrude, you told me your mother was little." I was sure that whatever else I had told Lucy, I had never even suggested such a thing. She was stout and now she was almost portly. Lucy never said anything to indicate whether or not she liked my mother. She guessed it was the picture she had in her mind; she had expected to see someone little and delicate... Sophie said, mentioning my mother, "I like her style awfully, but kid (she pronounced it keed), your father must have been a wonderful man."

"Tom" Sawyer, a business girl of considerable sensibilities and style, appeared to understand my mother better than anyone else. She invited us to luncheon at the most fashionable restaurant on Michigan Boulevard, and seemed delighted with "Jedge's mother." "Tom" was full of slang, but sometimes my mother would match her with a phrase just as racy which she had learned from my brothers. To her my mother was a frightfully good sort; they laughed and talked like old pals. If my mother used a phrase like "putting one over" or "hitting below the belt," "Tom" would roar with laughter. "Now, Jedge, I know you taught her that," she would say in an accusing voice. We visited Sarah in her little flat near Sheridan Road. I felt Sarah had taken a critical attitude, and in my embarrassment I talked at a terrific rate all evening, telling them my experiences at New York, Boston, Niagara and the like; I sounded as though I could "talk the horns off a billy-goat."

I showed her the city and she spent the money she brought shopping. My mother told of the new house she had bought at Abilene; it was the house across the street which I had wanted young Weakley to think was ours, when he drove me home from Simmons that time. The oil refinery at Abilene which was connected with the Ranger oil wells was going to keep Abilene on the boom for a long time. She was making money; it looked as though she was going to make more; and Roger was helping her. She carried home lace curtains, linen, etc.... She already had a few rugs and carpets and she was going to get more; "I'll tell you; I'll have fine carpets for you to put your feet on the next time you come home." She was going to buy a baby grand piano; "you are the only one who ever would play and sing for me"; Corrie would "fly off the handle" if she ever asked her to play and quit the piano. Yes, a piano, and I had to come home and learn to play and sing again; she had tears in her eyes.

One night we talked and I tried to tell her about Boyce; he had tried to kiss me. "Don't you ever let him come again," she said in a hoarse whisper. She explained that men like that would "work on a woman" until they found she was getting weak, then they would take advantage of her. In bed she talked about my father, "You know during all the years I lived with that man, he never once called me sweet names—some men call their wives sweetheart or darling," she was crying, "he never did." And if she ever tried to be affectionate with him, he would "give her just what she was looking for." I thought she meant to say he took her in sexual intercourse, perhaps when she did not want. "He was a beast," she went on, "there never was a meaner man ever lived." We were both weeping; I turned over repeating "my father was a beast" and went to sleep.

I went out alone one morning, and as I walked tears dropped in my handkerchief and my throat hurt. I was saying, "Oh God, I hate her, I hate her…" But I stopped myself; we had had no quarrel; what a disgusting person I must be! My mother was pleased with me: I had a better vocabulary than anyone whom I had introduced to her; I was getting better looking every day; she knew I would be like that; ugly children always grew up to be handsome old people: education sure did improve the human countenance; she had noticed it all her life; each time she had seen me during those years she had remarked the difference. Emma was not pretty anymore; her neck was long and full of wrinkles and she was getting fat and coarse. I was going to be the best-looking girl in the family after all. Why was I so narrow minded, so small? Why should I expect my mother to be like myself? We were quite different individuals.

After a day of sightseeing and shopping, both of us tired, we stopped at a restaurant on 63rd Street for an early dinner. How good the food was, my mother observed. Fresh sliced tomatoes and beef-steak. It just suited her tooth; she was beginning to have things to her taste at home, too. She did hope she'd get the two houses rebuilt and paid for soon; she did so want to get out of those old rooms; there was no rest as people often came all hours of the night to ask for rooms. She talked on, eating with relish and using her fork in a way which suddenly appeared to me she should not be using it. I merely looked cross or critical. She saw, understood, and was hurt. She saw through me; I really was ashamed of her; she knew it; she expected it, she had known it for a long time. She said nothing of this sort, but I felt a spasmodic desire to kill myself; I felt the blade of my knife in my own heart; I wanted to kill myself and I wish I had. She went on talking; she had lived alone so much; had had her meals "in any ole way" so long that she wasn't fit to be in civilized company. Then she'd been angry so much and "had been devilled so near to death" that she could see her face was all out of shape; sometimes when she looked in the mirror her own countenance astonished her.

What a difference it made when one worked with one's mind; she mentioned the time she took music lessons and how it had rested her nerves. (My mother sold the organ to a music teacher who paid for it by giving lessons to her and Alta. She learned the notes and could pick out the tune to "Nearer My God to Thee," this after she was past fifty years of age.) One ought to study and read and improve one's mind… But she had had some awful disgusting and disgraceful things to put up with in those old rooms; she would be "ashamed for the niggers to know what sorry people had come there to ask for rooms."

Once the grandson of Old Man W. rented a room from her and brought a girl there whom she evidently had been living with, for the girl had a miscarriage; the fetus was several inches long. "And not so long ago," she went on, "a nole devil of a man came up there asking for women...I was so mad I grabbed the gun and told him I'd learn him a lesson...he flew down the steps but I fired anyway, you've got to do something, you can't be devilled to death." Oh God, it had been hard, but she had been brave, had held out to the end; how I ever dared to be critical of a woman whom life had hurt and scarred as it had hurt my mother was incomprehensible. She had called the President of Simmons College and asked his advice; told him she had to make a living and yet, at that rate, she was going to lose her mind. He suggested that the incident should be written up for the *Abilene Daily Reporter*, but she told him she wouldn't have that done for anything in the world; it was such a disgrace. Anyway, she was living in hopes; she thought she was going to eat her white bread in her old age. She would sell those old rooms before very much longer.

━✳

The time came for Mother to go back to Texas; I arranged for a berth and found a place for her in the observation car. The same day I booked on a special train for Seattle, Washington. At least I wasn't going back to the grind in Chicago that year; I had a permanent certificate for Chicago; I could return if I wished but I didn't believe I ever should, as the high school teachers' examinations and appointments were too uncertain. Some of my friends were afraid

I would never be able to get along with old lady schoolteachers; a few even advised that I go in for a business career. I was a practical person and I would likely make a lot of money. I promised them and myself also that if things didn't go to suit me in Bellingham, I was going to raise hell; you had to kick and kick hard in this world. I would have given my Chicago principal a hectic time, if I hadn't been tied up with University work and night school—I would never have put up with her nonsense as long as I did. "Watch me! from now on I'm going to tell people what is what. A wishy-washy life isn't worth a damn!"

On the train a woman inquired about a book I was reading. It was one of Ellen Key's. I loaned it to her, and we talked about it. I told her a little about Emma Goldman's lectures and we talked about socialism too, from the standpoint of making the world happier and more intelligent. She said there were radical professors at the University of Washington; I should get to know them.

I carried on a flirtation on the train with a young officer who was just returning from France; it began while I was in conversation with this woman. Why was I coming to Washington? the officer asked. I told many tales: I was the wife of a cattle-puncher in Idaho, and was going to my husband; I was a "lady Senator" or a congresswoman from such and such a state. But I finally stated that the person with whom I had been talking and myself were going out to the State Normal School at Bellingham to teach psychology. That was more like it, he thought. My friend would be head of the department and I was her assistant. The woman, who was the wife of a Seattle banker, liked our jokes and invited me to come and see her.

The officer and I became warm friends; he told me about the West, "God's own country," and we wore out a good deal of shoe leather pacing the sidewalks at the stations in Montana and Idaho. I promised to write, and we exchanged letters during the following year. I had to have someone to write to; fancy living in a Godforsaken place like Bellingham, after having had five years in Chicago; letter writing would constitute a leisure occupation.

North Dakota, Minnesota, Montana, Idaho; they were not new to me; I had seen the plains in Texas. But by and by we came to the Rockies. I began to compare but there was really no comparison; I had crossed the Alleghenies, too, that summer. What a queer attitude seizes one in the presence of gigantic natural phenomena. One grasps for support a little as the religious cling to their gods. Seattle and then Bellingham and the Normal School. The Puget Sound country is perhaps as beautiful as any in the world; it is almost as picturesque as the Crimea. I settled down to work in the midst of a charming nature.

—←✳

A few weeks passed at Bellingham and I had to go to the doctor. The ache in the back of my head and neck came back more acute than ever and I had terrific pains at menstruation. My shoulders and spine were sore and appeared stiff again. The boardinghouse lady recommended her family doctor and told Miss K. one of the supervisors, she should go with me. I took five treatments, Lota K. accompanying me each time. The doctor questioned and examined me; the genital organs were not functioning properly. Perhaps I didn't want to hear it, but it was a fact: the thing to do was to get married and have a baby and then I would be cured. The only other thing he could suggest was the insertion of a cotton packing and suppositories to make the womb lie straight; its being slightly out of position caused the monthly pains. I had to do something; I could not afford to be ill or miss a single day at school; I was $200 in debt; I had borrowed of the Citizen's Bank of Abilene which had to be repaid. I took the treatments. One day as I was getting dressed the Doctor told Miss K. that he doubted that I could conceive, as my womb was about the size of a twelve-year-old child's. The treatments helped me a great deal; I moved in a room next door to the Normal to avoid climbing the hill two or three times a day and carried on. I told Miss Earhart, the head of the Training School, of my illness and explained that I had lived a strenuous ten years, having studied each summer but one since I was seventeen. She understood thoroughly; she had had it herself; nearly all women who worked with their brains shared my difficulties.

I wrote limericks, rhymes, verse, and free verse at odd times, and letters to my family, friends, and sweethearts. I say sweethearts, I should have liked to have had about a dozen, men who cared enough to send telegrams and special letters and knew how to make love in writing. In such a case I would probably have ripped them open saying: I wonder what this poor fish has to say! what does this nut find to wire about? and would have seen unusually long ears. But, as a matter of fact, none of them were ardent enough for me. There was Boyce who had transferred his work to the University of Southern California; Whitacre, still with the *Chicago Daily News*, and Neely, the returned officer, who lived at Spokane. I wrote to all of them first, and made love, as much as I dared without being too ridiculous, to Boyce and Neely. If I recall rightly, I teased or coaxed or asked Boyce and Neely right out to come to Bellingham to see me; but they weren't fish. Their letters were extremely tardy. I don't remember that Whitacre ever aroused any emotion in me, perhaps it was too delicate for memory; we were like two school children.

During long walks in the outskirts of beautiful Bellingham alone, between mountain and sea, a perfect Eden of flowers, I dreamed and wept for Boyce. One day, when I was sitting in my office, a vision appeared to me; I was suckling a child; it was Boyce's son. That evening when I had returned to my office in the Training School to read and to play the piano in the next room, I became absolutely saturated with the idea of being in love with Boyce. Instead of playing the school songs, I played and sang sentimental old love songs. The sweetest one I could think of which I was able to play the music for was: "Last Night the Nightingale Woke Me."

I went back to my desk in the office and began to write; I wrote partly out of curiosity—how would it sound on paper?; partly for relief of my feelings, as a sheer experiment; and partly because I believed in my emotions and wanted to express them. It was in a way similar to the frame of mind I was in when I began writing this book. Here it is, I found it among my papers:

I think of you always alone; in my walk when the air is soft with mist, and as it presses against my face, I feel it, your breath. You don't write...I hate you with a hatred that burns and shames me, and then I dream that you are sorry and with your face pressed in my breast, I forgive you. I am a worm in the dust when with you, I despise being inferior in your eyes and, yet, I know that I am so inferior so unattractive to you that you loathe not only my body but my soul. Would you care if you knew I battled with my soul after leaving you one night? I said within my secret heart with hands rigid, "I want my son to be happy and not ashamed...I want him to find life sweet in a love such as I have for you." He will not desire learning or fame or glory...only love, that which you have never experienced—at least not for me; and I doubt whether you have ever known the meaning of love. I sit here and write about you and whisper...a darling! and see you near and feel your own son at my breast, and you don't care, never think of...I'm incapable of comforting you or letting you see my own soul. I feel cold now and I wish for you—you could warm my heart and make my soul tremble. I love you, I love you, I love you with my soul...

the soul of a woman…it shall last forever. I love loving you even though you are unmindful. I didn't let you kiss me that night because you didn't care…I was afraid, afraid of your lips and their sting, and when you left I pitied and would have caressed and smoothed your hair. At the dance that night…my hand touched yours…and that sweet sensation! I felt and liked it and tried to let you know and I believe you did understand a little, but you have never told me anything definitely…with your lips and with warm caresses which I would not try to avoid.

Another paragraph:

And you…you are my sweetie. My cheeks burn and my heart beats warm when I wish on a star about you. I want to hear from you tomorrow. Are you going to be mean and scoldy? I see you now…you are sort of wondering as you did by the lake that time. I'd like to know the truth about you. Why must I wait? Are you ever going to care enough to be gentle and tender and warm? Tell me a secret when you write…I'll bet you could say a lot if you cared to speak…

—✶

Hume Whitacre and I once paid a visit to the I.W.W. headquarters in Chicago. I talked with and questioned some of the men, but, as often happened on such occasions, I was not so talkative in the presence of a third party. Whitacre thought I was dressed too well; he declared that every time I opened my mouth, I put my foot in it...I was reminded of this occasion when I.W.W. literature reached me in Bellingham. Red ink splashed on the paper; it stirred me; "With drops of blood the history of the Industrial Workers of the World has been written." I read it: "I.W.W. members have been murdered, imprisoned, tarred and feathered, denied the right to organize, of free speech, free press, free assembly, etc." My eyes grew smaller, mist and the brightness of resentment and anger vied with one another; my fists clinched. Yes, this was a relic of the war, the damnable war which all of us had been forced to shout for in some way or other. In Chicago we had to read Woodrow Wilson's speeches in the classroom and carry on a daily campaign for Liberty Bonds and Red Cross funds. I had been forced to buy Liberty Bonds when I felt I couldn't spare the money; finally I had revolted and told the damn fool principal I wouldn't buy anymore. The workers were not the only people suffering from this insane hysteria; the whole country, that is the people without sufficient money or power, was paralytic with fear. Democracy, bah! we were living under an autocratic regime equaled only by Czarism. The people of my own profession were a lot of sheep; you could scarcely find a fearless schoolteacher.

One evening I sat in my room reading; it was the first time in my life I ever felt conscious that people were unnecessary to me. I had rather sit there, my feet on a chair near the radiator, reading, than to talk to anyone in Bellingham, nay, any person whom I could think of. I was reading Judd's *Genetic Psychology* again. It delighted me as books seldom do; it was charmingly written; the ideas were first rate. What a good thing I had done to come out to Bellingham; there was an excellent library at the Normal: 25,000 volumes, 150 current publications. I had barely started my education; I had absolutely raced through the University; why, I had left passages in Heine, Hauptmann, Herbert Spencer, and whonot, to run for my train when I was teaching at Highland Park. Sometimes I had skimmed through required reading and had not found the point. But now a new era was dawning in my life; I could be absolutely happy in my room or the library alone. I was going to enjoy my study now.

One of the Supervisors at the Normal School met a young man in the country whom she gave my telephone number. He called and jollied me about being from Texas; mimicked the native Texan's manner of speaking; asked when I was going to graduate; and made an engagement. I was going to graduate the coming May, I said; very well, he would be along with the roses, what color did I prefer? He came in a taxi and we went to the show. Another time in a telephone conversation, he called me sweetheart; I told him not to use mushy names like that in referring to myself; he coaxed: "Don't speak so loudly the landlady will hear you and she won't let you go out with me." Once we made up a foursome and went to a granger's dance not far from Bellingham. I nicknamed him Jimmy (he was about twenty-one years old) and the younger teachers all knew him by that name.

They were immensely interested in my flirtation at the Normal School, which, so far as courting and social engagements were concerned, was little better than a nunnery.

Towards Christmas we succeeded in persuading the President to give his permission for a faculty dance. It was like pulling teeth; I made a big, private speech on personal freedom; it was a hellva note that faculty members of one of the institutions of higher learning of the State couldn't dance if they wanted to. I invited Jimmy to the Faculty Dance; the Domestic Science Teacher called him "Jimmy" and he was insulted; he said it wasn't his name at all; she apologized and said that was what I called him... He found out that night that I was a member of the Faculty; I thought he perhaps already knew it; the Normal School President took us home in his Sedan. Jimmy never called again, I imagined he thought I had been laughing at him; so I had, but I expected him to laugh too. The Domestic Science Teacher thought I had made a terrific hit that night. Someone had said I looked about nineteen years old.

The younger faculty members used to go to dancing classes at a dance hall downtown; often we stayed for the dances in the evening or sneaked away from the boardinghouse without letting the landlady know where we were going and went there. Sometimes students went with us or else we found them there, but we never reported them as we were not supposed to be there ourselves. Once I met a young salesman from Seattle who held me tight and told stories while we danced. One story I did not quite understand; but I was pretty sure that it referred to sex in a particularly obscene light, which some people delight so in putting it; yet I was not certain; I could almost have wept. Why was one such a fool as to come to a public dance hall anyway? I could not say that I was studying the people there; I knew already their mentality; and the caliber of their conduct; I was frankly looking for pleasure; but he had evidently told me a story which men tell in a bawdy house. Afterwards he became friendly; told me of the girl whom he was engaged to in Seattle; they had had a quarrel and he was glad business was keeping him away for three weeks; they would make up when he went back; it was much sweeter after a quarrel. They were both graduates of the University of Washington.

—←✦

I wrote several articles on the teacher's salary and other school problems which were published in Bellingham and Seattle newspapers. The President and some of the faculty at the Normal School gave me a lot of trouble about them. In an article on teacher's organizations, published in the *Bellingham Journal,* a conversation between Gladstone and the Pope was quoted in an effort to show the importance of consultation among teachers, boards of education, and the State. The Editor said several people had come to his office asking if I were not an Irish Catholic; someone had called me an Irish Catholic agitator! The Editor himself thought I looked Irish enough; his family beginning with the father had all been English Protestants back to Adam. I told him that some of my people had come originally from the north of Ireland, but that I had never heard of a Catholic in the whole line; though there had been several fanatical Protestant ministers.

After my dispute with the faculty over the newspaper articles, I told the Editor what one of the teachers had said about someone's hatching up something against my character in securing an excuse for giving me trouble or putting me out of the Normal School because they disagreed with my articles. He said he would not put it past some of them. There were a lot of fools out there. I suggested that I ought to write to the best people at home and my professors and school heads where I had been for recommendations. Such letters would tell who I was if people began to attack me with their obscene lies. The Editor thought it a good thing, he added, "Your father was Governor of Texas at one time, wasn't he?" No, my father had never held office. The Editor thought he remembered the name Beasley as a one-time Governor of Texas.

In March or April, I went back to the Doctor to secure a prescription for a tonic. This was several weeks after my articles on amelioration of conditions in the schools had appeared in the papers. He said he had been wanting to see me; had I been trying to burn down the building on the hill? The Normal School President had telephoned him several days before and asked if he would supply him with a certificate of the condition of my health. The Doctor had told the Normal School President that he would do nothing without my permission, he said. He talked on about the ethics of the medical profession. Then the President asked the Doctor if he had read my articles in the papers; the Doctor had read the one which appeared in the *Seattle Times*. The School Head pointed out to him that the articles were hysterical or extravagant or radical, I believe, and quoted Miss K., the supervisor who accompanied me to the Doctor's, as saying that the Doctor had said I was extremely nervous.

The Doctor thought the school President was trying to find an excuse for dismissing me and he warned me against Miss K.; "that was the way with a damned woman"; she was not my friend, he declared; she had probably put the idea into the Director's head. I thought also that Miss K. had probably used this to try and curry favor with the head of the school; I had known teachers like that before. I thought immediately of the words of another teacher on the staff and told the Doctor that Miss M. once told me that these people would "attack my character" if they thought it would help them to oust me. I wanted to know: did the President ask or suggest anything derogatory about my character, that is about sexual morality. "Absolutely not," said he, "why, Miss Beasley, if I were you and they started a thing like that about me, I'd take a gun and go up there and clean up on them." I felt worried and went back and asked the Doctor to repeat the whole story and I took it down verbatim. Then I wrote a stinging letter to Miss K. asking her what it all meant. I have no copy of the letter, but I recall one of my friends said, "What a terrible letter to write to anyone with whom you have been friendly!" But I was sick and tired of the School Head and all his satellites. Miss K. replied, "Whatever I have said or done had been said and done as your friend." There was never any explanation and I believed I surmised right about Miss K. She meant to help the President get something against me.

Afterwards I called on the Doctor who had given me two or three electrical treatments of the spine during the year; had he been quizzed also? No, not a word. This Doctor had once been employed by the Normal School as physician or physiology teacher or in some such capacity. He said all this meant that I was going to be fired. The President had fired him, moreover, he was "black balled" and couldn't get a job in the whole state. He had decided that the thing for him to do was to try to get back into the Normal School. This fool talked in the most depraved way I had ever heard. Yes, I was losing my job in spite of everything; the Board would never hear me, he said; the only course open to me was to go to the President and apologize for my articles and propaganda which I had carried on against him. "Before I would do such a thing, I would starve to death in jail," I said. He opined that I would probably starve all right. He believed I was already "black balled," he doubted whether I could get another job in a higher institution in the entire United States. He said my high-sounding phrases were like Woodrow Wilson's but my method of attack was that of Theodore Roosevelt, and like Roosevelt I had attacked only the branches. I imagined many things after I left him. One of them was that he was trying to get me to talk for he wanted to act as talebearer to the Normal School Head. I had not been clever;

I had not sat tight and chosen the right moment; I had not been a politician, a talebearer, a backbiter, or a damn fool…I left in a heat of anger and I never spoke to him again; I felt in him the quality belonging to a snake; no one had ever dared use such low talk in my presence before; his advice: go and apologize! I never heard that this teacher secured a position in the Normal School; but I was pretty sure he was trying for a place.

In a day or two the President called me to his office. He was going to make recommendations to the Board, but he didn't want to recommend anyone who was "out of harmony with the school." Perhaps he was wrong, but he had felt that I was unhappy and out of harmony with the institution. He said I was extremely critical; I had written articles criticizing almost every phase of schoolwork in the whole state. But, I protested, criticism is the chief aim of higher learning; Professor Parker at the University of Chicago held that the chief aim of a University was to make students critically minded… He went on discussing my articles; I had attacked the policies and regulations of the Board of Trustees and they were not going to stand for it. Why, I had quoted Mark Twain showing them up as idiots or lower than idiots, and I had made an attack on my own contract. If the Board of Trustees did not like what I had to say about the teacher's contract, it was their business to show that I was wrong, I told him. "You have no right to take my bread and butter away from me merely because you disagree with me," I called out, pounding the table with my fist. "Let me appear before the board," I challenged, "I will defend myself."

He went on. My comparison of teachers' salaries with other types of work was entirely overdrawn and the questions which I had prepared asking for a stand of presidential candidates on the school question were presumptuous, even silly. What had I meant by asking: Do you believe the school was made for the child? The question was absurd. I said that question was the most important one in the whole school situation. I explained... He thought it looked as though I was trying to represent the Normal School, as the name of the school had been placed after my name in the articles. I said all school people had the same privilege; I cited Dr. Judd's books and articles in which the name of his department and University were always placed. Anyway, I had never written the name of the Normal School on my articles, the editor had put it in. I told him his point had no significance whatsoever. He went on, saying that he thought my health was not very good and he had called my Doctor. I knew all about it, I told him; I pulled out a paper, the Doctor's conversation with the President of the School. I remember that I talked to him in a very severe way. At first he returned by saying, "How did I know what was the matter with you?" "I told you I was sick and that was sufficient," I said.

Mind you, the illness which the School President referred to happened in September and this was April or May, I can't be sure of the date; it had suddenly dawned upon him to investigate why I was ill! If I recall correctly, I threatened the President. I told him I didn't have to put up with his nonsense and his underhanded methods; I was no fool; I would defend myself. I repeated the Doctor's conversation about the ethics of the medical profession; I believed that under the law he would find a heavy penalty for securing information by such a method. I told him I had been fair and square and open with him; I had disagreed with him in faculty meeting; I had given him my ideas openly about the salary situation and teachers' organizations, etc., etc., and if he had wanted to know about my health he might have asked me. The President grew quiet and said he admitted he had been wrong in telephoning to the Doctor; he apologized. I thought I had scared it out of him. But, he stated, there were other counts against me which had to be cleared up during the next week or two before the Board met for reelections...

Towards the end of May the papers announced the reelections. The Editor's wife telephoned the good news at noon. My name appeared among the administrative group as an unassigned instructor.

All faculty members received the same form of letter. The salary was at the rate of $1,800 for the ensuing year, that is for forty-two weeks of teaching, provided additional appropriations were available; everyone knew they would be. When I asked what my work would consist of, no one dreamed that it would be anything other than it had been; I would continue as a Supervisor in the Training School. I thought I understood what the President had done, he had been passing the buck; I had seen it done so many times by Chicago principals and heads; it was the chief characteristic of the Chicago system; it was the American system. The President wanted it to appear that the difficulty had arisen between the head of the department and myself;

that he had gone to the bottom of the trouble and found me all right. It was all pretense, all shifting of responsibility. The President was being criticized by his "superior" at Seattle and was afraid of losing his own job now. Another row might turn him out of office.

I try to recall exactly what I had in mind in carrying on the teachers' campaign for higher salaries and better conditions and what the effect upon me was. I remember how proud I felt upon seeing my name in print; there was egotism, impudence, and sheer experimentation in it too. But from the experimentalist's point of view, there was very little of the pragmatist's idea that it was all right if it worked; on the contrary I felt a sense of pleasure in learning something as I worked. For I was convinced in the beginning that I was right…I was pleased with myself when I thought of the way in which I took the head of the school to task, defended myself against his talebearers, and challenged him upon every occasion to prosecute my dismissal. I went to see Directors of the Board and a State senator too, to whom I presented my side of the dispute. I felt glad of every impudent phrase I had uttered in their presence and went home calling myself brave…

There was considerable hysteria too in the background of my mind and conduct with reference to the attitude of the President and Faculty, which reached its height in the conversations about the condition of my health. I was extremely afraid that some of the Normal School staff or other tenth-rate persons were wondering why I had to go to the Doctor for a complaint of the genital organs. Maybe they were thinking I was immoral; maybe they were gossiping merely out of malice. I marvel now that a woman twenty-seven years old could be so distressed and hurt by the thought of such gossip. I was possessed of a vain superstition with regard to sexual virtue which outweighed even my loathing for liars and petty tattlers. Then the attitude of my colleagues pained me too; during this dispute, most of the teachers of the staff, faculty members with whom I had been friendly, refused to bow to me in the street. Although from the day of my reelection they renewed their smiles and conversation. I understood them thoroughly, but the sheer asininity and insincerity of their conduct hurt me deeply... But there was more than hysteria, impudence, egotism, and vanity connected with the writing of the articles about school teaching. I really believed everything I wrote. It was all a "righteous cause"—the securing of adequate salaries, protests against the lack of free speech and press for teachers, and the teacher's rights as a citizen and a member of the community—and I meant to stand by my guns until I had either convinced the enemy or been routed by them. I thought the articles were disinterested and courageous.

—≺✶

My work as Supervisor was absolutely the most pleasant I had ever had; I had liked my work in Texas too when I was rid of the bad boys who came to tease teacher and break up the school. But there were no bad boys at the Bellingham Training School; some of the children were a little dumb and stupid, but on the whole, there was much interesting material to work with. About fifty young teachers came under my supervision during the year. I met them for frequent conferences, marked their lesson plans, recommended professional books on the teaching of their subjects, and lectured to them once a week at a general conference. I gave them as much opportunity as possible to do as they pleased; besides I was glad to be rid of them; I knew they would like me for it. I had had enough interference from Principals, Superintendents, and Special Teachers in Chicago during the past five years to deter the most stupid from their mistakes. I had no desire to be like any schoolteacher I had ever heard of. I gave demonstration lessons only when I felt like it; it was glorious being able to leave the classroom as soon as you felt the slightest inclination towards boredom. The teachers under my supervision liked me; the President told me towards the end of the year that the teachers who had taught in my department were fond of me and proud of their work under my supervision. Of course, the student teachers were not fools; they knew we had a marking system and that they would each call on me sooner or later to recommend them for positions. I am unable to recall a case of friction with any of them, and very few instances of discipline from the children under my direction…

By the middle of the school year I had paid all my debts, including the balance of my endowment pledge to Simmons College which was made when I was sixteen years old. Although I had paid several installments for interest, it still amounted to forty dollars. At home, affairs were going better than they had ever gone before, financially. It looked as though my mother was going to own two houses very soon; then there was a small plot of land which her father had left her near Ranger, Texas. From time to time, we had been greatly excited over this quarter or eighth or so of a section of land as an oil well had been dug within a mile of it. I used to amuse my friends with this story, suggesting that before long I would be rolling in wealth.

My dream of going to Japan recurred many times during the year, and I began concrete steps for its realization. The passport department informed me that I required a birth certificate. I wired my mother who sent an affidavit as there were no official records.

Some explanation had to be made about my parents; they were not living together, or a similar point was raised, and I felt called upon to clarify the question; but I was so sheepish and stupid in my talk and attitude that the clerk finally dismissed it by informing me it was none of her business. Why didn't I say directly, "My parents are divorced" and consign those who inquired further to the devil! No, I was still possessed with the idea that my parents' divorcement was a disgrace. The same attitude seized me in making an affidavit connected with my passport in Seattle. And how I loathed myself for being such an idiot!

I made a reservation on the "Empress of Japan" which sailed from Vancouver, and made the inquiries and preparations which I required. Two large suitcases held the necessary clothes for the journey; the other things together with my papers and precious notes on the Normal School squabble were packed in my trunk. There was the revolver which I had taken to Chicago with me the first time; it had lain in my trunk nearly six years. It shamed me; once when I was at the boiling point about the school President's conversation with the Doctor, I had a vision, a disgusting picture in my imagination of gun play. It was a terrible thing ever to have resolved to kill, for as soon as a thing stings one deeply it was so easy to be on the verge of resolving again. I was not the kind of person to be entrusted with a gun; I might lose my head and use it some time. The whole theory of guns, armaments in general, as a protection, was a fallacy; the idea was revolting.

At midday on the 23rd of June, 1920, the "Empress of Japan" left the harbor of Vancouver, ploughing through the northern course towards Japan. I was happy, as happy as a person of my temperament is capable of being. A secret wish bid in my heart; I hoped I was going to find someone...

FURTHER READING

Almon, Bert. *This Stubborn Self: Texas Autobiographies*. Fort Worth, TX: Texas Christian University Press, 2002.

Baym, Nina. "Eleven More Western Women Writers." *Resources for Literary Study* 36 (2011): 62–82.

Beasley, Gertrude. "I Was One of Thirteen Poor White Trash." *Hearst International-Cosmopolitan* 80 (January 1926): 90–2, 168.

"Euthenics: It's Not What You Think." *New Yorker*, July 21, 2015. https://newyorkerstateofmind.com/tag/gertrude-beasley/.

Fox, Jena Tesse. "A Different Woman." August 16, 2005. https://www.broadwayworld.com/off-off-broadway/article/A-Different-Woman-20050816.

Graham, Don. "A Woman of Independent Means." *Texas Monthly*, July 2000. https://www.texasmonthly.com/articles/a-woman-of-independent-means/.

———. *Lone Star Literature: From the Red River to the Rio Grande*. New York: W. W. Norton & Company, 2003.

Holland, Dick. "2003 Texas Book Festival Preview: King of Texas: An Interview with Don Graham, Editor of 'Lone Star Literature.'"

Austin Chronicle, November 7, 2003. https://www.austin chronicle.com/books/2003-11-07/185093/.

Marshik, Celia. "Sexual Violence as Founding Narrative: Edna Gertrude Beasley's *My First Thirty Years.*" *Feminist Modernist Studies* 4 (2021): 71–92. https://doi.org/10.1080/24692921.2021.1880 247.

McMurtry, Larry. Afterword. *My First Thirty Years*, by Edna Gertrude Beasley. Austin, TX: Book Club of Texas, 1989.

Mencken, H. L. "A Texas Schoolmarm." Rev. of *My First Thirty Years*, by Edna Gertrude Beasley. *American Mercury*, January 1926: 123–5. Accessed May 4, 2012. http://www.unz.org/Pub/AmMercury -1926jan-00123.

Specht, Mary Helen. "The Disappearance of Gertrude Beasley." *Texas Observer*. Ed. Jonathan McNamara. May 17, 2011. Accessed April 23, 2012. http://www.texasobserver.org/culture/the-dis appearance-of-gertrude-beasley.

Streitfeld, David. "Overlooked No More: Gertrude Beasley, Who Wrote an Uncompromising Memoir, Then Vanished." *New York Times*, December 19, 2018. https://www.nytimes.com/2018/12/19 /obituaries/gertrude-beasley-overlooked.html.

Taylor, Lonn. *Turning the Pages of Texas*. Fort Worth: Texas Christian University Press, 2019.

ABOUT THE
AUTHOR

Edna Gertrude Beasley (1892–1955) was an American educator and journalist. After an impoverished and abusive West Texas childhood, Beasley earned a teaching degree from Simmons College in Abilene, Texas, and a master's degree from the University of Chicago. An ardent feminist and sex education advocate, she worked as a foreign correspondent in East Asia, the Soviet Union, and Western Europe. Her frank 1925 autobiography, *My First Thirty Years*, was published in Paris to some acclaim but ran afoul of U.S. and U.K. obscenity laws. Customs officials and Texas law enforcement confiscated most copies, and Beasley was deported from the U.K. in 1927. Within days of her return to the United States, she was committed to the Central Islip Psychiatric Center in New York, where she remained for the rest of her life. Beasley died of pancreatic cancer in 1955.